THE ANNOTATIONS OF JOHANNES BUGENHAGEN, THE POMERANIAN,

ON TEN EPISTLES OF PAUL,

namely,

TO THE EPHESIANS, PHILIPPIANS, COLOSSIANS, 1 AND 2 THESSALONIANS 1 AND 2 TIMOTHY, TITUS, PHILEMON, HEBREWS;

and

THE HARMONY OF THE EVANGELISTS ON THE RESURRECTION AND ASCENSION OF THE LORD
(1524)

THE ANNOTATIONS
OF JOHANNES BUGENHAGEN, THE POMERANIAN,

ON TEN EPISTLES OF PAUL,

namely,

TO THE EPHESIANS, PHILIPPIANS, COLOSSIANS, 1 AND 2 THESSALONIANS 1 AND 2 TIMOTHY, TITUS, PHILEMON, HEBREWS;

and

THE HARMONY OF THE EVANGELISTS ON THE RESURRECTION AND ASCENSION OF THE LORD (1524)

as translated by
The Rev. Dr. Richard J. Dinda, Prof. Em.

Repristination Press
Malone, Texas

A translation of Johannes Bugenhagen, *Annotationes Ioan. Bugenhagii Pomeraniin X Epistolas Pauli, scilicet, ad Ephesios, Philippenses, Colossenses, Thessalonicens pri. et secu., Timotheu prima et secunda, Titum, Philemonem, Hebræos. Item Concordia Evangelistarum de Resurrectione ac Ascensione Domini. Argentorati Apud Iohannem Hervagium Mense Maio Anno M.D. XXIII.* Copyright 2013 by Richard Dinda. Published by permission of the translator. No part of this publication may be reproduced, stored in a retrieval system, or transmitted in any form or by any means, electronic, mechanical, photocopying or otherwise without the prior written permission of Repristination Press.

ISBN 1-891469-72-X

Published in 2016.

REPRISTINATION PRESS
P.O. BOX 173
BYNUM, TEXAS 76631

www.repristinationpress.com

TABLE OF CONTENTS.

Ephesians 7
Philippians 39
Colossians 63
1 Thessalonians 91
2 Thessalonians 121
1 Timothy 149
2 Timothy 191
Titus 211
Philemon 227
Hebrews 235

The Resurrection and Ascension of Our Lord Jesus Christ
According to the Four Evangelists 279

ANNOTATIONS OF JOHANNES BUGENHAGEN OF POMERANIA ON THE EPISTLE OF PAUL TO THE EPHESIANS.

THEME OF THE EPISTLE.

This epistle includes in a few—but wonderfully rich—words a summary of the full preaching of Paul and therefore of the Gospel so that one can add nothing more. In the first three chapters, he declares very clearly the Gospel and the freedom and efficacy of the Gospel. However, in the remaining chapters, after the faith by which alone we receive justification, he takes up (as is his habit) the Christian life which is the fruit of internal faith, that is, of justification. There he advises what each and every person should follow. So much for the theme.

ON [SPECIAL] PASSAGES.

However, there are outstanding passages in this epistle. The first concerns divine predestination: that we were predestined before the creation of the world according to the good pleasure of God the Father (ch. 1–3), that we may have something over which to rejoice, namely, salvation, which He has given freely. But let us not consider that this [predestination] is something over which to boast, for who has given first to God and it is not repaid him?

((Our practical judgment is cursed.))[1] The second concerns our cognizance of this grace (ch. 1). Paul wants us to recognize (as he does almost everywhere in his epistles) the power of the Spirit of God, who is at work within us. His grace, you see, is boundless. From it, you possess as much as you can believe, but you cannot believe except through the power of God; namely, that by which He raised Jesus from the dead and exalted Him above all things. The third passage is the same as the prior one (ch. 2); namely, that works accomplish nothing for this grace, so that it remains the glory of God alone. The fourth (ch. 2 and 3) is that if not for this grace we also belong to the Gentiles, something which had been unknown before but has now finally been revealed. This passage must strengthen us as much as possible.

The fifth outstanding passage concerns the abrogation of the Law (ch. 2), for the Gentiles could not have gathered together into one body with the Jews had not Christ removed the intervening wall. ((The abundance of this [demonstration] is the Epistle to the Colossians.)) We have the same passage in Col. 3 (Eph. 4), concerning the unity of spirit and the unity of doctrine. After we have become one body, let us not be carried about by every wind of doctrine. The seventh passage concerns the unity of Christ and the Church under the type of carnal marriage. The eighth passage (ch. 6) concerns not contending and, in fact, not wrestling with any human powers against the mighty snares of the ancient serpent whom we overcome by the Word alone.

---

1   Trans. note: Words enclosed in double brackets are marginal statements. To keep them in the margin would perhaps double the length of this treatise, and would also make the typing so much more difficult for me. Some few, which seem unnecessary, I have omitted.

CHAPTER 1.

[v. 1:] "Through the will…"
    Paul says: "…through the will of God," not as the pseudapostles who came of themselves without a call. (Read in Acts 19 concerning what happened to the Ephesians.) [In v. 2,] "grace" is the free remission of all sins but "peace" is the acknowledgment of that grace by which the conscience rejoices in the Holy Spirit that sin has been forgiven, etc.

    He calls God "our Father" [v. 2] so that you would not be fearful about approaching such great majesty, for He wants us to call Him "Father." Furthermore, he calls Jesus "Lord" so that you do not despise the fact that He bore the cross for you, etc.

[v. 3:] "Blessed…"
    He immediately begins with joy and preaches the Gospel; that is, the remission of all sins and the inheritance of eternal life through Jesus Christ inasmuch as we have not only become righteous through faith in Christ but also the children of God. ((He wants us to believe the subject of predestination, for it is incomprehensible to the flesh.)) Here he immediately inserts divine predestination with many clear words, which produces very great comfort for the faithful, who know that all things are in God's hand, and that whatever happens to them is the good will of God. After all, what is sweeter for me than to know my salvation and that (in addition) my life is in the hand of God?

    He says: "No one will snatch any believing sheep from My hand, and no one can snatch them from the hand of My Father" (John 10). Otherwise, if salvation were in my hand, it would have perished a long time ago already.

((Know this: If you have believed that you were predestined, you truly are. This is a very great thing!)) Read about predestination in the *Loci* of Philip [Melanchthon].[2] This is such a clear locus that almost nowhere can it be more clear, even if you have grasped this everywhere in Scripture. Whenever the wicked hear of predestination, they turn it into themes of wickedness. But, as this very thing did not frighten Paul, so let it not frighten us. In fact, let us confess freely that, as God created all things, so also He governs us with His hand.

((When we bless God, the words exist; but when He blesses us, the blessings actually exist.)) We say that God is blessed in the same way that we say He is holy, for He both blesses and sanctifies. However, we are said to be blessed because we receive the blessing, and we are said to be holy when we are sanctified. Yet, the prayer is a simple one: "Blessed be God," that is: "Praise to God; I give thanks to God."

In every blessing there is a multiplication or increase. Blessing is a physical thing when God offers physical things. Blessing is spiritual when He offers invisible things such as grace, peace, and the heavenly inheritance.

[v. 3:] "…in heavenly places."

Paul posits this three times in this epistle; that is, "in the superior places," or in matters which are above us and which are invisible and not apparent to the judgment of the flesh. I say this that you may understand what Paul says at the end of the epistle: "…against spiritual wickedness in high places." You see, in that air which we also call "heaven" the wicked spirit is not active, as Paul says not just once in this epistle, etc.

[v. 3:] "…in Christ."

[2] The first edition of Melanchthon's *Loci Communes* was published in 1521.

This is a dative, so that you understand this as "to Christ" or (as others read it) "in Christ," that is "through Christ" or "through faith in Christ."

Scripture speaks not only about God, but also about the works of God, in human fashion. Thus, it attributes ears, eyes, mouth, and hands to God. It also speaks about His works as if about the works of humans, as: "Your hands have made me, O Lord"; and about the world as if about the creation of the world it says: "He laid the foundations of the earth" (Pro. 8); and in the psalm: "…for He set it upon the seas"; also: "You, who founded the earth upon its own foundation." Scripture does the same thing here, although Job nevertheless said most truthfully: "He hangs the earth upon nothing."

[v. 4:] "…before Him…"

That Paul may condemn the world very greatly, he here condemns hypocrisy as well as feigned faith, when he adds: "…through love," that is, "through mutual love among us." Here you have a brief summary of the entire Christian situation, namely, that we be holy in the presence of God. Among ourselves, however, let mutual love join us together. By nature, Jesus Christ is the Son according to His deity, and through adoption He is the Son through His humanity, just as we are children [of God] through Him. And in Him (that is, for Himself), that is, that we may be His children and He Himself our Father.

[v. 5:] "…according to His good pleasure, etc."

Thus, it is not according to some merit of ours, so that the glory is not ours, but His.

[v. 5:] "…to the praise of His glory, etc."

That is, that the glory may remain that of His grace alone, by which grace He made us dear to Himself through His beloved Christ.

((He rendered us His children though His Son.)) This He could have done most appropriately in this way: He rendered us beloved through His Beloved, just as He said about Christ: "This is My beloved Son in whom I am well-pleased," so also He says about individual believers.

[v. 7:] "…richly…"

He gave the Law to one people, but He wanted grace to be published to all so that you may know that He preferred being Father to being Judge. He speaks in this way in Eze. 18: "I do not want the death of a sinner, etc." He poured this grace out abundantly. Let us simply accept it. He gave not only grace, but also the understanding of grace—but these are the same.

[v. 8:] "…in wisdom…"

"Wisdom" here is spiritual understanding and "prudence" is that by which we are careful not to fall again into unbelief. Wisdom makes us understand what the things of God are; prudence causes us to remain in them persistently so that various doctrines not mislead us again, etc.

[v. 9:] "…the mystery of His will…"

That is, the Gospel.

[v. 9:] "according to His good pleasure…"

To be unable to understand this mystery is to be unable to believe it unless God should disclose it to you, and this not because of our interest or merit, but according to His good pleasure alone. Rev. 21: "Behold, I make all things new." Heavenly things had split away from earthly ones because the peace which existed between them had been destroyed through the sin of man. When through the blood of Christ that sin had been removed, all things became renewed in heaven and on earth, for the ancient peace returned. ((Be careful of the fictions of Origen!)) You read in Col. 1: "You became pacified through the blood of the cross, etc." For this reason, at the birth of Christ the angels sang: "Glory in the highest, etc."

[v. 10:] "...all the way to, etc."

That is, until the dispensation in the fullness of time (that is, when the times were completed which God prescribed for the revelation of His Gospel) in which He arranged and distributed this mystery throughout His entire household, that is, in all the world. We read the following in Gal. 4: "When the fullness of time came, etc." The grace of the Gospel existed at all times. Through it, all the saints before the incarnation of Christ were saved. However, that grace had to be revealed through Christ at a time which the Father had predetermined. Paul speaks in this way everywhere about the mystery revealed, the hidden Gospel, etc., as He did in Galatians: "...shut up in that faith which was going to be revealed." ((The revelation of the face of the Lord.)) Paul desired this greatly everywhere: that day by day and more and more this grace would be revealed to the eyes of our hearts, as he says later: "I therefore, etc.," that we may advance from faith to faith, from strength to strength, from glory to glory, just as from the Spirit of the Lord. Obviously, this mystery He had set forth in Himself and He kept it as a secret within Himself.

[v. 11] "...that finally [*ut summa*]..."
That is, at the same time.

[v. 12] [...that we may be to the praise...]

With this periphrasis, namely, "we who first placed our hope in Christ," he signifies the Jews who believed in Christ; for instance, they believed along with the other apostles and disciples who believed or hoped in Christ before the Gentiles. The Ephesians belonged to the number of these, for later they hoped and believed by the preaching of Paul. With reference to these, Paul adds: "In whom you also obviously believed who heard the word of truth, that is, of the Gospel of your salvation, etc." This is the true understanding of this passage if you should consider what the whole Gospel requires; for it teaches that Gentiles as well as Jews belong to this revealed grace of Christ, as you see also in ch. 2 and 3. Therefore, we now read in a corrupted way in the Greek "ἐν ᾧ γε ἡμεῖς - in whom we also..." instead of "ὑμεις - in whom also you..."[3] The context of the discourse itself shows this, not to mention the rest. The old interpreter also reads it in this way, and Ambrose and Jerome interpret it thus: "You were the first," that is, "before the Gentiles in whom you hoped," namely, you Gentiles, in whom, that is, "through the word of truth."

[v. 13:] "...you were sealed..."

This is just as you see in 2 Cor. 1. Here we have "the Spirit of promise." There we had: "This is the promised Spirit," whom Christ promised believers, as you often read in John. Because He was given in our hearts, He is the sure earnest [or pledge] that God does not fail in the rest of His promises, that God accepts us as righteous, and that even now He deigns to dwell in us. Look also at Romans: "The Spirit Himself bears witness..."

[v. 13:] "...until the redemption of the purchased possession," as he says.

That is, "that our inheritance which we have acquired through Christ may be redeemed that we may praise His glory as a result." Thus, we read in Gal. 3: "This alone I wish to learn from you, etc. ... He therefore who ministered, etc."

---

3   "...ἐν ᾧ καὶ ὑμεις..." (Stephanus 1550 edition)

[v. 14:] "...who is the earnest [or pledge]..."

The earnest that we may be certain about receiving our inheritance, "until the redemption, that is, of the possession of our inheritance acquired through Christ," which is not a result of the glory of our own merits.

[v. 15:] "Therefore..."

I have spoken about this earlier. Note carefully the distribution of Paul. We must deal with God by faith; we must deal with our neighbor in love. We deal with God *by faith*, and we are one with Christ. Moreover, we deal with our neighbors *in love*. It is a matter of wisdom that you *know*, and a matter of revelation that it be *revealed* to you. It is hope, namely, of our inheritance, to which hope He has called us. It is a matter of His power by which He works in us.

[v. 19:] "...which is surpassing..."

Here you see how immense His power is and how effectively the Spirit of God works faith within us, to wit, by which He raised Jesus from the dead and causes Him to rule over all things. ((We are saved without works, that is, without our works but with the work of Christ.)) Therefore you know that those who think they can believe easily (as if by their own powers or will) have nothing of faith. In this way, they magnify their own works with their contempt of faith and this to the injury of our Savior (whose works alone save us). What Paul says in the chapter following speaks contrary to these: "You are saved by grace through faith, and this not of yourselves, for it is the gift of God that no one should boast."

[v. 21:] "Above every principate..."

That is, above everything which is lofty whether in heaven or on earth, just as Christ Himself says: "All power has been given Me in heaven and on earth." What do we dread under that King and, in fact, under that Head with whom we are one (namely, as His members)? For we ourselves also can do all things in Christ, and we are the lords over death, sin, hell, and all things, for "who will separate us from the love of God," etc.? Paul says these things in ch. 2 in this way: "He has brought us to life again with Christ, etc."

CHAPTER 2.

When carnal people hear the preaching of faith they live neglectfully as if they are already the sort of people God wants them to be. They lay hold of the freedom of the flesh instead of the freedom of the spirit which does not exist except where the Spirit of the Lord is (2 Cor. 3). But where the Spirit of the Lord is not present, there the slavery of the Law is still present and, therefore, also the curse of the Law. 1 Tim. 1: "The Law has been given not for the righteous but for the unrighteous, etc."

((Where is the Spirit of God?)) Moreover, the Spirit of God is in that place where He always knows who we are and what we have become. We have not been what we are by this or that work alone, but we have been by nature the children of wrath and of the curse. Do not think that there was any good in you for which reason you may usurp anything for yourself. Tell me, please, what tree was able to produce any fruits except evil ones?

Thus you see that free will is nothing. We used to be led according to the lusts of the flesh, as we read in Rom. 1, according to every will of the prince of this air, that is, of this world, whom Paul elsewhere calls "the god of this age." That prince is still acting in those who are not obedient to the truth but to the lie, as we read (2 The. 2); just as the Spirit of God acts in the godly (Rom. 8).

However, because God does not impute our sin for Christ's sake, we have become not only righteous, but we have also become the lords of all, exalted as we now are over all things along with and through Christ at the right hand of the Father in the heavens, as we said in the chapter preceding. This has happened by no work or merit of our own and, in fact, while we were still dead through our sins and were by nature the children of wrath, as we read in Rom. 5: "...while we were yet His enemies." That's how far we are from having been able to deserve this. Thus the Spirit accomplishes two things in us to recognize Himself within us. With the one, He causes us not to live in security (as if we have already become sated with the grace of God), because the Spirit here always demands indescribable groans on behalf of the saints and makes us say: "O, unfortunate fellow that I am, etc.!" As regards the second thing, He causes us not to despair with respect to any sins, however great those are of which we are aware.

The one causes us not to be thankless; the other, that we persist before God, knowing that this [work of the Spirit] is not a matter of our work but of the grace of God. In the one, we see ourselves as publicans, sinners, and prostitutes; in the other, we see that we have obtained mercy in Christ. Paul wants us to acknowledge these everywhere: the one, that we may turn back to Him; the other, that we increase in Him daily as we advance from faith to faith until (as we shall say later) we all reach the stage of being the perfect human, etc.

Next, when the good tree, enlivened as it is by the Spirit of God, grows gradually in Christ, how will it happen that it not also produce good fruit of its own free will at its own time? That those may finally learn to be embarrassed who say that God forbids us good works when we teach according to the truthfulness of the Gospel that no one is justified on the basis of works; good fruits do not cause the tree to be good, but indicate that it is a good tree. However, the good tree does not indicate, but produces, good fruits.

For this reason what Paul here says ("We are His workmanship"), he says not about our creation (by which we are born the children of wrath because of Adam's sin), but about our rebirth (by which we are born as the children of God by grace through Christ for good works, not which those workers offer to God but which God has prepared that we should live in those works). Those are works of love, joy, peace, etc. (See Gal. 5.) We ourselves do not accomplish such things in ourselves. Rather, this is the work of the Spirit of God within us, through which work our nature is changed into grace and we produce fruits not of the flesh, but of the Spirit.

[v. 11:] "Therefore, etc."

This is an outstanding passage. It is dependent on the preceding passages; namely, that the Gentiles also belong to the blessing of the seed of Abraham, that is, of Christ, for Abraham receives the promise in this way: "In your seed all the kindred of the earth will be blessed"; and: "I have called you the father of many nations." This is something which was "not made known to other generations," just as we read later in ch. 3. The Jews who were not learned kept imagining that this meant the kingdom of the Messiah, and that the blessing belonged to them alone.

Next, although they saw in Scripture (as we see often in Isaiah, the Psalms and the prophets) that the Gentiles were also going to receive that call, they nevertheless kept dreaming that they, as better people, were going to be placed ahead of them. We see this in the epistles of the apostles, etc., that the pseudapostles who were of the Jews perceived this. In the meantime, then, let me not say that they were imagining this on the basis of many passages, namely, that they were going to have a carnal rule over the nations, as we have that in Psa. 4:6: "He will subject the people to us."

Therefore, this great mystery had still not been revealed, namely, that the nations also belonged to the seed of Israel through faith in Christ, for they were strangers to the covenants of the promises of God through which their inheritance was preserved and were people who were without the true God. In this world, however, this mystery still lay so hidden that not even Peter knew it even after he had received the Holy Spirit. Indeed, he learned this from a unique revelation, as you read in Acts 10 and 11. For that reason we have the addition there: "And the believers from the circumcised were astonished, etc." Paul and Barnabas interpret this in this way on the basis of Isaiah (Acts 13): "It was necessary for the Word of God first be spoken to you, etc."

[v. 11:] "…which circumcision…"

According to Rom. 2:29, this is a circumcision of the heart, not of the letter but of the Spirit.

[v. 14:] "For He is our peace, etc."

Therefore because the Gentiles along with the Jews were going to be one body under one head, Christ, they would also be one building constructed upon the foundation of the apostles and prophets which was placed upon the Rock, which is Christ. Thus it could not have happened unless the intervening space which separated the two very different peoples were removed. That was the Law which he calls "enmities against the flesh of Christ," that is, against the Jews. This Law, I say, was not only ceremonial, as some people interpret it, nor only of judgments, but also of behavior (("Thou shalt not kill… Thou shalt not steal.)). As Paul says here, it is the Law of the commandments which is situated in the decrees and statutes of God and of which all people are guilty and which holds all people under its curse. Gal. 2[:14]: "He blotted out the handwriting which was against us through its decrees, took it out of the way and attached it to His cross, etc." God consecrated this Law through circumcision.

Those who had received circumcision would separate themselves from the uncircumcised as unclean according to the

Law. In addition, all the burdens of the Law kept following circumcision, as Paul says to the Galatians [5:3]: "I bear witness again to every person circumcising himself that he is a debtor to do the whole Law." Peter says (Acts 15[:10]) that "neither we nor our fathers were able to bear these burdens." Also, Paul says Acts 13[:39]: "You could not have been justified of your sins in the law of Moses." He says that in the Law it is not in ceremonies alone. Also, Rom. 8[:3]: "What was impossible for the Law, etc."

Therefore, it was necessary that the Law be taken away, so far was it that the Law also be imposed upon the Gentiles. The Jews trusted in the Law, but, when that was taken away, they saw that they were not a bit better than the Gentiles, because Scripture has included all under sin. The Gentiles, you see, were openly wicked and as a result were themselves found to be sinners after they understood that the works of the Law do not justify them.

Next, because this was the Law of God, they could not abrogate it unless they satisfied it for ever. If we could not satisfy it, as it has been said; then it was necessary that that person be subject to the Law and fulfill it who owed nothing to the Law. This is Jesus Christ, who through the blood of the cross made the Gentiles and Jews one body for Himself and made Himself our sanctification, righteousness, and justification. Whoever clings to Him by faith is one with Him and has whatever Christ Himself has. Therefore Christ's satisfaction is mine so that the Law cannot condemn me, and the sin which is left to me in my flesh is not counted against me because of my faith in Christ. Hence, the Spirit of Christ is already causing in those who believe that they love God and their neighbor, something which the Law indeed requires but cannot grant because it was the letter and not the Spirit.

Furthermore, in whom the Spirit of Christ is not dwelling they boast foolishly of the abrogation of the Law. All the rest of the things which are not contained under the heading of the love of

God and of one's neighbor are means so that, regardless of whether or not they are in the Law of Moses, you may omit them, provided you avoid offense and that you not place the process of our salvation in them. Also, the things which here pertain to the abrogation of the Law you have in passages of Philippians. Therefore, the covenants and the promises of God, belong equally to us as to the Jews, etc.

CHAPTER 3.

The signal testimony of true preaching is to not deny the name of Christ in persecution. As regards all who have heard the Word, it is clearer than light that the Spirit of God in the hearts of those who have learned it has strengthened this Word because of which they fear no bonds. When the hearers of the Word have received strength from this testimony, they can boast to themselves that they are certain that they have heard the Word of God. "Therefore" and "for this reason, I ask, etc." "For the good shepherd gives up his life for his sheep, but the hired hand, etc." [John 10:12]

[v. 2:] "…the dispensation…"
Acts 22[:21]: "Go, because I shall send you far away to the nations." And to Ananias, Acts 9[:15]: "That man is My chosen vessel."

[v. 3:] "…according to the revelation…"
((The words are not Paul's but Christ's.)) Gal. 1[:6]: "I make known to you the Gospel, etc." He wants himself known everywhere that he is a minister of the Word whom God has sent, just as you see clearly in 2 Corinthians, that we might be absolutely certain that this Word which Paul is preaching is the Word of God, etc. This is not seeking your own glory but the glory of Him who

has sent you, etc. Thus Paul descends to himself and adds [v. 7]: "To me, the least of all the saints has been given this grace," as if to say: "God wanted work through me, although I am the least important."

((By what logic Paul calls himself "the least of the apostles")) "I am the least because not only have I persecuted the Church of God (as he says elsewhere), but also because I am nothing of myself. However, these works are not matters of human powers that the glory of God may appear to be greater when He accomplishes such amazing things through the weak vessels of human frailty. Let no one, therefore, raise his hand against a person when the power of God works through a person who is despised in every way. We have the following words in 2 Cor. 4[:7]: "We have this treasure in earthen vessels that the sublime character of that power may belong to God and not to us."

[v. 8:] " ... unsearchable..."

Below [v. 18]: "...what is the breadth, etc." Psa. 50 [51:6] speaks about this: "You have revealed to me the uncertain and secret things of Thy wisdom."

[v. 9:] "...the fellowship..."

Obviously because he must distribute the Gospel not only to the Jews but also to the Gentiles. That is, the Gospel must become common to all people.

[v. 10:] "...to the principalities and powers..."

Take these to mean the same about which you read later in ch. 6. These are words burning with the Spirit, as if he were saying: "We are bringing out into the light this mystery which we have believed in such a way that the whole kingdom of hell perceives it; and we say to it: 'Take away your gates, you princes, etc.'" And that they may perceive how many are in the military service of the empire of darkness and how many the very light of the truth has overcome successfully, let them battle against the kingdom of light. The devil began to suspect or even to know that by the preaching of the Gospel it would come to pass that mankind be redeemed. Who, however, could know that very diverse and unknown wisdom of God, namely, that God was going to lead the foolishness of the world to wisdom, to glory through a cross and to life through a death, as you read in 1 Cor. 2. Had the princes of the world known the wisdom of God, they would never have crucified the Lord of glory.

We explained earlier what he adds here; to wit, in the heavenly places, that is, in the upper air or in the world in which we live. That is why the devil is called "the prince of the world."

[v. 14:] "For this reason…"

((You have as much as you acknowledge.)) This is what we have said above; namely, that Paul wants us to acknowledge everywhere the limitless and incomprehensible grace that, fortified as we are by the Spirit, we understand the heights of this grace, for it penetrates the heavens, as well as its depth, for it penetrates hell, and its length and breadth, for it fills the whole earth so that you understand that it is now known not only in Judea, just as we read in Psa. 75: "The earth is filled with the mercy of the Lord"; and Psa. 118 and 8: "O Lord, our Lord, how wonderful is Your name in all the earth."

[v. 15:] "…of whom, etc."

This very Person is the Head, Christ, just as you have it in Corinthians. Next, He gathers all things of heaven and earth into one and is Himself the *paterfamilias* in heaven and upon the earth. He is the Governor of His own, and from Him flows forth every spiritual relationship. He Himself is the Father of all things. Those, therefore, who are united with Him through faith do not dread Him as their judge but have Him as their Father, etc.

[v. 16:] "…in the inner man."

That is, that the inner person may grow in the Spirit and become strong. See later, ch. 4 [v. 13]: "Until we all shall have reached, etc."

[v. 17:] "… rooted…"

That your love not be feigned, as he says elsewhere, but be steadfast and enduring, even if those whom you love treat you poorly. When this love is so steadfast, it is the indication and fruit of a steadfast faith within.

[v. 17:] "…and founded…"

Look at what Paul calls "the foundation," namely, the inner man strengthened as he is by the Spirit of his faith, which inner man produces the fruits of unfeigned faith. This must proceed from faith to faith that our knowledge of the incomprehensible glory of the grace of God may increase in us from day to day with the result that we judge that we have not grasped it falsely. Read this also in Phi. 3.

[v. 19:] "…that you might know, etc."

((Just as there is one God, so there is one Mediator. Thus there is no additional intercessor.)) We cannot know the grace and mercy of God except through Christ, as you have it in 1 Cor. 1. We cannot achieve this knowledge by any merit of our own but because He loved us fervently and beyond measure so that He gave up His life for us, a love than which there is no greater, as He Himself says in John. Oh, how few there are who recognize so great a love of Christ in us! However, knowing this is not an insignificant matter but (as Paul says here) one which stands above and surpasses all human understanding and knowledge.

[v. 19:] "…that you may be filled…"

That is, that you may grow into all the things which are of God so that you lack nothing of spiritual perception and grow into the perfect man, etc., as we said earlier.

[v. 20:] "Now unto Him…"

We suffer no frustration in our prayers for we have an omnipotent Father who can do beyond measure all things for which we ask even before we ask for them, etc. Thus the Lord says in Luke: "Because you are evil, etc." According to His might by which He Himself acts within us, let us not attribute anything in this grace to our own effort because the glory belongs to Him alone, but thanksgiving for it is our responsibility.

[v. 20:] "…be glory in the Church…"

Just as all salvation descends from God to us through Christ, as also all glory again rises to God from us through Christ.

[v. 21:] "…for ages of ages…"

That is, of that age which will never have an end as the ages go one endlessly. That Hebrew periphrasis commonly expresses eternity, as you often see in Holy Writ.

CHAPTER 4.

After such great mysteries of faith, we have an admonition to good behavior, as is usual, which advises that those whom God has honored with so sacred a calling live in a holy way (as you read in 1 The. 4). God has not called us to uncleanness but to sanctification. ((No one plants a good tree to produce bad fruits.)) See above in ch. 2: "We are His workmanship, etc." That he may accomplish this, Paul first touches on the main point of all Christian behavior; namely, that the unity of the Spirit be preserved in the gentleness of peace. After all, only one spirit can control and give life to a single body.

Furthermore, he commends to us in unity all things on the basis of which we are Christians. He says [v. 4]: "One body, etc." Those break down this unity who establish new religious scruples with their chosen works and who fall away from the unique and genuine teaching of Christ with their various human teachings. From those [works and teachings] new religions spring forth: superstitions, sects, and heresies which completely extinguish faith in Christ when each person places himself ahead of others with diabolic arrogance, as we see has happened. Such things had begun among the Corinthians, to whom Paul writes, 1 Cor. 1: "I beseech you, brethren, etc." Unity of doctrine follows unity of the Spirit, and through the former we increase in the knowledge of Christ until we become perfected men so that we are no longer children, etc.

Next, nothing stands in the way of this unity because the Holy Spirit has marked some people with some of His gifts and others with other gifts of His. These gifts, you see, are nothing other than the labors [*ministeria*] for building unity. If you benefit the Church with these, you have them correctly, and not only these gifts but also grace will have increase for you. If, on the other hand, you do not provide advantage to the Church with these gifts, but neglect the gift which the Spirit has given you or abuse it to increase your arrogance, profits, or even an offense against your neighbor, then you do not have that gift correctly, and in His just judgment God will take both His grace and His gift from you.

You have that in this way in the Gospel (Mat. 12:12): "To everyone who has it will be given, and he will have an abundance; but, from him who does not have, even what he appears to have will be taken from him." Paul expressed these words in this way in 1 Cor.

12[:7]: "To each has been given the manifestation of the Spirit," and this not for his own utility but for that of the Church, "for to one is given by the Spirit, etc." There [v. 11] he says: "The Spirit divides to each individually as He wills."

As a result, because grace is given to each person according to the measure of the gift of Christ, Christ and the Holy Spirit work together as one and have one will. Hence it happens that Christ makes some apostles whom He sends into all the world; some prophets, that is, interpreters of Scripture; and some evangelists, that is, ministers of the apostles and of the Word. Where the apostles are not present as preachers, there are some pastors, that is, bishops in individual cities; some are teachers, that is, people who teach faithfully the subjects which others receive. In whatever way you may have distinguished these, Paul is signifying ministers of the Word of God so clearly that no one is able to understand his words in a different way, for he adds: "… for the perfecting of the saints, etc." (Eph. 4:12) Therefore, they should not think that those have been included here whose nature only titles and names have inflated for the usefulness of the Church. Paul is speaking here about the unity of the Church and about her various gifts. Elsewhere, however, he inserts some things in passing which we shall look at separately.

[v. 8:] "…He led captivity captive."

We explained in our commentary on Psa. 67 that Paul is not citing this passage because of this brief sentence but because of that which follows: "…and He gave gifts to people." The gifts are those of which we spoke above. Rather, he inserts this on the occasion of this citation in which we read: "When he ascended on high, etc." The righteousness of no one is acceptable in the presence of God except the righteousness of Him who descended to justify us. We read the following in John 3[:13]: "No one has ascended into heaven except Him who descended from heaven, the Son of Man, who is in heaven." And in the last chapter of Luke, [v. 26,] He said: It was necessary for Christ to suffer and thus enter into His glory that He might fulfill all things." He also said after His resurrection [Mat. 28:18]: "All power has been given Me in heaven and on earth."

[v. 13:] "…into the perfected man…"

Some people have related these words to quantity and to the time of the rising again of bodies on the last day, namely, that we are going to be raised again in that age when Christ died. It is, however, shameful to refute so obvious an error of this misunderstood text, despite the fact that it speaks very clearly about the teaching by which we increase to a perfection of our knowledge of Christ or by which we grow fully into Christ so that we finally attribute nothing to external matters as we used to do when we were still infants and were hand-led (so to speak) by some works and ceremonies. (For the Law is a schoolmaster into Christ.) Rather, let us acknowledge fully and with full faith that Christ alone is our salvation. When you have come to Him in this way, you have turned out to be the perfect man, etc. Note here that the many subtleties of the doctrines of men strive to hinder this edification and perfection, etc.

[v. 15:] "…the truth…"

In the Hebrew manner, Paul is calling the faith "the truth." We have here, then, an elegant connection in that the people speak the truth in love. "The truth," "sound doctrine," and "faith" are all the same, and love is their fruit.

[v. 16:] "…in whom the whole body…"

This happens just as the life-giving spirit flows into all the members not equally but in proportion to the measure and utility of the member, etc. Read the metaphor of the members of the body and of the head as Paul describes that elegantly in 1 Cor. 12.

[v. 17:] "This, then, I say, etc."

He is returning to that which he said at the beginning of this chapter, that, renewed in spirit as we have become, we should walk in newness of life.

[v. 17:] "... in vanity..."

See what the signs of wickedness are in that place where there is no illumination of the Word, just as you read in Rom. 1. The punishment for wickedness is blindness. The fruit of blindness is obstinacy and carelessness. Isa. 28[:18]: "We have struck a covenant with death, etc.,'" and, "He will turn away from the face, etc."

[v. 21:] "...the truth is in Jesus."

Falsity, lie, vanity, blindness, faithlessness are all things of the old [as opposed to the new] person. In opposition to all these, Paul places the truth of Jesus. We must understand this not only in the words but also in the deeds which are Christ's and God's. That is why we had earlier, [4:15:] "...speaking the truth in love." We also read in John 3[:21]: "But he who does the truth, etc."

[v. 24:] "... of the truth..."[4]

He adds this against the righteousness and holiness of vanity, of hypocritical faith, and of specious superstition; for he is calling (as is his wont) faith and the knowledge of God "the truth."

[v. 30:] "Do not grieve the Holy Spirit..."

This should not happen among you or among your hearers. You see, godly minds are in the habit of grieving if those in whose hearts the Spirit of God dwells hear shameful things. Scripture attributes human emotions to God, for it cannot speak any differ-

---

4   The Latin reads: "*in justitia et sanctitate veritatis* - in the righteousness and holiness of the truth."

ently to us. As it therefore says that God rejoices over our salvation (as you see in the parable, Luke 15), so also it says again that God grieves over our sins, for He hates them. Gen. 6[:5]: "God saw that the wickedness of man was great, etc." He frightens us sufficiently away from shameful activities with that admonition, etc. (("The mouth speaks out of the abundance of the heart," [Mat. 12:34.] If you wish to deny yourself, you make God a shameful liar. As the spring is, so also is its water.))

[v. 30:] "...you have been sealed..."

See above, ch. 1:[13]. But why is it that Paul adds here "unto the day of redemption," that is, unto that day when you shall have received your full inheritance and are fully redeemed, that is, until the day of the coming of Christ? See Rom. 8[:23]: "We ourselves groan within ourselves as we await our adoption as the children of God, to wit, the redemption of our body."

CHAPTER 5.

"Be imitators of God." This is explained in Mat. 5[:44–45], that you attend not only your friends but also your enemies with kindness. As Christ says: "...that you may be the children of your Father who is in heaven, who makes His sun, etc." And Paul adds that highest model of love, v. 2: "...even as Christ, too."

[v. 2:] "...an offering..."

After this one offering of Christ, there now is no longer an offering for sins. This offering, after all, sanctifies forever, as we read in Hebrews: "Christ delivered Himself, etc."; and in Rom. 8: "The Father delivered Him over"; and in Isa. 53: "He offered Himself and was offered." Why, then, do we, for whom so great a price was paid, fear? Paul is writing this that we who have been delivered and made the children of God may pay back love to our brothers.

[v. 2:] "…as a fragrance of fine bouquet."

He is alluding to the offering and to the incense which they formerly used in the temple or in the tabernacle of Moses.

[v. 3:] "Let it not be named, etc."

The godly person does not speak such things, nor does he listen to them willingly. See to it, therefore, that you do not sin against yourself and that you do no harm to the conscience of your hearer nor cause him to be offended. Read Mat. 12. One recognizes a tree from its fruit.

[v. 4:] "…the giving of thanks."

That is, from what source does such talk which does not hallow His name praise God? Earlier [4:29] we read: "If anything is good for edifying, etc."; and later [5:19] we shall read: "Speaking to each other in psalms, etc."

[v. 5:] "…wantonness…"

God hates this. Sufficiently terrible examples of this are the Flood and the destruction of Sodom.

[v. 5:] "…greed…"

Paul writes almost everywhere that greed is slavery to idols, and he does this so that you may know that this militates directly against the true God. For this reason, Christ says: "You cannot serve God and mammon." He who places his trust in money cannot place his trust in God. Thus we read in 1 Tim. 6[:6] that they think that "godliness…is profit."

[v. 6:] "**Let no one deceive you…**"

These are the people who today shamelessly say that simple fornication is no sin, although Paul nevertheless does condemn it, because of which we must avoid it. He wants each man to have his own wife. As Christ says in Mat. 19, from the beginning God instituted marriage for this: that they be united with an inseparable bond so that the two become one flesh. There are those who defend greed and laugh with wicked words at, or hold in contempt, the providence and concern of our Father God toward us. They say to Him: "If You will not have provided, who will provide for You?" They also say with Juvenal: "No one has a source from which to seek these things, but you must have them."

[v. 13:] "**But when all things therefore are brought forth, etc.**"

As happens to you for your salvation that your darkness be uncovered by the Word of God that, embarrassed as you are, you may recover your senses; so also it will happen for the salvation of those who are still living in their shameful activities, if the Word of God discloses to them their sins and errors so that they acknowledge their filthiness and come to their senses. This is not something dishonorable but the wound by which the Word of God bites into the conscience of its hearer. You therefore read in 1 Cor. 14[:25]: "The secrets of his heart are manifest, etc."

[v. 14:] "**He, (namely, God), says.**"

We do not find this in Scripture, but Paul seems to be saying this after the custom of the prophets, for "they say" frequently means: "The Lord says."

[v. 15:] "**See, therefore…**"

And this not in the manner of the heathen but in the light of the wisdom of God (as we read later), understanding as you do what the will of the Lord is so that you follow His, and not your, will.

[v. 16:] "Redeeming the time…"

That is, you should seek whenever you can the opportunity to do good and to care for those things which are of Christ so that at any time you are promoting the business of Christ and the work of godliness, "for the days are evil." That is, not only does external persecution fill them, but much more do deceit and the hindrance of both godliness and the word of the Gospel do the same. You see, the devil is trying in every way to hinder the business of the Gospel. Here Paul has called the days "evil," just as in 2 Tim. 3[:1], he called the times "perilous." So, too, in Scriptures days are called "days of salvation," "days of ruin," "days of wrath," etc., not because of the times (because God created them as good), but because of those things which happen to some people in those times.

[v. 18:] "And do not become drunk with wine in which, etc."

That is, do not become drunk with anything or with any inebriation of wine, so that you relate this to wine alone, for this would be condemning a good creation of God. In wine there is extravagance, that is, excess and no necessity. From such excess follows superficiality, foolish talk, empty tales, jokes, filthy songs, unseemly behavior because of which you do no other wickedness more greatly and are despised. But, when our behavior is despicable, who will have correct feelings about us? This situation, therefore, inclines to blasphemy of the title "Christian." In addition, drunkenness turns you away from God. The Savior therefore warns, Luke 21[:34]: "Take heed to yourselves that you not overburden your hearts with gluttony and drunkenness and the cares of this life, and that day come upon you suddenly."

[v. 18:] "...but be filled with the Spirit."

He is opposing this to the inebriation from wine. That is, rather strive earnestly to be drunken with the Spirit (that is, with the affection of God), that the things which are of God may appeal to you, so that, if you come together to comfort each other, your gathering involves the Holy Scriptures, psalms, and other praises of God and that you sing a spiritual song in your hearts to the Lord. Tell me, what would be sweeter to our conscience than if our conversations were like this? Not to mention what a great promotion of the Word of God this would be when we not only assist each other with our saintly behavior but also summon many to the hallowing of God's name! This is having the sort of servants against whom no foe would have anything to justly rebuke.

[v. 21:] "Subjecting [yourselves] to each other…"

[Do this] wherever that ancient serpents lies in ambush and when each of us comes in contact with Scriptures. He also wants us to be prudent in other matters more than in the rest of the things from which contentions and disagreements stem which violate Christian love. ((("Surpassing each other in honor."))) Paul therefore adds [v. 21]: "Submit yourselves one to another in the fear of God, that each fear God and trust his brother." Should it happen that a brother err, let him know no more than is necessary. In Rom. 12, he says: "Surpass each other in honor." On this occasion, he also adds more about the rights of being master and being subject: first, regarding spouses; second, between children and parents; and third, between masters and their servants.

[v. 22:] "Let wives be subject to their own husbands…"

If you should throw all the arguments of teachers of oratory into one place, you would not have persuaded spouses to have mutual love as much as Paul does here. The natural man judges that this is of no benefit; but see how greatly Paul has magnified this so that, in the meantime, he depicts for us that incomprehensible unity of Christ and the Church and the limitless love with which Christ has attended us on the basis of the unity of husband and wife. (With reference to this very matter, read Luther "On Christian Freedom.") You see, the devil (who promotes fornications and loves adulteries, and whose teaching is, as Paul says, that prohibition of marriage which has provided a foundation for the celibacy of priests to propagate lusts more freely, as we are seeing) tries with his remarkable talent to separate what God has joined together and always attempts with his ordinances to overturn what God has ordained.

We certainly have experienced our own evil, namely, what punishment of blindness those must suffer who want to improve on the things of God which they despise. However, the more that the devil sows his seeds of disharmony between spouses who are held together by no love for God, the more horror we see and the more souls perish when there is no spiritual person to aid with his holy counsel those who are struggling. For this reason, we must deplore our times in which even violence forbids us from supporting with some advice those who are about to perish. It was for this reason that Moses once permitted the Jews a bill of divorcement because of their hardened hearts (Mat. 19, etc.).

CHAPTER 6.

Not only does he say "love" but also "honor," for honor has connected to itself respect [*timor*], just as he said above that a wife should respect [*revereor*] her husband. He also wants children to obey their parents in all things and to serve their will and, if there is need, to serve even their necessity. This is not simply the first commandment but the first commandment in promise, that is, which has a natural promise connected to itself (namely, "that it may be well with you and you may live long on the earth," as you see in Exo. 20[:12]). As a result, accept the fact that Christians should not despise the carnal promises, and believe God's Word that you may be justified. With reference to this subject, read more in passages of Philippians.

At the end of this epistle, he is warning us diligently not to be neglectful. After we have been justified, let us live; for these are not visible enemies but invisible and powerful ones who are attacking our salvation with both ambushes and open warfare. Thus you also read in 1 Peter 5[:8]: "Be sober, etc." You cannot resist these with human force, because these are not flesh and blood, that is, human beings, just as Christ has it in Mat. 16[:17]: "Flesh and blood has not revealed this to you." ((That is, you have not learned this from a human being.)) However, we have this work with courage of our spirit that we may resist this with our spirits and spiritual clubs, namely, with the Word of God, as we cling to it with strong faith, just as we read in the Psalm [5:12]: "Its truth will surround you as with a shield."

[v. 14:] **"Stand therefore…"**
Scripture often and freely uses military terms.

[v. 14:] **"…with the belt…"**
They were in the habit of covering the part around the loins with a leather belt in warfare. The prophet says about Christ in Isa. 11[:5]: "Righteousness will be the belt of His loins and faithfulness the belt of his reins."

[v. 18:] **"…in every prayer…"**
See here with what great boldness we must call upon God, that is, without ceasing and with very great fervor and eagerness,

especially that He send workers into His harvest (Mat. 9[:38]), and not only this, but also that He give the power of His Spirit to the same workers that they may speak the Word with confidence and freedom of their spirit. When Paul demands this, he is certainly faulting the rashness of we who are taking all things for granted. For this reason, the disciples pray, Acts 4[:29]: "And You, O Lord, look upon their threats, etc."

[v. 18:] "…with sincerity…"
That is, with sincere feeling and understanding which have a taste for the pure Christ, and not corrupted with foreign teachings which not only obscure but even erase Christ. Amen.

38

THE ANNOTATIONS OF JOHANNES BUGENHAGEN OF POMERANIA ON THE EPISTLE OF PAUL TO THE PHILIPPIANS.

This epistle was written to those who had been justified through faith in Christ. In his chains, Paul therefore advises them to continue to grow in their faith in Christ and mutual love for each other. The preachers or teachers of human righteousness lay severe waste to both of those.[5] You see, when they have taught us, we attribute righteousness and salvation to our works and lose our true righteousness and salvation, that is, Christ. For Christ is of no use to us if righteousness comes from works, Gal. 2[:21]: "If righteousness comes through the Law, Christ then has died in vain"; and Gal. 5[:4]: "Christ has become superfluous to you," that is, of no use. Whoever you are who are justified through the Law, you have fallen out of grace. But when we have embraced the righteousness of works; tell me, please, what harmony can there be among us? After all, it cannot help but happen that, if we neglect true righteousness, some prefer their own works to others, while others prefer their works to ours, some will not judge others and others will not judge us, some will contend with others, etc. From this stem hatreds, rivalries, sects—the sort of fruits we have been seeing so far; and Christian love we have been seeing nowhere. Cursed, therefore, be the righteousness of works which has produced such fruits!

In this epistle, therefore, he condemns workers of evil and these preachers of human righteousness because of their egregious

---

5   That is, the false teachers undermine both faith in Christ and love of the brethren.

disgrace and commands us to be careful of them, namely, of these who are destroyers of the entire Christian edifice. If the righteousness of Christ not save, we remain that which we are; that is, blind and condemned. If, on the other hand, we believe in Him, He saves us.

Next, if we truly believe in Him, we shall become His brothers, something which He became for us so that, just as He has dwelt among us, so also we have become subject to one another in the fear of God through love.

Notice that, when the apostles command the works of God, they are commanding nothing other than those which necessarily are the companions of faith and which the Spirit which possesses our heart requires by His own nature. Therefore, Paul calls these "the fruits of the Spirit" (Gal. 5[:22–23]), for they are the living testimonies of the living faith within. Thus the apostles command, or rather advise, that we not be sluggish and try to despise the things which are of the Spirit, but that we learn from the Word of God in what direction to go and often sigh to God, without whom we can do nothing, and who gives us both to will and to be able to do according to His good will. That good work which He has begun in us, He will complete until the day of His coming, as he says in ch. 1 and 2.

Here you see that Paul is attributing nothing to our efforts, not even the beginning of our faith. When, however, the false apostles command works, they command them in such a way that they teach us to seek righteousness in those works and, in fact, that those works are righteousness itself and not the fruit of preceding righteousness. They teach rather the contrary order and want to produce the tree from its fruits. Furthermore, they especially teach and magnify the works which the Spirit Himself does not require. At the same time, they forbid those which are not at all opposed to the Spirit. This is something they do in such a way that they take care of their own glory and belly. These people Paul calls "the enemies of the cross of Christ whose god is their belly and whose glory is in their shame" ([Phi. 3:18–19]).

[v. 1:] "Paul and Timothy, the servants of Jesus Christ…"
   This is the true title of Christians and ministers of the Word of God.

[v. 1:] "…along with the bishops and deacons:"
   Look: there is more than one bishop in one city. They, therefore, are "ministers of the Word of God and stewards of the mysteries," as Paul calls them (1 Cor.[4:1]). Moreover, deacons are servants of the saints whom the Church has chosen for this duty, namely, the dispensing of the goods of the Church to the poor whom they serve as the need arises. The Church should select citizens of the best reputation to do this: people who care faithfully for her property lest that happen just as we see today when people neglect the poor and busy themselves with the goods of the Church when they ought to be the distributors thereof. That is the way the apostles discussed the matter when they were about to elect deacons, Acts 6[:2–4]: "It is not just for us to abandon the Word of God and wait on tables. Therefore, brothers, consider seven men of you who have a good reputation and are filled with the Holy Spirit, and appoint them over this task. We, however, shall be instant in prayer and in the ministry of the Word. These words pleased the whole crowd." (With reference to bishops and deacons, read 1 Tim. 3.)

[v. 2:] "Grace to you and peace, etc."
   To "God" (which is a title of majesty), he adds the title "Father," that you not be fearful of the title of majesty, for you are hearing that He is the Father and *your* Father. To the name "Jesus Christ," however, he adds a title of majesty and calls Him "Lord,"

that you not despise Him as base because He has become a human being on your behalf.

[v. 3:] I thank my God in every, etc."

It is the duty of the genuine apostle not only to preach but also to pray that the Spirit of God work in the hearts of his audience and also to thank God continually as he perceives that he has promoted the Word of God. Such a person, you see, shows that God has truly sent him both to seek and to thirst for the salvation of his hearers. You see an outstanding example of this in Paul.

[v. 6:] "...having the conviction as I do of this very thing..."

Here you see that which we said earlier is very far from the truth, namely, that in the matter of salvation we are attributing something to our judgment, powers and plans. You cannot even begin anything which is good, unless God grant this. After all, He is "our Alpha and Omega, the beginning of all things." [Rev. 1:8] Next, the first good work is faith. John 6[:29]: "This is the work of God, etc." The next is love, that is, the fruit of faith.

[v. 6:] "...He will perform it until the day of Jesus Christ."

This marks perseverance, for, unless you will have persevered, you will not reach the finish line. Between the beginning and the end, however, you will experience how much more necessary Christ is to you. After all, unless He be the Shepherd of all the foolish, who among so many mishaps and so many temptations of mind and body would persist? Psa. 37[:23]: "The Lord directs a person's steps, etc."

[v. 7:] "Just as is rightful to me..."

The person who truly loves in Christ cannot have bad feelings about his brother. However, he can respect his brother, and love accomplishes this very thing. You have here, therefore, an example of the true shepherd who, after the example of Christ, gives up his life for his sheep and, even in chains, loves them not with some carnal affection but with Christian love. This, Paul says, is "in the bowels of Jesus Christ." [v. 8]

[v. 9:] "This I pray, namely, that your love, etc."

He wants mutual love to grow among us, that is, "in all knowledge and wisdom," that is, in faith and the knowledge of Christ, that we not place works themselves ahead of faith nor take them as righteousness. This is what he says in Romans [1:17] ("...from faith to faith") that we may be spiritual and pass judgment on all things. He says, [v. 10]: "...that you prove the things which are excellent," that is, the things which please the will of God. This is something which he says in this way in Rom. 12[:2]: "...that you may approve what is the good and acceptable and perfect will of God," so that whatever is well-pleasing to us and even on whatever occasion, whether that happen to us because of the Gospel or because of our sin, we know that we are receiving that from the hand of our kind Father and Shepherd. These things, therefore, are excellent: that we place God ahead of all humans and that we place love ahead of all precepts, laws and works, just as Christ teaches often in the Gospel and shows by His very example.

[v. 10:] "...that you may be sincere..."

First, sincere in faith, that you not allow your knowledge of Christ to become mixed in with human traditions and teachings. Next, sincere in love, that your affection toward your neighbor be of such a quality that he also knows that you are tolerant of his weakness that we [sic] not cause an offense in some way. After all, "love bears all things," [1 Cor. 13:7] just as we see that Christ kept secret and bore many things in His weak disciples. In sum, he wants us to be wise in such a way that we are not abusing our knowledge. 1 Cor. 8[:1–2]: "Knowledge inflates; charity builds up. If anyone thinks that he knows something, etc."

[v. 10:] "…until the day of Christ."
He is again noting perseverance.

[v. 12:] "Furthermore, brothers, I want you to know…"
Because he loves them, as he makes known to his friends the things which have been happening to him, Paul at the same time warns them through this that this persecution which he is suffering should not become an offense to those who still have weak minds, until they learn that the cross must glorify us, regardless of whatever is imposed upon us. He speaks in this way in Eph. 3[:13]: "I beseech you that you not fail in my tribulations on your behalf, which is your glory." As we have it in Romans [8:28]: "All things work together for good to those who love God," even those things which indicate a very wicked flesh. Thus, when confessors of the Gospel receive the attacks of curses, persecutions, and death, those things are so far from harming them that through such things that cunning God of ours is promoting the Gospel so that it happens to unbelievers and those who are still unknowing of the Gospel that something is occurring of which they perhaps have not yet heard. Also, those who already believe are receiving strength when they see that the preaching (for the sake of which the preacher now is willing to die) was not deceptive.

[v. 15:] "Some indeed … through envy…"
He is saying here nothing about those preachers who preach something other than the teaching of Christ, although the world is full of such preachers. But how would Paul rejoice about them? He himself also expresses this sufficiently when he says:

"Christ nevertheless is being announced." Paul, then, is saying about them: "Those are preaching the teaching of Christ." Some of these are indeed doing this very thing with an evil spirit, namely, that Paul not be released, for he is the instigator of a sect of such a type that he is causing an uproar everywhere and upsetting the tranquility of the state because of it. However, he is not describing four kinds of preachers here, as some think. Actually, he is describing only two, for the two latter ones which seem to be types are only an explanation and clarification of the two preceding ones. Here you have it that many preachers announce the actual truth but nevertheless not truly, so that you always recognize that "the kingdom of God is not in word but in power." [1 Cor. 4:20]

[v. 23:] **"For to me to live is Christ…"**

He is explaining what he had said, [v. 20]: "Christ will be magnified"; for, whether I shall have lived, I shall have lived for Christ and not for myself, and I shall preach His glory and produce fruit with my work of preaching. That is, I shall be useful to those who are going to hear the Word from me. We read the following in Gal. 2.[20]: "I live, and yet I no longer live, etc." And whether I die, my dying is to my gain. You see, if I have died because of the perils of this life or because of my duty, I shall be crowned with Christ on that day, just as he says in 2 Tim. 4[:17]: "I am now delivered, etc." Although the latter would be better as far as I am concerned, nevertheless the latter is necessary for you. This is the sublime affection of the saints, which we, still uncultivated as we are for spiritual subjects, cannot understand. Nevertheless, we read them usefully for this purpose: that we may see and recognize our weakness; to wit, how far distant we, who flee from and shudder at the cross and death as things most damnable, still are from the kingdom of God. Nevertheless, when Paul was handed over, he said, as we read later in 3[:12]: "Not that I grasped perfection and already was perfect, etc." Where, then, are those who have judged that perfection is theirs because of their cold works, ceremonies, and sects, etc.?

[v. 25:] "…for your advancement and joy…"

This is the joy of your faith; that is, that your faith may cause you to rejoice and exult richly and with full joy through the Spirit of Christ. I say, may you glory in me or about me that I have returned. Note the mutual joy of the saints. They glory over Paul, and Paul glories over them, just as he says in the following chapter, [v. 16]: "…that I may rejoice in the day of Christ, etc." This is not carnal rejoicing but that which happens, as he says, "in Christ Jesus." He writes in this way in Rom. 1[:12]: "…that I may take common comfort in you through your and my mutual faith simultaneously"; and in 1 Cor. 12[:26]: "If one member is glorified, all the members rejoice together with it."

[v. 27]: "…as much as becomes the Gospel…"

From this passage all the way to that passage in the following chapter where he says [v. 24]: "Moreover, I hope in the Lord Jesus, etc.," he commends very highly mutual love among themselves. This, however, cannot happen unless we subject ourselves mutually without strife and have the same feelings unanimously. This will happen if we preserve the teaching of Christ unmixed and pure, not admitting the teaching of humans who glory in their works and wretchedly tear at the sacred body of Christ (because they are dogs). You see, when we allow that human teaching rather than the pure Word of God, it cannot help but happen that we dispute; that we boast in ourselves; that we pass judgment on others; that we place ourselves ahead of others; and that we become separated by sects from the body of Christ. This is just what the Lord says in Isa. 1[:21]: "How has the faithful city become a whore, filled with lying? … Righteousness lived in her, etc."

We certainly have been suffering until now the punishments of great blindness and monstrous sins because of our contempt of the Gospel and our acceptance of human teachings. Our Savior says about these, Mat. 15[:9]: "In vain do they worship Me, as they teach the doctrines, etc."; that is, they are truly committing idolatry and are lifting up something other than God in place of God, as they worship human things rather than divine ones.

However, where the Gospel is pure, there faith is without complication and love is sincere. After all, those cannot disagree who hold onto one Word of God; who rejoice over each other; who know that they have received all things through the mercy of God; who indicate to one another that they always know that; and who stand or fall in the Lord. Here, although their gifts and works and exercises and crosses differ, nevertheless no one condemns the interests of another, for whatever individuals do pleases all. They tolerate the weaknesses of others, they use their gifts mutually for purposes of utility. One comforts another, and one helps another. In brief, each person submits himself to others and neither equals or prefers himself to others. That's the way true Christians feel.

That Paul may convince the Philippians of this, he uses the very great example of Christ, who arrives at the heights of His glory by casting himself down and submitting Himself very greatly. This he does here to shame deservedly those who arrogate for themselves the name "Christian," and who with empty strife look to and pursue their own glory, but are never going to reach true glory and are the stumbling blocks of Christians rather than members of Christ. They finally become the authors of human doctrines who used to boast about having the Gospel.

[v. 28:] "…and this from God."

That clearly means that He is the cause of your salvation, that you cannot ascribe merit to yourself because you are suffering.

((Suffering is the gift of God.)) For you have here this passage that one cannot suffer on behalf of God, just as one cannot believe in God, unless God give him that faith. We know that Peter paid the penalties for his presumption when he kept denying Christ. The Lord says: "Watch and pray, etc." [Mark 14:38]

CHAPTER 2.

He is continuing what he had begun earlier, to wit, not just advising but confirming [or swearing] by all the sacred situations of Christians and by adding the example of Christ that we not experience arrogant feelings, etc.

[v. 5:] "Let this feeling be in you…"

Paul is speaking about Christ the Man, whose example he is presenting to us. It was not His attempt nor thought nor wish to snatch glory away from God, although He nevertheless truly was in the form of God; that is, although He was truly God. You see, He attributes to the Father glory and all things, as you see in the Gospel of John. Rather, He set Himself aside from the glory of His majesty and came down not only *to* people but even *beneath* people that for our sake He might become obedient to the Father unto even the most shameful death (Isa. 53). All power in heaven and on earth, therefore, was given to Him (Mat. 28). He received the name in which alone we must be saved (Acts 4), and whom all peoples, tribes and languages serve (Dan. 7), so that even the gates of hell tremble at such great glory of Christ, as we read in Eph. 3: "that the manifest wisdom of God might become known to the princes and powers in the heavens through the Church, etc." God raised Him from the dead, placed Him at His right hand, etc. (Eph. 1) Why, then, do we (who are nothing) not submit to our brothers when such great majesty submitted itself? Why are we forgetting those words: "He who humbles himself will be exalted, [Luke 14:11]? — or those words: "He who thinks that he is something when he is nothing is deceiving himself" (Gal. 6[:3])?

[v. 6:] "…the figure…"
That is, the appearance or form, as in Heb. 4. "He was tempted in all things" (Heb. 2[:18]).

[v. 12:] "Work out your salvation…"
That is, do the things which are involved in your salvation and not those which are involved with other matters, so that you all have the same feelings and are not seeking your own advancement, etc., as we said earlier. In this way, you will behave worthy of the Gospel of Christ, etc. He says: "Do this with fear and trembling," namely, before God. It is a certain thing that those who behave otherwise do not have the fear of God. He says the same thing in Eph. 5[:21]: "…submitting yourselves to each other in the fear of Christ." However, lest you claim free will from this because he says: "Work our your salvation," he adds: "…for it is God who works in you, etc." What he adds, however, namely, "in proportion to the good pleasure of the heart" (as if God does this very thing in us because of *our* good pleasure) does not agree. So that I do not say that Paul is attributing something to our own pursuits, how does it agree that God works in us in proportion to our own will? Paul writes that it is given to us to will. The Greek reads: "ὑπὲρ τῆς εὐδοκίας - in proportion to the good pleasure," that you may understand *His* good pleasure and not *ours*, as we read in Eph. 1[:9]: "… according to the good pleasure of His will, etc." The good will, you see, is His, because He (and not our effort) works in us through His grace.

[v. 15:] "…in the midst of a corrupt nation…"
1 Peter 2[:12]: "…having your conversation, etc."

[v. 15:] "...as lights..."

Mat. 5[:14]: "You are the light of the world." And elsewhere [Luke 12:35]: "Gird about your loins, and have your burning lights in your hands." Also, [Mat. 5:16]: "...that they may see your good works, etc." However, take care here that the light within you not be darkness. I say, you are the light because of the word of life which you are carrying for the illumination of the nations. The psalmist writes,119:105: "...a lamp for my feet, etc." Both the ignorance of God and death, where the Word of Life does not exist, are pure darkness, although all things may appear very holy. As a result, Paul says that you are permitted to boast until the day, that is, until the coming of Christ, because through my Gospel, God is accomplishing something in you, whenever I hear: "Well done, good servant, etc." I rejoice or glory so much about this that I am going to rejoice even if I am sacrificed, that is, even if someone slay me for God because of your faith which you have received through my preaching. For this reason, you yourselves cannot help but rejoice. See again here the outstanding love and sublime affection of the saints!

Notice that he is calling the behavior of the Philippians "the sacrifice and service of your faith," and thus signifies to them that they are a fine fragrance to God in every place (2 Cor. 2[:15]), just as you read often about carnal sacrifices in the ancient Law, as in Num. 18[:17]: "You will offer their fat for a sweet fragrance to the Lord." You also read about the sacrifice of Christ in Eph. 5[:2]: "He has given Himself, etc." The behavior of Christians, however, is "the sacrifice and service of faith," because whatever you may have thought or said or done as something good; "it is still impossible to please God without faith" (Heb. 11[:6]). Those things are "the offering of Cain," about which the Law says [Gen. 4:3]: "The Lord had respect for Abel, etc." For "whatsoever is not of faith is sin" (Rom. 14[:23]). Also: "To the clean all things are clean" (Titus 1[:15]).

((Works without faith.)) Your works are without faith when you do them contrary to conscience, that is, when you do not believe that they please God or when you doubt whether what you are doing pleases God. Those works are without faith when you live in hatred of your brother, and for that reason you hear: "When you offer your gift at the altar, etc." [Mat. 5:23] They are also without faith when you seek to be justified through such works, for only faith in Christ justifies, as you read later in ch. 3[:9].

[v. 23:] "Moreover, I hope, etc."

See with what diligence he commends his messengers, as we said earlier about deacons! For those who have the care of the preaching of the Gospel and the support of the poor must be not only approved of God but also beyond every suspicion of greed. (See Rom. 12.)

[v. 26:] "…all…"

We must interpret his prayer in the common manner.

CHAPTER 3.

He does not rejoice in the Lord who rejoices and trusts in his own righteousness, in his own wisdom and in his own wealth—in sum, who finds something in himself in which to trust. For the poor have the Gospel preached to them; that is, they receive the good news. That is, the Gospel belongs to those whom Christ addresses as "sinners," when He says: "I have not come to call the righteous but sinners, etc."[Mat. 9:13] For this reason, Jeremiah writes [9:23]: "Thus says the Lord: 'Let the wise man not glory… but let him glory in this, that he knows Me.'" You see, you will always and forever be upset unless you have learned by faith to glory in God alone (something which Scripture advises everywhere).

A conscience in temptation will be unable to stand up in the presence of God in advance of that terrible day of judgment, because we are sinners and actually sin itself, unless we believe that God has made Christ to be for us our wisdom, righteousness, sanctification, and redemption (1 Cor. 1[:30]). This is the joy of Christians that, when they look down within themselves, they find nothing except condemnation, for "the One who handed down His Only-Begotten for us, how has He not with Him given us all things?," (Rom. 8[:32]). But here at the same time rises up the brood of vipers of that ancient serpent, and, at the same time, the ravening wolves and shameless dogs are tearing at, and keeping busy cutting off the Lord's flock from the body of the Lord, as they try to lead away their minds on account of their lack of guile, just as the serpent led the young lady Eve off, as we read in 2 Cor. [11:3].

Those truly are teaching us to trust in our works, in our righteousness, and in our merits. For this reason, they are making Christ useless to us as He was to the Pharisees, whom Paul later calls "the enemies of the cross of Christ," that is, who teach not the glory of God but are seeking their own gain and glory to their eternal destruction and confusion. After all, what else were they gaining who have their belly as their god and are unwilling for us to be justified solely from faith in Christ? They are shameless dogs which are never sated, as we read in Isa. 56[:11].

They are workers of evil who conduct their own business in the imperial harvest but not in that of the Lord. At the judgment of God they hear: "Depart from Me, you workers of iniquity"; and this, despite the fact that they wanted to boast: "Lord, haven't we prophesied in Your name, etc.?" These boast that they are the circumcision, although they actually are not the circumcision before God but the cutting up and laceration of the teaching of the Gospel.

Notice here, therefore, that the well-known pseudapostles of that time who were of the flesh of the Jews who kept boasting that they were the people of God to whom He had made the promises, whom He had honored so often and of whose blood Christ also had been born; I say, notice that they kept teaching that the works of the Law were necessary for salvation.

Paul verbally attacks them very bitterly and with sorrow, as he does nearly everywhere; for, if you have sought justification through works, Christ is not your righteousness. Therefore this is denying Christ and putting up the Antichrist in His place. 1 John 2[:22]: "He is the Antichrist who denies the Father and the Son." ((They are not denying Christ openly, but His power.)) If this, then, is true about those who were trying to introduce the works and righteousness of the Law (the author of which was God), what shall we say about our own people who battle over purely human and fictitious laws and traditions as they teach the doctrines and commandments of humans as well as the doctrines of demons, as the apostle calls them?

[v. 3:] "For we are the circumcision…"

Here you have the spiritual circumcision, the spiritual seed of Abraham, who believed God, and it was imputed to him for righteousness. The circumcision of the flesh was not righteousness, but only a sign of faith, as we read in Rom. 4[:11]. Those, then, who do not have the actuality (that is, the righteousness of faith) are carrying around only an empty sign of circumcision. You see, it has to be a circumcision of the heart in the spirit and not in the letter. (See Rom. 2.) Moses speaks about this in Deu. 30[:6]: "The Lord your God will circumcise your heart and the heart of your seed so that you love the Lord your God with all your heart and with all your soul, that you may be able to live."

This spiritual circumcision is not only a cutting away of some impure affections so that your ears do not listen willingly to shameful things, your mouth does not say them willingly, and your hands do not do that; but it is also the cutting away of faithlessness, which is the course of all sins. You have begun to be justified, that is, to be circumcised, but you are not yet perfectly justified; that is, you do not yet believe perfectly. For who will boast of this when Paul says that he has not yet reached this point, despite the fact that God is imputing this very thing to you who have already begun to believe?

You must always be advancing from faith to faith, as the Spirit teaches you within. That is, you must be experiencing circumcision at all times and be receiving Baptism by fire and the Holy Spirit that ultimately all the old corruption is finally thrown out and burned. After all, there is no one in whom there is no hypocrisy and who does not attribute something to his own righteousness until that fiery Spirit burns all that so that you finally can, as a perfect man, meet Christ, as we have it in Eph.[4:13]. While you still cling to some external things, you cannot be united with Christ perfectly. This Spirit acts gradually in a wondrous manner so that all things fail in which we seemed to have some confidence. The result is that you finally acknowledge that Christ alone is your righteousness and Mediator and that you are beloved in the beloved Son of God.

Those who magnify external righteousness do not know Christ. This is what Paul here is calling "boasting in the flesh," that is, in external things and in the works of the Law. We learn of that circumcision and of that Spirit of Baptism as God reveals these in us every day. Let us only ask God that He comfort us with His Spirit and that we go forward and not turn around and go backward.

[v. 3:] "...the Spirit..."

John 4[:23]: "God is a Spirit, etc." He is of not of the flesh, not of the letter, that is, of external things, but of a good will of His heart which God gave through His Spirit and which Christ earned for us if we believe. Psa. 1[:3]: "[His delight is] in the Law of the

Lord." See how carefully he casts away confidence in the works of the Law so that we rejoice in Christ alone. He says: "Ahead of all the pseudapostles, I can glory in the flesh of the Law as a saint and very distinguished Jew, but I have counted everything as dung because of my knowledge of Christ, who surpasses all things."

You see, the more you have learned to know Christ, the more all those works and all the righteousnesses in which people trust topple down. You are continually receiving more illumination and have been strengthened to such an extent that even the gates of hell cannot prevail against your faith. You remember only to bear still the weaknesses of others. You also remember that you still have not grasped everything, that you are not yet perfect, that you still are ignorant of many matters. In fact, you are compelled to condemn all your past, as the truth demands. Just as Christ bears your lack of wisdom, so also you must bear that of others. The condition of those who are still straying is better than that of those who think they have already grasped everything. We are still lacking in many areas; but Paul here is comforting us, and says: "If you perceive something differently within yourselves, God will also reveal this to you."

((Why God permits the saints to sin.)) God permits the saints to be ignorant of many things. In some matters, they have even sinned. After we have discovered our sin (because of God's grace), let us learn not to trust ourselves. We are foolish little lambs, but, under the hand of Christ, our Shepherd, we cannot perish.

((The true worship of God.)) We worship God in Spirit, if we are carried by our faith and trust in Him and fear Him.

The person who knows that Christ is ruling and is triumphing over death, sin, and hell knows the power of the resurrection of Christ by which same power we believe, as we read in Eph. 1[:19–20]—I say, that person knows the power of the resurrection of Christ. Therefore we read in Rom. 4[:25]: "He was raised for our justification" and that we might be righteous; and in Eph. 2[:4]: "God, who is rich in mercy, etc." We cannot understand this without the Spirit teaching us, for this is true, Christian faith.

We recognize our sharing of the afflictions of Christ when we understand that all the afflictions or Christ are ours, too; and again, that all our afflictions are Christ's and have been blessed in Christ, and that whatever happens to us is the good will of Christ. Col. 1[:24]: "I am now rejoicing, etc." By such a sharing of afflictions and temptations we finally arrive at our full resurrection, just as Christ reached His. Blessed is the person who understands this! The Christian does not see how far he *has* run (otherwise he would ascribe it to his own righteousness), but how far he *still must* run. In fact, he condemns his own past so much that he rejoices solely in the righteousness of Christ through which he believes he must be saved.

[20:] "For our conversation…"

The elect are called "the kingdom of Christ," "the kingdom of God," "the kingdom of heaven," in which God Himself rules. Therefore it is also called "the kingdom of light." On the other hand, and on the contrary, the kingdom of the world is said to be "the kingdom of darkness," etc. Therefore we read, Col. 3[:1]: "If you be risen along with Christ, etc." And here Paul speaks of your "conversation which is in heaven."

"What is left, my brothers, etc."

We also have this very witness often in the Gospel that Christ will return from heaven to deliver us fully from the body of this death. 1 John 3[:2]: "We know that when He shall have appeared, etc."; and [v. 3]: "Everyone who, etc." You read about our resurrection and our body which is going to be glorified in 1 Cor. 15. Therefore, the Savior says, Mat. 13[:43]: "Then the righteous will shine like the sun in the kingdom of their Father." Lest any natural person ask: "How will bodies which have been consumed in earth, in water and air and by beasts rise up again?" He adds another effective agent: "Every word will not be impossible before God. Thus God is willing and able." The unbeliever argues the contrary, but the believer says with John [1.2:2]: "We know that when He will have appeared, etc., we shall be the children of God"; and with Paul, Rom. 8[:22]: "We know that the whole creation groans, etc."

CHAPTER 4.

[v. 3:]   "…σύζυγος"

This means "spouse" and "partner." People therefore take this to mean Paul's wife who, he says, is his "*germana*,"—that is, his true and sincere partner, for she was a Christian and promoter of the Gospel, as was Paul.

[v. 3:] "…whose names are in the book of life."

These are the people whom God knows as His own, as we have said. We read in Psa. 90[:14] and Mat. 5[:12], "Rejoice and be glad, etc." But we read about the damned, Psa. 68[:28]: "Let them be erased from the book of the living."

[v. 4:] "…again…"

He says this because he cannot preach sufficiently this very joy to weak consciences.

[v. 5:] "…moderation…"

This is that moderation with which you do not support your perception but by which you accommodate others as with God, although in all things. Paul wants you to show this not to some but to all people, even to your enemies and those who can appear to be your inferiors. As you see, he teaches this moderation throughout almost this entire epistle. Here the flesh responds: "If I shall have preserved this moderation, people will hold me in contempt, they will harm me and take my possessions away from me, and no one will respect me, etc." Paul responds: "The Lord is near you. He will take care of everything for you. Do not worry about anything, but only ask God for the things you want and thank Him for the things you have received. Oh word of faith which you have believed in every necessity of body and spirit! May it be sufficient against every temptation of our unbelief!"

[v. 7:] "The peace of God…"

This is that peace which God gives to believers so that, rejoicing as they do about the forgiveness of their sins and the grace which God has given them, they embrace each other with mutual love. It surpasses every understanding, for human reason cannot comprehend it. Reason judges that sweet things are peace as far as the flesh is concerned. Moreover, the peace of God also rejoices in tribulations(Rom. 5[:3]), for it knows that everything that happens pleases God and that all things yield to our salvation. This is peace of conscience which, he says, protects us through Christ in faith and oneness, about which I have spoken much.

[v. 10:] "I have rejoiced, etc."

This is a passage of thanksgiving for a gift received and concerns the alms received from the Philippians. See here how the spiritual person gives thanks with many words (but without base flattery) and how much teaching abounds. First, he shows that it is the responsibility of the good preacher to require nothing of his hearers. Next, it is the function of his hearers to alleviate the needs of their preacher. Furthermore, that the preacher not offer pseudapostles an opportunity, he must also abstain from some things which he is owed by right, just as Paul stayed away from taking anything from the Thessalonians and Corinthians. Also, things which people give in this way must give way to the convenience of those who are the givers; and these things have been their sacrifice which is acceptable to God (Heb. 13[:15]). Such sacrifices placate God. Paul also says that God will return abundantly to those who give (2 Cor. 9[:6]). Finally,—do not neglect this—the saints are content with the things which they have and, safe as they are, they rejoice under the providence of God, just as a small child is happy under the hand of his father and remains unworried, whatever happens. For his father has said: "I have taught you, etc." (Pro. 4.) May your behavior be without greed, and may you be content with your present situation.

OUTSTANDING PASSAGES IN THE EPISTLE TO THE PHILIPPIANS.

CHAPTER 1.

1. The love of the godly and evangelical pastor; "I thank my God, etc." [v. 3]

2. Where he intermixes that he is not even permitted to begin a good thing without God: "He who has begun, etc." [v. 6]

3. Some indeed preach the teaching of Christ but not in a Christian way: "I want you to know, etc." [v. 12]

4. The disposition of the saints who want to die: "For to me to live is Christ, etc." [v. 21]

5. To suffer for God is a gift of God: "But to you it is given, etc. [v. 29]

CHAPTER 2.

1. The unanimity of the teaching and disposition of Christians, after the example of Christ: "If there is anything, etc." [v. 1]

2. Such behavior is the service and sacrifice of faith: "In fact, even, etc." [v. 17]

3. Those who distribute alms should be free of any suspicion of greed: "I hope, etc." [v. 23]

CHAPTER 3.

1. Be careful of ravening dogs which are turning you away from the righteousness of faith: "Beware, etc." [v. 2]

2. The righteousness of faith is nothing, but the righteousness of faith and the circumcision in the Spirit is salvation: "For we are the circumcision."

3. [v. 12]: "We have not yet grasped," that is, that we are fully justified, so that we are always hungering and thirsting after righteousness: "Not that I apprehended, etc."

4. The behavior of Christians is not earthly, for "our conversation, etc." [v. 20]

CHAPTER 4.

1. We must always rejoice in the Lord, for we have left worry to Him: "Rejoice, etc. [v. 4]

2. Thanksgiving without flattery is filled with very Christian teaching: "I have rejoiced, etc." [v. 10]

THE END.

THE ANNOTATIONS OF JOHANNES BUGENHAGEN OF POMERANIA ON THE EPISTLE OF PAUL TO THE COLOSSIANS.

This epistle is almost the same as the epistle to the Ephesians, except that this is shorter and that he here condemns the teaching of human philosophy, that is, of human wisdom and logic. These know nothing except the elements, that is, the external things of this world in which reason imagines through hypocrisy a worship of God and justification, although God alone justifies and not our works or satisfaction. God also wants to receive worship in spirit and has no need of our good works. After all, there is nothing so opposed to our faith, that is, to our salvation, than when we begin to evaluate the things which are of God on the basis of human reason.

Sometimes human reason will not deny that God made man and that He was made, suffered, died, and rose again for you. It sometimes tries to persuade that there is no forgiveness of sins (because deeds cannot become corrupted). Sometimes it will be persuaded that there is life after this one and that there is a resurrection of the flesh after the destruction thereof. About all these, it will have to give a reckoning in the judgment to come. However, it does not even believe what it nevertheless sees present in some people, namely, that the Spirit of God can change a person in this life so that he clearly is different from what he was before.

Briefly, "the natural person does not perceive the things which are of God, for they are foolishness to him," [1 Cor. 2:14](as James himself calls them). This is earthly, natural, and diabolical wisdom, a wisdom which produces for us various kinds of worship and observances according to the elements of the world, to all of which, were we truly Christians, we would be dead in Christ and celebrating a happy Sabbath that we who have Christ alone might have all things; that is, that we might judge nothing as necessary for salvation except Christ alone and that all other things are free for our use and for that of our neighbors either to do or to omit.

Tell me, please, why do human traditions trouble us? After all, we ought to know that Christ has abrogated on the cross the Law which God once gave—not so that it does not exist, but so that it cannot condemn our deeds nor make us guilty. Indeed, we have learned from God that our righteousness is not the works of the Law but Christ.

Furthermore, those fictitious revelations lead to the greater seduction of the world, for they lead to the new growth of superstitions and strange worship of angels and saints and man-made superstitions. We have learned to hope and trust in these to the great harm of our Creator God and Savior, Intercessor and Mediator, our one Lord Jesus Christ. ((He intervenes for us (Rom. 8[:27]). He is the one Mediator (1 Tim. 2[:5]). He is our Priest (Heb. 4[:14] and 6[:20]); and our Advocate (1 John 2[:1]).)) That we may strengthen those false religions we have abused the ministry of the Word, twisted Scripture, and turned the truth of God into a lie.

We still see relics of this (after Scripture ceased to be preached) in those chants and public readings which the Church sings and chants about the saints according to the ordination of the Church, as they say. We are thinking especially of the ones about the Blessed Virgin Mother of our Savior, about whom we read almost all the things which were written about Christ and the wisdom of God, as well as the abuses we have done to the Sacrament of the Body and Blood of Christ, when we celebrate Masses in commemoration of St. Anna, St. Sebastian, and St. Peter, and for the dead. We have abused it contrary to the institution of Christ, who wanted this Sacrament not to be *offered* to the faithful, but to be eaten in remembrance of Him. But we have made a marketplace of Christ's Sacrament.

For these reasons, I believe that Paul truly called that cursed celibacy "the worship of angels" [2:18] or "the angelic life," as they call it, just as its fruits show today. What is this strange celibacy, and with what sort of great sanctity of its works and ceremonies have they adorned that made-up hypocrisy so that people do not see this demon even at midday nor that the angel of Satan has been transformed into the angel of light? There once were holy martyrs and godly people, celibate virgins and chaste individuals according to the gifts of the Spirit of God. But they did not feel that their unique gifts were necessary to all and common according to the necessity of salvation.

Therefore the devil took care that out of the unique gifts of God, wicked people made statutes and mandates commanding us to have in our flesh the angelic life which God did not give to us, just as if those laws commanded us to put off our body and fly into the air now like birds, ordering us wickedly, I say, to do what God has not commanded. Do you think that this is "the religion of angels" about which Paul is speaking?

He does these things that they may understand that not only are they calling that life "the angelic life" but also that Paul is speaking about foods and perhaps even about marriage, just as he says elsewhere [1 Cor. 7:1]: "It is good not to touch a woman." He says: "Do not touch," and: "Do not taste, etc." Because these two forbid marriage and [command] abstinence from foods, he says to Timothy that these things will be taught in the last days by those who are abandoning the faith and paying attention to the spirits of error, who are not from God, and that what they teach is the doctrine of demons. They are speaking hypocritically the lie of a feigned religion, they have a cauterized conscience, and are ignorant of what they are affirming. As he says here, they have not seen that which they have understood.

All these prodigious signs and lies have come in line with the operation of Satan upon those who are perishing, as we read in 2 The. 2[:9–10], "because they have not accepted a love of the truth in order to be saved." [Col. 2:10] Therefore he says: "God has sent them workers of error" [v. 11] that they might believe their lie and that all who have not believed the truth but have consented to iniquity might be judged. The apostles of God could have foreseen easily that these things were going to happen, for, when they were preaching, the righteousness of works began to appear to them to the harm of the grace of God and Christ.

We are not unaware of how bitterly the apostles resist this, for we learn this from their writings. They have seen by the Spirit, whom they have (so that also today the spiritual person could see this easily), that this is the very kingdom of the Antichrist but which is going to be revealed in the last times, as we read in 2 The. 2[:7]: "The mystery of iniquity is already at work" that it may be revealed at its own time; and in 1 John 2[:18]: "Little children, it is the final hour. As you have heard that the Antichrist is coming, now many Antichrists have been fashioned, etc." These things which we have now been saying in this epistle, therefore, are extraordinary and take precedence over those which Paul wrote to the Ephesians.

If you wish outstanding passages: in the second chapter are those things which we have been mentioning; namely, the condemnation of human traditions, of the righteousness of works of the Law, and of feigned religions. The first chapter contains the full preaching of the Gospel, that is, of the power and use of Christ, as in the Epistle to the Ephesians. The third and fourth chapters have an exhortation to Christian behavior.

CHAPTER 1.

[v. 1:] "…by the will of God…"

Paul is not like the pseudapostles who, although not called, intrude into preaching and teaching. We read in Jer. 23[:21] "I did not send the prophets, and yet they began to run; I was not speaking to them, and yet they began to prophesy."

[v. 2:] "…to the faithful in Christ…"

That is, to those who are believers and Christians not through someone other than Christ. He summons the Father of Christ whom he earlier called "our Father." We have, therefore, a common Father along with Christ. Thus all the things which belong to God also belong to us. Let us pray that the Gospel is beneficial in its hearers. We give thanks as it advances.

[v. 4:] "…we have heard…."

Paul had not come to the Colossians, but they had heard the Gospel from Epaphras, as you see in this first chapter [v. 7]. They also now had Archippus as their apostle or pastor, as you see at the end of the epistle [4:17].

[v. 4:] "…the faith…"

He says that he has heard of their faith in Christ and of their love for all the saints because of their correct distribution. Now we are perverting all things. We have faith and confidence in works, not only good works, that they may be seen, but also puerile works. We do no work well for the saints, that is, for our brothers, as he called them earlier [v. 2]. In Scripture, love is our duty over against our neighbor. Faith is to cling to God alone through Christ according to the promise of His Word, whenever temptation comes upon you.

[v. 5:] **"Because of the hope, etc."**

Paul is making love and our works toward our neighbor mercenary because we receive a reward in heaven on account of good works, although Scripture removes from us all merit, as we read in the Psalm [143:2]: "Enter not into judgment, etc."; also [Psa. 71:2:] "Deliver me in Your righteousness, O Lord"; also: Psa. 119:24: "Teach me Your statutes," and Isa. 64[:6]: "All our righteousnesses are as filthy rags."

((Concerning the reward for works.)) Paul is not at all saying all these things. Scripture does at times speak as if a reward is offered for a work and as if you deserve a reward if you perform a work. This is despite the fact that, if you examine Scripture correctly, it says a reward will be given for a work but not that it is earned, just as it was paid to those who had come into the vineyard at the eleventh hour and had worked for one hour. Here we are certain that the payment for the entire day was not due them, but they accepted the will of the head of the household not because of their merit but for their work. He said: "I wish to give to this last just as I did to you. Am I not permitted to do what I wish?"

God does not need our good works. What, then, is the source of your merit? Nevertheless, He does want us to work and to serve each other mutually without pay and with love just as carnal brothers serve their weaker brothers with a hope for receiving a reward from their father, for their father promised to do this or that. Otherwise they still would serve, even if he would give them nothing because they love both their father and their brothers.

You see that this is not mercenary servitude but love. Christ speaks in this way in John 14[:31]: "But that the world may know that I love the Father, etc." And Paul says to the Romans (8:18), "Inasmuch as we suffer...that we may also be glorified." He speaks in this way as if God owes us glory for our suffering, just as Christ also says: "It was necessary that Christ suffer and enter into His glory." [Luke 24:26]

As I have said, however, we must not look here at our work or suffering but at the good will of God our Father who wishes His Son to receive glory through disgrace. That is the way Paul explains himself in the same chapter: "They are not worthy, etc." [Rom. 8:8] What people generally throw around about merit from other passages we have resolved from this one passage with which we are now dealing. That is how far we are from confirming "merit" here. We show love to the saints because of the hope which is laid up in heaven. You develop this hope from the promise of God, who has promised heavenly things if you do this or that. If, then, I were to promise you a hundred dollars if you were to go to the market for me, this is something which Paul would say clearly here. You had heard about this hope first through the true speaking of the Gospel. You see that we have done good things because of our hope, not because God has *owed* us something for our work, but because He has *promised* something for our work. Therefore we must do good works because of our confidence in the Word of God alone, and we do that to please God so that we do all things as a result of our faith.

[v. 5:] "...through the true word of the Gospel..."

In the Greek, we have here a Hebraism. It is much more effectively significative than "in the word of the true Gospel." He is saying that the Gospel is the word of truth, not only because it is true in itself, but much more because it creates true people and the sort of hearts as it itself is. Otherwise, without the Gospel, all people are liars. Moreover, it is the Gospel of the knowledge of the grace and mercy of God through Christ, etc. This is what he is adding: "You have heard and learned of the grace of God through the truth." Hearing through the truth or "in the truth," (as the Hebraism reads in the Greek) and learning of the grace of God. This is not hearing in vain, not knowing in vain and reading in vain the grace of the Gospel. Rather, we understand by faith the promises of God. The Spirit of God imbues this faith and understanding and fills our hearts so that the Gospel may bear fruit in our hearts. If it is truly in us, the Gospel cannot exist without fruit, for the seed which has fallen onto good ground produces a hundred other fruits, etc. Otherwise, faith is feigned and love pretended, as Paul generally calls them. Here he calls faith "the true word of the true Gospel" which produces fruit when we hear it, and the knowledge of the grace of God through the truth and love in the Spirit, that is, not carnal nor pretended love, etc.

[v. 9:] "For this reason we also…"

This [ceaseless praying] he demands in Eph. 1 and almost everywhere. The person who begins to believe indeed knows through the grace of God that he truly does believe but that he never sufficiently and perfectly believes, so that he is always hungering and thirsting for the righteousness which is of faith, until he is filled. This is something which will not happen in this life. 1 Cor. 13[:12]: "Now we see through a glass, etc. … but then we shall know even as we are known." And, Phi. 3[:13]: "I do not judge that I have grasped, etc." Spiritual circumcision always cuts around, and the Baptism of Spirit and fire always burns and consumes the flesh until the flesh is consumed. Here, however, we see the obedience of the Christian heart which in the presence of God is concerned not only for itself but also for others that they may grow in their knowledge of God "until we all reach Christ in the perfect man" (Eph. 4[:13]). All this is that we may differentiate between the will of God and our will, for God rules over us with His will against our will, Rom. 12[:2]: "…that you may prove what is that will, etc."

Such great grace happens through Christ that we never can understand nor believe it. In fact, this is the very thing that we believe and that we believe in faith. That happens without our ability or eagerness but through the limitless power of God as He works within us and by which He raised Jesus Christ from the dead, etc. (Eph. 1[:19–20]). This is something which he says here [v. 11] in this way: "Strengthened as you have been in all might according to the power of His glory"; and in Eph. 6[:10]: "Be comforted in the Lord and in the power of His might, etc." Also, 1 The. 2: "God works in you who have believed." This clearly is the power of the Gospel, that it is the power of God through Christ against sin, death, and hell. That is obviously the power of faith, that is, the knowledge of the mercy of God.

[v. 9:] "…wisdom and [practical] judgment [*prudentia*]…"
When Scripture posits words absolutely, these are not empty words, as they are among the philosophers. Rather, they signify true things, that is, not the wisdom and judgment of the world, but that which he adds here: "…in all wisdom and spiritual judgment." It is wisdom that you know the things that are of God. Eph. 1[:17]: "…that the God of our Lord Jesus Christ, the Father of glory, give you the spirit of wisdom and revelation." However, practical judgment is that you know how to be careful of whatever is opposed to this wisdom, namely, human teachings and traditions and all the snares of your adversary who is endeavoring to lead us from the simplicity by which we simply cling to the Word of God, as happened to Eve, as we read in 2 Cor. 11:3. This judgment is no less a work than the aforementioned wisdom, as the Lord commanded that we be as prudent as serpents and that we always be vigilant. For this reason Paul says, Eph. 6[:12]: "For we are wrestling not, etc."

[v. 11:] "… for every tolerance…"
The power of God is at work in us, not only that we may believe, but also that we may suffer on behalf of the Gospel, and this

with joy, that is, with a free spirit, as Paul writes, Phi. 1[:29]: "...for it has been given to you, etc."

[v. 12:] "... giving thanks unto the Father..."
This is the magnification of rejoicing by which Paul is describing the Gospel, that is, the greatness of the power and mercy God has shown us through Christ, as we read in Eph. 1[:3]: "Blessed be God, etc." He says: "Blessed be God, who has made us and not our merits fit that we may be sharers of the lot of the saints," that is, that we may have a sharing of the inheritance with the saints, which is in light, that is, in the knowledge of the Gospel.

However, where that knowledge of Christ does not exist, there is darkness and error. 2 Cor. 4[:3]: "But even if our Gospel be hidden, etc."; and, Eph. 5[:8]: "Once you were darkness indeed, etc." The kingdom of Christ is the kingdom of light; the kingdom of the world is the kingdom of darkness. Christ is the light of the world; the devil is the blinding of the world, "in whom the god of this world, etc."[2 Cor. 4:4] Thus, in the Gospel, because those who seemed to be in the kingdom of the light as believers do not have the faith which alone this kingdom requires, they are cast into outer darkness, that is, into that darkness which is outside this kingdom. You see, I do not agree with those who think that is called "outer darkness" because, as they say, there is also some inner darkness. Rather, I understand this simply to mean that inside there is light but outside there is darkness, and the person who is cast out of the fellowship of light tumbles into the darkness which is outside.

[v. 13:] "He has transferred us into the kingdom of His Son, etc."
Therefore, God cannot help but love us who are in Christ because He loves Christ into whose kingdom He has transferred us and of whose Head He has made us members (Eph. 1[:7]). He has

made us beloved in His beloved Son. Thus it follows: "…through whom we have, etc."

[v. 15:] "…who is the image of God, etc."

He hurries ahead still more broadly with his amplification and makes Christ the head and beginning everywhere, whether you are looking at His works of creation or works of the new creation and of redemption. There He is Himself the Firstborn ahead of every creature, and the Creator and Lord of every creature. Here, however, He is the Firstborn ahead of every glorification of the creature. He was the first to be glorified with a resurrection, He is the Creator and Lord of the new creature and the Head of the body which is the Church, etc. Because it thus pleased the Father (lest anything be attributed to the merits of people) that all things be in Christ through whom, as all things were created, so He also gave new life to destroyed things through the blood of the cross and the body of His flesh which He had taken on. All these things confirm our faith with great persuasion. For the Father commands us not to be neglectful in His Son, for He gave us His Son and with Him all things that He has (Rom. 8). For this reason he wrote, Heb. 1[:2]: "[The Father] has established His Son as the heir of all things and through Him also created the worlds, etc."

[v. 15:] "…invisible…"

John 1[:17]: "No one has ever seen God." No one will know God except through this living and (so to speak) substantial image, that is, Christ. "No one knows the Father except the Son" (Mat. 11[:27]). The Father, you see, inhabits an inaccessible light which reason cannot approach, "which no human has seen and which he cannot see" (1 Tim. 6[:17]). The Word, therefore, became flesh so that through our foolishness we know God, who could not be known through wisdom (1 Cor. 1[:21]).

[v. 15:] "…the Firstborn of every creature."

That is, He was born in His divine nature before every creature, because all creatures were created through and in Him or because of Him, and all things are preserved through and in Him, as we read in Heb. 1[:3]: "…upholding all things by the word of His power."

[v. 16:] "…without thrones, etc."

That is, even whatever power may exist, whether in heaven or on earth or in hell, as we said in our notes on Eph. 1. Thus it is to no avail that some people are hunting from this and similar passages for the names of the angel choruses without a decree of Scripture.

[v. 18:] "…the Firstborn from the dead…"

In 1 Cor. 15[:20], Paul calls Christ "the firstfruits of those who are sleeping." Through Him is the resurrection of the dead, just as death came through Adam. Christ was the first to have been glorified by the resurrection that He might glorify us all with the resurrection. Rom. 4[:25]: "He died for our offenses and rose again for our justification." Indeed, there were some who were once raised again before the resurrection of Christ, but clearly to the natural life which they had had before and which they had to put aside again through death. However, the resurrection is a renewal by which the natural body becomes spiritual and the mortal body becomes immortal (1 Cor. 15[:44]). It is of this resurrection that Christ is the Firstborn.

[v. 20:] "…making peace, etc."

He created this peace for our conscience that there may now be peace with all creatures, whether those be the things which are in heaven or the things which are on earth and, thus, also with

Him, the Creator of creatures. See Eph. 1[:9]: "He has purposed in Himself to restore, etc."

[v. 21:] "And you, who once…"
See Eph. 2.

[v. 21:] "…enemies in [your] mind…"
That is, people who are ignorant of God, despisers of God, blasphemers against God, etc., so that you know not only those gross dispositions and fruits of ungodliness, but also the actual ungodliness and root of sins (that is, the actual Adam) hiding deep within.

[v. 22:] "…holy…"
That is, purified in spirit, and "blameless," that is, without hypocritical righteousness; "irreproachable," or who need no excuse, that is, however great sinners they may be, nevertheless they cannot be accused—not even by the Law of God—because of their faith in Christ, who is the righteousness of those who believe.

[v. 22:] "…in His sight."
This is a wonderful addition, for there are those who appear to be holy in the sight of people, but who are not holy in the presence of God. Again, the glory of the saints is condemned in the presence of the world, but it is glorious in the sight of God. In His sight, the saints are far from displeasing, so that even this very thing which seems very bad to the world, that is, death, is turned into salvation for them, as we read in the Psalm [116:15]: "The death of the saints is precious in the sight of God."

[v. 23:] "If indeed…"
Here you see the foundation upon which Paul wants us to stand everywhere. Everything else is nothing without faith and hope.

[v. 24:] "Now I rejoice…"
Phi. 2[:17]: "In fact, even if I be sacrificed, etc." Eph. 4[:1] "I beseech you that you not fail, etc." Paul is rejoicing because with his affliction and suffering or with his chains he is confirming the Gospel to the Colossians and to all the faithful, etc. With this image (that is, with the cross), he commends that he is a minister of the Gospel—just as he says elsewhere.

[v. 24:] "…and fill up, etc."
Do not take this to mean that Paul has minimized the sufferings of Christ so that it was necessary for Paul to suffer for us (something you would say very inappropriately and at the same time wickedly as well as contrary to Paul), who said above : "…pacified through the blood of Christ, etc."; and in 1 Cor. [1:13]: "Was Paul crucified for you, etc.?" Rather, take this in this way: Christ suffered, and all the saints are suffering in imitation of Christ, according to those words which say: "Those who want to live in Christ in a godly way will suffer persecution." Also, we are certain that the saints who are going to suffer have not yet suffered, just as Paul had not yet suffered when he was still about to suffer. This certainly was still lacking which had not yet happened but which had to happen.

Furthermore, the afflictions of the saints are the afflictions of Christ, as He cried out to Paul: "Saul, Saul, why are you persecuting Me?" What comforts us especially is that our sufferings are those of Christ. However we suffer them, they please God the Father just as Christ's sufferings pleased Him. Let us have no doubts but that we are going to be glorified with Christ if we suffer with Him. Paul is suffering these afflictions for the Church, that is, for the Gospel which He preached to the very Church and which He confirmed with his own sufferings. Just as "no one lives for himself nor dies for himself" (Rom. 14[:7]), so no one suffers for himself, for all things turn out well for the chosen, etc.

[v. 25:] "…according to the dispensation…"
He is saying this against the pseudapostles whom God did not call.

[v. 26:] "…the mystery…"
This concerns the mystery that the grace of the Gospel also belongs to the Gentiles, as Paul said to the Ephesians not just once.

[v. 27:] "…the riches, etc."
These include that He forgives sins freely; that He does not impute the remnants thereof; that He makes all things, even the most evil ones, give way to good; that He causes us to sit down together with Christ in heaven.

[v. 28:] "…perfect…"
That is, that we may present everyone as believing and trusting in God alone through Christ, because that which He has begun in us is counted to us as perfection. Phi. 3[:12]: "…not as though I have grasped or that I have already been perfected, etc."; and, v. 15: "presently, as many as have been perfected, therefore, etc." For this reason, he adds here emphatically: "…perfect in Christ Jesus," in whom you who have nothing in yourselves are lacking nothing.

[v. 29:] "…for this…"
That is: "It is for this that I carry out my duty." See here how Paul has sensed the effectiveness of the Spirit of God within himself that those whom no zeal of their spirits is touching may not presume to teach without having any concern for the sheep, etc.

CHAPTER 2.

We mentioned the things which this chapter contains before the preface to this epistle. It is a complete disputation against human teachings and traditions.

[v. 1:] "...anxiety..."
Paul's anxiety is that the wolves (that is, the preachers of human righteousness) not sweep over the innocence of the flock of the Lord. These wolves are false apostles. Paul speaks in this way to the bishops of the Ephesians, Acts 20[:29]: "I know that [grievous wolves] will enter, etc." That is why in 2 Cor. 11[:28] he counts among his labors also his concern for all the churches.

[v. 2:] "...that they may receive comfort..."
Perhaps this should rather be: "...that those who are one in love may be strengthened," that is, that they not allow themselves to be divided by sects of works, just we see happening today after we have withdrawn from the simplicity of the Word of God to the doctrines of works. He says: "...that they may be confirmed for all very certain riches or abundance of understanding so that they dare to say from their heart: 'Even if an angel from heaven should preach a different gospel, let him be a cursed.'" [Gal. 1:8] This obviously is to believe truly and to understand the mystery of God the Father and of Christ. This is unknown to the world; that is, to flesh and blood. Because the kingdom of God and His Christ in us is not in external things but in the Spirit, and because "in Christ are hidden all the treasures of the wisdom and knowledge of God" [Col. 2:3]; therefore, once you know Christ, there is no need to have a taste for, nor to know, anything outside of Christ.

In fact, whatever you may have desired to add to this wisdom and knowledge, that is empty and opposed to Christ. You see, you are doing Christ an injustice, as if that person who is wise and prudent in Christ is lacking some wisdom and knowledge. For this reason, Paul very contemptuously rejects human doctrines as well as the carnal righteousnesses of the works of the Law and says [v. 4]: "This I say…," that is: "It is to this that I am directing my words, etc."

[v. 4:] "…credibility [of language]"
That is, with trifling sophistry and rhetorical arguments as if very similar to the truth-like fluff of human reason, as if in other polished fora and appearing on the surface to be righteousness in holy matters and not in solely the knowledge of Christ, that is, in faith. 1 Cor. 2[:1]: "My speech was not in the persuasive human words of wisdom, etc." Notice what things he says there about true wisdom and human wisdom.

[v. 5:] "Although in the flesh, etc."
He writes in this way to the Corinthians, 1.5[:3]: "As absent in body but present in spirit," that is, in heart, will, and affection.

[v. 8:] "…the elements of the world…"
He calls these "external" things, that is, non-spiritual ones, which are not of the Spirit, whether they are works which humans have invented or even works of the divine law according to the flesh, that is, according to the external coating of knowledge, as you see clearly in Gal. 4[:9–10]: "How will you turn again to the weak imperfections of the world which you want to serve again? You observe days, etc."

[v. 8:] "…not according to Christ."
His kingdom and righteousness are in the Spirit and not in external things or works. Christ says: "My kingdom is not of this world," [John 18:30] and: "God is a Spirit." [John 4:24]

[v. 9:] "For in Him dwells all the fullness of the Godhead bodily."

Earlier [2:3], Paul said: "In Christ are all the treasures of the wisdom and knowledge of God," so that there is no need for any other wisdom and knowledge. Here, however, as if adding more, he includes all things in Christ and says: "For in Him, etc." You do not need to think that there is another righteousness outside of Christ. When you have Christ, you truly have God, not in figures nor representatively (as once in the ceremonies and works of the Law). This is why he says "bodily"; that is, truly, not in a shadowy way, that you may distinguish the body not from the Spirit but from the shadow. Before, they had only a shadow and figure of this grace of God which we now have in Christ, as he says later [v. 17]: "…which are a shadow of things to come, but the body is of Christ."

[v. 10:] "You are complete in Him…"

That is, in Him you lack nothing. It is in vain that you look for anything outside of Him. After all, in heaven and on earth there is nothing so sublime which does not belong to the Lord Himself, for He is indeed truly God. Therefore He is also Lord of the divine Law, lest anyone make this objection that he who abrogates the Law is not from God, as the Jews charge falsely. He who fulfills the Law and does whatever the Law requires is not the destroyer of the Law. They preach circumcision to you to make you answerable for the whole Law (as we read in Gal. 5[:3]), but you have been circumcised of your sins and have died to Christ through Baptism that you may no longer live according to the flesh nor in the elements of this world, as if there is a righteousness in such things, as we shall see later. You now have risen again with Him through the faith which God works in you through His power by which He raised Jesus from the dead, as you see in Eph. 1[:19–20]. (We spoke about circumcision and Baptism in our notes on Phi. 3.)

[v. 11:] "…you, too,…"

We have the same passage in Eph. 2[:11] and similarly regarding the abrogation of the Law. "…[T]hrough circumcision," that is, in being Gentile because of which you were living in the flesh, truly dead before God. This is the circumcision where that spiritual circumcision has not yet begun nor taken place.

[v. 13:] "…forgiving you all [your sins]…"

When the Law reveals sin to our heart, that is, when it causes sin for the conscience and confuses that conscience; it therefore inscribes this very sin of ours upon our heart or conscience in such a way that we cannot blot it out. As a result, it happened that some people committed suicide. But others (as we read in Eph. 4[:19]), after they reached the point of ceasing their sorrow, "handed themselves over to lasciviousness to perpetrate all uncleanness with greediness." Now you see that, because the Law is only the knowledge of sin (Rom. 7[:7]) it can accomplish nothing else than confuse, condemn, and cause despair. You see, "The strength of sin is the Law" (1 Cor. 15[:56]).

Who, then, will deliver us from this unhappy conscience except Christ alone? If you believe in Christ, the righteousness of Christ is yours, and immediately your sin will be nothing and the whole army of hell which was declaring you guilty vanishes like smoke before the wisdom of this faith. Thus you are able to scoff at death, sin, and hell and say: "Death has been swallowed up in victory" (1 Cor. 15[:54]). You see, Christ has overcome these, and He has overcome them for you, provided that you believe that they have been overcome. For, as we read here, He Himself has forgiven us all our sins through His sanctification, something which we were incapable of accomplishing.

He Himself made satisfaction for us freely, and erased the handwriting, that is, the writing of our conscience, which will be blotted out when you believe that Christ is your righteousness, [Col. 2:14]. This handwriting "was against us through the ordinances," that is, through the Law of God which was declaring us guilty. Christ removed that Law and nailed it to the cross. If, then, you believe that the Law was satisfied on the cross for your sins, no longer will the consciousness of your sins, however great, condemn you. Instead, your conscience will have peace, and you will rejoice that you have been saved in Christ, who was condemned in you, unless you should think that the salvation of Christ is not more powerful than your damnation.

Here Christ is leading the lords of death and princes of darkness, who are the torturers of consciences in the triumph which He Himself has gained, something which is impossible for us or our pursuits to accomplish. Again, you are seeing here an outstanding passage of Christ abrogating the Law, a passage which you also have in Eph. 1. As a result, Paul says here: "Why are your consciences bound by the decrees and statutes of the Law, as if those either hinder or profit your righteousness?" [Col. 2:20–22]

[v. 17:] "...which are shadows, etc."

The Law forbids eating unclean things (Lev. 11). This meant that the people of God ought to be clean, Tit. 1[:15]: "All things are clean to the clean." The feasts of the new moon and of the Sabbath (Lev. 23[:3]) used to signify the joy of the conscience, the renewal of the person, and that Christian Sabbath when we rest from all our labors and do not do our own will but that of God, who is at work in us through His Gospel which we believe.

In addition, Paul calls these "shadows and figures of things to come," that is, of the coming grace which is through faith in Christ. Isaiah also rejects these (1[:10ff.]) because those who were using this hypocrisy of the Law were unclean in the presence of God (that is, they were unbelieving). I say, these were shadows, but the body—that is, the actual sanctified body and very truth of the matter—is of Christ, that is, in Christ or in the grace of Christ, which truly justifies us.

[v. 18:] "Let no one steal the prize from you…"

That is, let him not do that by deceit, that the prize not be given to you, and that you not arrive at the predetermined goal, etc. The word in the Greek here means "to intercept the prize" [or "cheat out of the reward"]. Those who teach a righteousness other than that of Christ are doing this and transferring far from us the Christ who became Man for us in His Blood. Those who do this are especially those who do their works with pretended humility and modesty, and with the superstition of feigned revelations seduce you from the angelic life and who are driving almost the whole world crazy, as we said earlier. They are arrogant because of their saintliness (which is the hypocrisy and that leaven of the Pharisees), who are affirming those things which they do not understand and who are not holding up the head, that is, Christ. After all, they are ignorant of the righteousness of Christ. Therefore they have nothing more of life than a body without a head. In turn, their ruins lie open to the assaults of storms, and they become a house without a foundation. "The head is the life and increase of the body" (Eph. 4[:16]).

[v. 18:] "…from his fleshly mind…"

((What "flesh" means to Paul.)) Here you see readily what Paul is in the habit of calling "flesh," namely, whatever does not proceed from the Spirit of God, which does not pertain to the Spirit, or which is completely different from the Spirit, because you also see that "flesh" is attributed to the mind, etc.

[v. 20:] "If, then, you have died with Christ…"

The argument is as follows: You have died with Christ. Why, then, are you willing to serve the elements of the world, as if you are still living? That is, why are you seeking the righteousness of God in external things? Why are you permitting yourselves to be bound by human laws from which Christ has delivered you in conscience? Why do you allow yourselves to be told: "Don't touch this, etc."? All these things perish through use because they are human traditions. To touch, taste, and handle these otherwise would not exist as either good or evil.

We also read the following: "All these perish by their very use," [v. 22] that is, they are consumed with their using, as if Paul were saying: "The righteousness of God is eternal. Whatever perishes by use, as are all external things, is not eternal. The righteousness of God, therefore, is not in such things, etc." Indeed, they appear holy, but with a pretended holiness and humility (that is, with hypocritical devotion), so that they do not even attribute necessities to the body or keep them from the body. Look, you have the religions of the brothers, even of those who cannot help but judge that they, in their own opinion, are saints, and such are those who commend to us with such a great appearance of goodness fasts and disciplines, and pawn them off to us as merits.

Indeed, fasting is necessary for chastising the body lest it become proud against the Spirit, but we should not fast according to a prescribed rule. We must pray, but not according to an ordinance or statute but according to the desire of our heart, etc. Thus Paul writes as follows, 1 Tim. 4:8: "Train yourself in godliness, for physical exercise, etc." They do not understand "mortification" correctly, but Paul interprets it for us in the following chapter [Col. 3:5]: "Mortify, etc."

CHAPTER 3.

This also pertains to the preceding words. The argument is this: you have risen again with Christ and died to this world and to the elements of this world. Therefore, do not put your righteousness and trust in any external and worldly things which one can see. Care for heavenly matters, that is, for spiritual ones, which one does not see. The kingdom of Christ is not of this world. Whatever pomp and external righteousness it shows us is hypocritical dressing, because, just as Christ is hidden, for "no one knows the Son except the Father and him to whom the Father wanted to reveal Him," as we read Mat. 16:17; "Flesh and blood have not revealed this to you, etc; and no one knows the Father except the Son and him to whom the Son has revealed Him," as we read in Mat. 11:24; so also true Christians are hidden, and "God knows those who are His (2 Tim. 2:19). Indeed, they are the children of God, but they will first be revealed in the coming resurrection (1 John 3:2 and Rom. 8:14). Again, therefore, whatever eternal things the world reckons as righteousness or the kingdom of God is a pure lie and the deceit of the world.

It also follows that those are something less than true Christians who up to this time have been peddling themselves as Christians. ((This example is about Abel and Cain.)) In fact, not even this is of great importance, namely, that they wanted to be more than Christians (that is, more perfect than the rest), because in spirit, where that Christian righteousness is, there is no difference in lesser or greater works, for all works which are compared as great or small are equal in the presence of God, as Paul says later [Col. 3:17]: "Whatever you do in word or in deed, do all in the name of the Lord Jesus, giving thanks to God the Father through Him." He also says, 1 Cor. 10[:31]: "Whether you eat or drink or whatever you do, do all things to the glory of God." Also: "In the Spirit or in

Christ, there is no difference of persons." That is, as He says later to the Romans [10:12]: "There is neither Greek nor Jew, etc."

From what source, then, do Christians have those names such as "Franciscan," "Augustinian,"[6] etc.? From whence do those black and white habits come, which no one is permitted to change under penalty of an eternal curse? Isn't this imputing righteousness to trifles? Finally, from whence do "layman" and "cleric" come? Ministries and the different gifts of the Holy Spirit exist among those who are truly Christians, as we see in 1 Cor. 12. Such a variety of sects, however, are a figment of the mid-day demon and of the angel of Satan transformed into the angel of light, so that the world is deceived by lying signs and portents, many of which the wicked preachers have poured out onto the world from the phial of divine wrath so that people who are unwilling to take up a love for the truth so that they may be saved will instead believe a lie. We now are finally seeing what the words of Paul (which are filled with the Spirit) can accomplish. You see, the devil can no longer hide in the face of the light of those words whenever the Spirit of Christ will give this very light that we may see these things still more clearly.

[v. 5:] **"Mortify, therefore, your members…"**

Now, after having treated faith, he writes an admonition to Christian behavior, as is his custom, against those who, whenever they hear "freedom of the spirit," understand freedom of the flesh and think that they are permitted anything. He says: "Mortify, etc." Earlier he said: "You have risen again. You were dead." We must take these to mean: "You have begun to rise again, you have begun to die," just as we have already said about perfection, circumcision, and Baptism. Otherwise he would not say here again: "Mortify."

((Mortification.)) Furthermore, you see here what Scripture is calling "mortification," namely, the mortification of our will

---

6   Bugenhagen's argument concerns the tensions which existed between the various monastic orders.

and our denial of those things, not as the vigils, torments, and fasting which weaken those members which you see in your body, but the members of the body of sin like defilement, uncleanness, etc., which we can hold back temporarily from the external act with physical exercise, vigils, fasting, and hard work, as the poet says: "Venus grows cold without Ceres and Bacchus."[7] We cannot kill those, however, without the Spirit, as we read in Rom. 8:13[8]: "If with the Spirit you mortify the deeds of the body, you will live."

[v. 10:] "...which is renewed, etc."

Note here the restoration of the image of God which was lost in Adam. Already the light of God is being restored through the Gospel so that we may live as the children of God by imitation of God the Father, whom we blessed have until now been expressing in our blindness as the prince of darkness.

[v. 14:] "...charity..."

Paul speaks about this in Eph. 4[:15] and Phi. 2:10: "This is the bond of perfection" or of wholeness or the muscle which holds together the perfection and wholeness of the body of Christ, that is, of the Church, as members in the body of a living person, for there is no other bond which holds together the members of Christ. We can see this when Paul speaks (as he did a little earlier) about the flesh of a living creature: "...the bowels of mercies which are compassion, etc." [Col. 3:12] Now he appears to have alluded to the skin when he says, [v. 14]: "Above all, put on charity"; for, just as the skin holds everything together and, so to speak, gathers together all things that are in the body, so, at the same time, love holds together all the aforementioned things and cloaks the members of Christ in unity.

---

7   I.e, "Absent gluttony and wine, lust grows cold," Terence, *Eunuchus*.
8   The text reads "Gal. 5."

[v. 15:] "And may the peace of God triumph…"

    He says: "May the peace of God [triumph]," and then adds: "…in your hearts." The world does not know this peace. John 14:27: "My peace, etc." God causes this in His people with such power that no injustice at the hands of our neighbors, no adversity, no temptation can cause it to crash to the ground, as we read in Rom. 5[:3]: "We glory in our tribulations." It indeed happens that, whenever God sees us sin, we see not so much as a trace of this peace. But because this peace sends down roots more deeply, that storm cannot hammer it down. On the contrary, it rises up more strongly against those evils when we seem to have lost the victory. You have an example of this in Paul. [1 Cor. 7:15] However, where that peace has not existed, love in the Church cannot be preserved and, therefore, the Church will not even exist.

THE FINAL CHAPTER [4].

[v. 1:] "…what is fair…"

    That is, what you owe to them, what is honorable. Do this equitably. That is, don't favor one with pleasure and oppress another; or do not permit your servants to lord it over other servants—something which is intolerable where the Spirit of God is not present.

[v. 5:] "Walk wisely, therefore…"

    Obviously, that you not become an offense to anyone, and that the name of God not be blasphemed among the Gentiles because of you (as we read in Rom. 2[:24]), that is, among those who do not yet know the Gospel of Christ and the truth of God, against which those act who abuse evangelical freedom (without freedom) in an ugly way. They, you see, are the servants of offenses and are nothing but pure offenses. It is necessary, however, that there be such offenses where the Gospel is preached. Nevertheless, woe to that person who causes offense to come.

[v. 6:] "…that you may know, etc."

Do not say all things to all people. To the weak say some things, but to the perfect say others. To unbelievers say some things, but to believers say others. To some speak harshly; but to others, sublimely, etc. [Remember] what Paul said earlier about himself: "… as it is necessary for me to speak." [2 Cor. 9:5]

THE END.

ANNOTATIONS OF JOHANNES BUGENHAGEN OF POMERANIA ON THE FIRST EPISTLE OF PAUL TO THE THESSALONIANS.

THEME.

When the Thessalonians had heard the preaching of Paul, they remained constant in the faith. Still, Paul could not help but be afraid for them because of the pseudapostles who were encouraging the Thessalonians to trust in their works. You see, as he said elsewhere [2 Cor. 11:28], Paul had the care of all the churches. He begins, however, with a thanksgiving (as is his wont) and proclaims two outstanding passages, the first of which is the example of the Thessalonians and of himself and, next, reveals how effective, how certain, how persistent and steadfast the Gospel of Christ is in its hearers who are truly accepting that through the Holy Spirit. Nothing shameful, no loss nor injustice, and not even death is causing them to depart from the Spirit, whom they have perceived through the hearing of the Word of God. This, you see, in the whole of ch. 1 and 2, where we read: "Therefore, we also give thanks, etc." [1:2] To those chapters belong also those admonitions to Christian behavior which you see in the beginning of ch. 4 and at the end of ch. 5.

The second outstanding passage explains what sort of person a minister of the Gospel must be, and this he shows with the example of himself in ch. 2 and 3, and privately provides the marks of the pseudapostles; namely, that they are fawning people who are seeking their own advantages and honor.

There are also [excellent] passages in this epistle, as that which points to the fact that the wicked are always advancing to the worse until the completion of the wrath of God. This passage, however, Paul expresses more briefly with these words (2:16), where he says: "...that they may fill up their sins, etc." Also, in ch. 4[:5] there is a passage about fornication (which God hates) and about sanctification [v. 3] (which alone God wants); also about those who live without restraint [v. 1]: "Moreover, I beseech you, etc." (This passage he writes more expressly in 2 The. 3[:6].) In addition, you have here the mystery revealed about those who are sleeping and about the final resurrection (4[:10]) and about the uncertain day of the coming of Christ (5[:2]) where he also teaches that we must always be prepared for that day.

CHAPTER 1.

[v. 1:] "Paul and Silvanus and Timothy…"

Although this is one of Paul's epistles, nevertheless Paul himself does not disdain to name the partners of the epistle whom he has as his co-workers in the ministry of the Word. He does not arrogate lordship for himself alone as do those who seek their own control, for those three had learned from Christ: "Learn from Me, for I am gentle and humble of heart." [Mat. 11:29] For this reason, the apostles of God are concerned for nothing more than that they fulfill their ministry by preaching the Word to the glory of God, having no thought for their own glory or disgrace.

[v. 1:] "…to the church of the Thessalonians, etc."

Because we also read in Holy Scripture of the church of the wicked, the synagogue of Satan and the congregation of bulls and bullocks, etc.: Paul also adds this: "…in God the Father and the Lord

Jesus Christ." Thus this is for that Church or congregation in God, etc., which has the promise, Mat. 18[:20]: "Where two or three, etc."

[v. 2:] "Grace to you and peace…"

Paul always connects grace and peace so that those two things which cohere in this way cannot be separated. Grace is that God forgives us every sin through Christ without any merit of our own, provided we believe this. This grace must have the company of peace of conscience, which otherwise cannot remain at rest unless it believe that God has forgiven its sins.

[v. 2:] "We give thanks…"

This is the thanksgiving which rejoices over the progress of those who had heard the word of salvation. We learn from the example of Paul, Silvanus, and Timothy that it is the function of the good shepherd [or pastor] not only to feed the sheep with the Word (something which is especially necessary), but also to give thanks about the growth of the sheep so that he knows how to relate all of their progress to the source from which it came. It is also his responsibility to pray that they remain and grow in the faith and hope of our Lord Jesus Christ, so that he knows from what source all things truly are that he must ask for them, namely, from God. We have learned from Christ and seen in Christ all these things.

((What sort of prayers Christ's were.)) Christ's entire life was nothing else than teaching. He ministered to us the word of life (as Peter says, John 6:68), and contrariwise, on the basis of their preaching, He sometimes gave thanks to the Father and said: "I confess to you, O Lord, Father of heaven and earth, etc.," as in Luke 10:21. Furthermore, He at times prayed for entire nights, undoubtedly for our salvation. His prayers were that kind or like that very last one which you read in John 17.

So much for the theme.

[v. 3:] "...[remembering] your work of faith, etc."

He gives thanks for them for two reasons, in which he sums up the whole matter of their Christianity. The one is their concern over against their brothers, something which he calls their "work of faith and labor of love"; the other is that they have persevered in the faith, even when losses and injustices afflicted them, just as you see in ch. 2[:14], where we read: "You became followers, etc." You see, adversities test faith, as we read in Rom 5[:3-5]: "Tribulation works patience, patience, character; character, hope; and hope does not shame."

Next, those who fall in temptations and persecutions and deny what they had confessed earlier have only pure hypocrisy, as Christ says about them [Luke 8:13]: "They believe for a time and fall away in temptations." Or those people are still very weak, something of which they themselves are unaware, as you see in the denial of Peter. To have fallen will be useful for them, because they cannot be saved without such a fall. It befits them and thus it is necessary for their salvation that they learn to know themselves and to thirst for the salvation which they cannot have of themselves. It is for their consolation that Christ says, [Mat. 9:13]: "I did not come to call the righteous but sinners to repentance."

Here, then, Paul adds neatly: "...in the presence of God and our Father." In this way, he is signifying that the faith which they had first professed was not hypocrisy but that they were true believers in the sight of God, who is our Father. This is His kindness toward us. There us nothing which makes us more steadfast in all adversities than that we ponder and know that the will of our Father is good even when we suffer. As a result, our will is mortified, and we learn to embrace the will of our Father, just as we also pray: "Our Father...Your will be done."

((Love is the work of faith.)) In fact, we must note here quite carefully that Paul calls a beneficial act shown to one's neighbor "the work of faith and labor of love." He calls it "work" and "labor" against those who think that love is only friendly greetings, a pleasant lunch together, etc. This is the way John speaks, 1.3[:18]: "My little children, do not love in word nor in tongue but in work and in truth." Moreover, work belongs to faith; and alms (however copious) without faith are sin. Paul's statement is valid: "Whatsoever is not of faith is sin" [Rom. 14:23]; and in Hebrews [11:6]: "Without faith it is impossible to please God." Christ says: "An evil tree cannot produce good fruit" [Mat. 7:18]; and: "Without Me you can do nothing." [John 15:5]

The person who is without faith is without Christ. Just as you must do all your works as a result of your faith, provided you wish to please God, so also is the case with alms. It is, then, a work of faith which will hear in the last judgment these words: "I was hungry, etc."? [Mat. 25:35] After all, what else does it mean when He says: "…and you gave Me…"? "You did that out of your faith; that is, you were eager to please Me."

Next, Paul also calls that "a work of love," that is, a work which comes from love, that is, which you do well from your heart, for a needy neighbor. ((Feigned love.)) This is not a pretended nor feigned love and charity nor a love which always wants to be visible by a work revealed externally. I am not speaking only about those who today are keeping that love within themselves, for God saves up all their sins for them, as you read in the parable (Mat. 18[:23ff]). Rather, I am also speaking much more about those who want to be seen because of the pretense of godly love in the presence of people, against whom Christ teaches, Mat. 6[:1]: "Be careful not to do your alms, etc."

Furthermore, this work of faith and labor of love you will experience both differently and most greatly when you must actually love him who, as your enemy, has injured you, for then you will see what faith and love can accomplish within you.

[v. 4:] **"Knowing, etc."**

This is an outstanding passage, because those who lay hold of the Gospel are certain that they are in grace. This happens as follows: people perceive the Spirit from the hearing of faith, as we read in Gal. 3[:5]; that is, from hearing the Word of God and from believing by faith the Spirit is given in their hearts. This Word is the promise of God which freely promises the remission of sins through Christ.

Furthermore, the Spirit of God, perceived as He us from the hearing of faith, "bears witness and testifies to our spirit in our heart that we are the children of God," as we read in Rom. 8[:16], in which Spirit we cry out: "Abba, Father." This is Christian knowledge, this is the power, the efficacy and certainty of the Spirit, about which Paul, in essence, says here: "This is the Rock. A house built upon it does not give way to any storms, and not even to the gates of hell."

Are you surprised at this? And yet, when I ask you whether you believe that your sins have been forgiven, you respond: "I believe." Again, I ask you whether you believe that your sins have been forgiven you. If you hesitate here, you lied when you said: "I believe." If, however, you respond here from the heart: "I believe," I ask with what confidence you believe, because you are a sinner who deserves damnation. Here, however, you must feel this way: "If I look upon my works, I am a sinner and condemned. Works, I say, are not only evil but also good, because I cannot trust in them because, however much I may have fasted, prayed, and given alms, my conscience will never be at rest as if God has forgiven me my sins because of those activities. For there will always and repeatedly be one or two uncertain things which my conscience will want in my life and works. If, however, I look upon the promise of God, that is, upon grace or the Gospel, I ought to be as certain about grace and the remission of sins as I am that the One who has promised cannot lie. That faith He will count as righteousness for me. You see, when I attribute to God truthfulness, He will render me righteousness. This is the righteousness of God which saves me."

As a result, you read often in Psalms: "Deliver me in Your righteousness, O Lord." On the other hand, we read about human righteousness, [Rom. 3:20]: "In Your sight no living person will be justified." Behold, the apostle says this in Rom 4[:16]: "It therefore is not of works that the promise may be certain according to grace." This is the assurance and confidence of the conscience in the sight of God, the revelation of which the prophets once foretold. (With reference to this certainty, read more in the passages of Philippians about love and hope, etc.)

[v. 5:] "…as you know, etc."

As witness for himself he calls forth the consciences of his hearers. This is the great confidence of our teacher. He writes more on this subject in the chapter following.

[v. 6:] "…having received the Word, etc."

He is explaining what he said earlier, [v. 5]: "…not in word alone but also in power, etc." "For the word of hearing, unmixed with faith as it was, did not profit them," as he says in Heb. 4[:2]. Thus the Savior says: "Let him who has ears to hear, hear." [Mat. 11:15] "Receiving the Word" is nothing else but believing the Word; but, as if they received the Word effectively, he adds: "…with much affliction and with the joy of the Holy Spirit." Here you have, set as it is almost in a single word, that which appears in almost all Scriptures as a dissonance, for elsewhere you read that, as was Christ, so also the Christian people are wretched, miserable, poor, afflicted, and destined to die as sheep to be slain and nothing else except pure forms of the cross. But elsewhere you read that the same Christ or the same Christian people are glorious, rich, abounding in peace and security, for they are filled with immortal and eternal happiness. You see this often in this way in the case of the saints and prophets.

I am not forbidding this alone, namely, that Christ had to suffer and in this way to enter into His glory, and that Christians enter into glory of the life to come by the cross of this time, but also this, to wit, that that glory lies within the afflictions. Here Paul is speaking in this way: "…receiving the Word with much affliction with the joy of the Holy Spirit"; and in Rom. 5[:3]: "We also glory in our tribulations, knowing as we do, etc."; and [Rom. 5:11]: "We glory also in God through our Lord Jesus Christ through whom we have now received reconciliation"; and Gal. 6[:14]: "Far be it from me that I boast, etc"; and Heb. 12[:6]: "Whom the Lord loves He chastens, etc." Christ speaks in this way in John [16:33]: "In the world I shall be oppressed, but in Me you will have peace." Paul speaks in this way in Col. 3[:15]: "The peace of God will triumph in your hearts. You have been called to this peace in one body"; that is, even if you suffer some trouble from your brothers, that peace of God will triumph over that.

To be sure, affliction is part of the world and of the gates of hell over against the upright, as well as losses, punishments, upset of conscience because of sins and the judgments of God. That is, affliction is carnal and temporary. However, consolation, or joy, is not carnal but a gift of the Holy Spirit. Therefore it is very powerful, and the gates of hell cannot prevail against it. It is also eternal so that not even death interrupts it.

Where there is true faith that in Christ you have received the remission of your sins and that in Christ you have become a child of God and an heir of all things, you will easily receive with joy whatever the kind hands of the Father grant you finally at any opportunity.

Experience and not the letter will teach you those things, as Paul says in Heb. 12[:11]: "All chastisement for the present does not appear to be joy but trouble, but it later grants the peaceful fruit of righteousness to those whom the chastisement exercised." We have also seen these things in Christ, although His entire life was nothing else but the cross. He nevertheless rejoiced in the Holy Spirit over the progress of the Gospel, something which you read in Luke 10[:21]. He never was without this joy, for He was certain that He had a kind Father, although at times He was overwhelmed with such great evils that He was unable to feel this joy. He truly cried out from the depths of His heart that God had abandoned Him, something which you often see in the psalms. Do not despair, then, whenever you feel anything like this.

[v. 8:] "…your faith which in God…"

Your faith is not in works nor in your pursuits, not in any external things nor (as Paul) says "in the elements of the world." They also are not in gold and silver idols which are now mammon, nor in greed, which is the worship of idols. You see, in whatever things you place your trust, that is your god. It is impossible for you to have the true God if you place your trust in some *thing*, regardless of how holy that might be, or however saintly that person may be, for: "Cursed is one who trusts in a man, etc." (Jer. 17[:5]). According to the First Commandment, we must trust in God alone: "You shall have no other gods beside Me." He is the living God, the Creator and Giver of life, the truthful God, truly giving salvation to those who believe His promise, because He can neither lie nor deceive. Everything else belongs to death and is no less superior than what it promises.

[v. 8:] "…so that we need not speak to you."

In these two epistles, he does not deal with faith as he does in the other epistles, although all the things which he writes here and everywhere have to do with faith. When, therefore, he writes to the justified, he has no need to tell them to receive faith. Rather, they need only an admonition that what has been prepared for them not perish because of their neglect of the Word or that what has been sowed for them not grow, for they do not live by bread alone, etc. Paul says: "We need not speak to you," for those who have the Word have learned from God through the ministry of preaching, just as there is no need to speak to guests who have been invited to a grand celebration where all things are ready for them to eat and drink, etc. There is no other need than that the host who has invited them admonish them often that those who are his guests should attend to their joy, etc.

[v. 10:] "…and how to wait…"

This is the confidence of Christians, that they joyfully await their Redeemer whom others dread as their judge. As Christ says, Luke 21[:28]: "When these things begin to occur, etc."; and Paul says, Rom. 8:20: "…to vanity, etc."

[v. 10:] "…whom He raised…"

Paul says this that we not doubt that we, too, are going to be raised, and that we entertain no doubts about the power of Christ, our King, in whose kingdom we cannot perish and who, when He was raised, received all power in heaven and on earth, and "was set at the right hand of the Father over every principality and power and might, etc." (Eph. 1:20–21). Paul is always teaching the resurrection of Christ, because in it we always recognize truly the kingdom of Christ where, after triumphing over death, we Gentiles receive His inheritance and possession, namely, the ends of the earth, and where He makes both peoples one.

[v. 10:] "…from the coming wrath."

The wrath of God is eternal and it rests now already upon all those who do not believe. It has not yet been revealed, however, and for that reason Paul says that it is "coming." You see, just as "we are the children of God and it has not appeared what we shall be" (1 John 3[:2]), so unbelievers are the children of hell. This will be revealed then for the first time when the bidden things of darkness will have been revealed. No one will receive deliverance from that darkness except through faith in Christ, as John the Baptist says, John 3[:36]: "He who believes in the Son has eternal life, but he who does not believe in the Son will not see life, but the wrath of God will remain upon him."

CHAPTER 2.

Here you truly have a picture of the minister of the Gospel, of the follower of that Shepherd, Christ, who describes Himself in John 10[:11–16]. When Paul received ill treatment before, he did not stop preaching, but acted constantly in the Lord and still desired to die for the Gospel, if the situation called for that, as he later says [v. 8]: "We kept desiring to share with you, etc." Today, many people want to appear to have been called to teach and preach, but temptation will prove the truth. The hired hand runs away, but the shepherd stays and gives up his life for his sheep.

((Indication of a true calling.)) A true calling does not permit a person to do anything other than what is worthy of the Gospel. Furthermore, he remains steadfast in all adversities which he suffers for the sake of the Gospel. You see, he knows that he has been called to be the minister of God and to conduct God's business. Therefore, whatever happens to him is not his concern; he does only what God has committed to him that he may be found to be a faithful minister. He commits everything to God, who has sent him, knowing that this is what Christ says, [Mat. 10:40]: "He who receives you receives Me and Him who sent Me"; also, [Luke 10:16]:

"He that hears you hears Me," to wit, you who are preaching what I have commanded you, etc.

[v. 2:] "...treated shamefully as we were, etc."

This happened among the Philippians, after they had driven a demonic spirit from a woman, which you read in Acts 16.

[v. 3:] "...inasmuch as our exhortation..."

He says this because of the pseudapostles who, by deceiving their hearers, were trying to expose them to the fact that the former at times used evil arts through lying signs which until then were befouling all the books and preachers, just as Paul foretold was going to happen under the son of perdition (2 The. 2[:3]). Here Paul calls these arts "uncleanness." He calls hypocrisy, however, "deceit." He is saying: "I have not acted differently with my associates from what God has committed to us, for He made us worthy of this apostolic duty." Also, he often summons the consciences of his hearers to this with great confidence, as we have said earlier.

[v. 9:] "...for night and day, etc."

Their hearers owe their preacher or teacher sustenance according to the Gospel: "The laborer is worthy of his hire" (Luke 10:7); and 1 Tim. 5[:17]: "The elders who rule well, etc." Lest Paul, however, give the pseudapostles, who were seeking their own support, an opportunity, he often gave up his own right and used to support himself by the labor of his hands as a bishop worthy of God. He was far different from those who are bishops today who boast that they are successors of the apostles. That you may understand this passage, read all of 1 Cor. 9.

[v. 12:] "...who had called you into His kingdom, etc."

It is the glory of God by which He freely forgives us our sins through Christ, without any merit or work of our own, not that we may be able to glory, but so that the whole glory remains to God, as we read in Rom. 3[:23]: "All have sinned and come short of the glory of God." With reference to this, we read, Psa. [19:1]: "The heavens declare the glory of God."

[v. 13:] "…without ceasing, etc."

We certainly do not take this to mean the words of his mouth, but the disposition of his heart, as he said in ch. 1:2: "…always." Christ also said about prayer, Luke 18[:1]: "A person should pray always and not fail." This they say not about the muttering of the mouth as those who interpret take "always" to mean. Rather, we understand it as the desire of the heart, which God understands. After all, when you desire something from God or when you desire to be delivered from evils or when you feel oppressed, for a long time you are sure of what you want and you even pray continually with either words or sighs until you receive or are delivered. In such matters prayer does prevail, for the Lord hears the desire of the poor, and He hears the preparation of your heart with His ears (Psa. 10:17).

[v. 13:] "…because, when you had received the Word from us, etc."

Note here the circle which we believe is from God, who does this very thing in us "through His power by which He raised, etc." (Eph. 1[:19–20]), and this very thing returns to God. We believe nothing else than God and in God, for we do not tie our faith to human traditions nor to the elements of the world but to God and through God, without whom we cannot believe, something which Paul is saying here in this way: "You have indeed received the Word from us, but we have now been the ministers of God." Furthermore, the Word was not ours but was God's, and from it you were learning within, according to the words: 'They will all be taught by God,' otherwise our word would be empty. I say, you were learning from God, but what you were learning was nothing else but God Himself. However, the superstitious and misled were learning from the false apostles and prophets. They know many things and are involved in many things, but because they have not been taught God, they do not know God. You see, they cannot trust God because they have their trust in other things."

[v. 14:] "For you became followers…"

The believing Jews were suffering many things at the hands of unbelieving Jews. They were murdered, imprisoned, etc.; their properties were confiscated, and they worked in poverty. As a result, it was necessary for the churches of the Gentiles to send needed support to the churches which were in Judea, as you see in Rom. 15[:27] and 1 Cor. 16[:1]. The particularly wonderful caretaker of this task was Paul, as he says in Gal. 2[:10]: "…that we remember the poor," something which he was also concerned to do of himself. The Thessalonians were suffering the same afflictions from their fellow-citizens as the Jews were suffering from Jews, something which pertains to the constancy of their faith, as we said earlier.

[v. 15:] "…as people who killed the Lord Jesus…"

He is making a serious charge against the Jews. Here you also have a passage indicated in a few words that the wicked, because of the judgment of God, always advance to something worse. You see, just as all things work together for good to those who love God, so also all things give way into evil for the wicked, until the final wrath of God comes over them. Let Pharaoh be an example. He heard this, Exo. 9[:19]: "For this very thing have I raised you up, that I might show My power against you." You read about this in Rom. 9[:17]. As an example are also those about whom he speaks here, namely, the Jews who also hear from Christ, Mat. 23[:32]: "You, fill up the measure of your fathers!"

[v. 16:] "…who forbade us [to speak] to the Gentiles, etc."

Because they used to think foolishly that God had not sent salvation to the Gentiles and was not going to send it to them contrary to what had been written of them in the prophets, Paul treats of this mystery of salvation in Eph. 2 and 3.

[v. 17:] "Furthermore, brothers, we…"

He makes clear his affection toward them that you may have an example that the saints longed to see him in the flesh.

[v. 18:] "Satan got in our way."

Satan cannot get in our way unless God permits him, as we see in Job [1:12]. Furthermore, he hinders the Word of God that he himself may "fill up their sins always," just as other wicked people do. When, however, he abuses God, God hinders his wicked ministry lest the pearls be cast before pigs and lest the wicked listen and become saved, as we read in Mat. 7[:6] and Isa. 6[:10]. These are the judgments of God.

[v. 19:] "After all, what is our hope…"

He adds the reason why he desires so much that they become the raw material for his rejoicing in the sight of God at the final judgment. Thus, then, he may say: "Behold, my five talents, etc.," and to hear: "Well done, good and faithful servant."

CHAPTER 3.

These words declare with what great concern Paul burned for the churches. When he could not come because Satan stood in his way, he sent Timothy not only to learn about the situation, but also much more. Paul sent him to strengthen them with his words that they not become upset over the afflictions of Paul. Timothy was also to lead them back if perhaps Satan had tempted them through his messengers—the pseudapostles—and led them away from the way of grace to confidence in their works. Paul was so afraid of that falling away that you should not be surprised that in the meantime those evils had increased which completely erased the grace of Christ.

[v. 2:] "…with reference to your[9] faith…

Let no one think that we, wretchedly afflicted as we have been, feel differently from the way we felt before, just as those who believe for a time and in time of temptation fall away. Let no one take offense because we who are preaching the glory of God are enduring the disgrace of the world; for the very fact that we are suffering those things is the confirmation of our Gospel. Heaven forbid that such things frighten anyone, as we read in Eph. 3:13: "I ask that you not fail because of my afflictions which I am tolerating for your sake, which is your glory." Hear, however, that the life of Christians is the special cross of their preachers does have a place. He says: "You know that we have been placed for this function, etc." Mat. 16[:24]: "If anyone wishes to come after Me, etc."; and John 15:20: "The servant is not greater than his master. If they have persecuted Me, etc."

[v. 5:] "…he who tempts…"

That is, the one who is in the habit of tempting, that is, Satan, tempts people not only to impurity of the flesh by which he

---

[9]   Ms. reads "*nostra* - our" but Biblical text has "*vestra* - your."

causes faith to topple (about which see the chapter following), but all the more what we have said, through false preachers who restrain us so that our entire faith in God alone through Jesus Christ is taken from us. They lead us off to confidence in our works and then always into new traditions and worship or, as we read in Col. [2:10], they find "the worship of angels and the merits of holiness" or, as they call them, "devout exercises." Their teachings are without number.

Therefore it justly should happen to those who have abandoned the one way and truth (which is Christ), and have turned away to a different path and are never certain in their conscience where they are going, for they judge that this is the holiest path. After a short time, however, they despise it as an appearance of a different holiness. This is something which they know very well who earlier were superstitious but now have turned truly to Christ. You see, they now consider all things as dung, which before used to appear holy and distinguished, that they may gain Christ alone, whose disgrace they consider more glorious than any appearance of holiness, as Paul writes about himself in Philippians (ch. 3), where he condemns the righteousness of the Law that nothing of the righteousness of traditions and of the inventions of humans frightens us.

Notice carefully, however, what he is saying: "…that our labor not have been useless," by which he is signifying that the whole Gospel is of no advantage to those whom Satan is leading away into another path. Furthermore, you must preserve the Gospel about Christ alone in which you have all things and without which you have nothing, just as you see more clearly in Col. 1 and 2. You should have no doubts but that he spoke about that misleading, for see what he says in Gal. 5[:4]: "You who are justified in the Law have fallen out of grace." A slip of the faith is often the opportunity for greater faith under the care of God, because in such a case we easily grasp our error.

However, when we are led off into another Gospel, that is, a feigned one, as he says in Gal. 1:6, here Satan certainly rules because true faith, that is, our whole salvation, perishes and hope is not going to return, because we do not see our error. You see, the angel of Satan is transformed into the angel of light, and we cannot recognize the demon which is seen at midday. Preachers of works teach many things that we not fall into the sins of the flesh. Therefore we should watch more carefully here to seal off that source of faithlessness from which those sins flow, as he says in Rom. 1[:28]: "They did not approve having God in their knowledge. God therefore handed them over into a reprobate mind." This clearly is what he is saying in Eph. 6[:12]: "For our wrestling is not, etc."

[v. 8:] **"For now we are alive…"**

That is: "We rejoice and say a fond farewell, etc. Seeing that nothing else is such a concern for us than that you stand firm in your faith, I do not tarry in my afflictions."

[v. 11:] **"[May God…] direct our way to you."**

Obviously, whether or not Satan intends it, our good and pious intentions (as they call them) are nothing, just as they were nothing to Paul. Moreover, we must pray the Lord to direct all our ways lest the light which is within us become darkness. We must also pray that His will be done, etc.

[v. 13:] **"…in the presence of God…"**

Paul does not want hypocrisy to be in us but the righteousness of God, which He will then accept as our righteousness when Christ comes to the judgment along with all the saints, etc.

CHAPTER 4.

Paul is admonishing them about all the things he had taught them that they should walk in such a way that they abound all the more, that is, that they grow from faith to faith. He is warning them especially that they be holy in body and that this is the will of God, just as he says in Rom. 12[:2ff.]: "I beseech you...to present your bodies, etc." You see, God often has terribly condemned the evils of lust, as in the Flood, in the destruction of Sodom, and in avenging the sin of the Benjamites (Judges 19[:16ff.]). These are the abominations of the heathen, who do not know God, as you see in Rom. 1[:20ff.]. Moreover, Christians should possess their vessel, that is, their body, with sanctification, not with the lust of concupiscence, to the extent that each measures his powers, lest he fall into the shameful activities of the heathen; and let him consider marriage for himself, as Paul teaches (1 Cor. 7[:9]), as well as in Heb. 13[:4]: "Marriage is honorable in all people, and the wedding bed is spotless," for God will pass judgment on whoremongers and adulterers.

This sanctification will not fall to the ground provided that you consider that you have a wife and not a whore according to God, for a wife is a good creation of God, the use of whom you are permitted according to the creation and justification of God, as you see in the case of Paul, who, as also elsewhere, is condemning uncleanness of the flesh very greatly (1 Cor. 6[:1–5]). As he says here, 4:7: "God has called us not to uncleanness but to sanctification."

This sanctification is not for those filthy pigs who, when they hear "freedom of the spirit" (which only spiritual people know), change that to 'freedom of the flesh' and think that they are permitted anything, contrary to Peter (1 Pet. 2[:16]), who says: "As free people, not holding freedom as a covering of malicious activity, but as the servants of God." This is also contrary to Paul, who says, Gal.

5[:13]: "You have been called into freedom, but do not give freedom to the flesh as an opportunity."

((Contrary to the freedom of the flesh.)) Although the authority by which Paul commands this does belong to him, in the fashion of the Evangelists, he only appears to be beseeching them and adds: "The person who rejects these ideas rejects not man but God, for I have said that your sanctification is the will of God who gave His Holy Spirit to you that you not contaminate your vessel in which the Creator of all purity, so wonderful a host, dwells" (1 Cor. 3 and 6).

[v. 6:] "Do not go beyond and defraud…"

"Defraud" pertains to any business, matter, or reason. I relate to this especially that no one cheat the spouse of another, for the context appears to require this. Next, I relate it to all other matters pertaining to what you are not to do your brother what you do not want anyone to do to you. If you are unwilling to do without the love of your brother, something which the spirit of faith demands in Christians, then do without it in fear of the judgment of God, because He does avenge such things.

[v. 9:] "Furthermore, with reference to brotherly love…"

Here you are seeing what he said in the beginning of this epistle: "…because of your work of faith and labor of love." For this reason, as he said in ch. 1:8, there was no need for him to write to them about faith, so also he says that he does not need to write to them about the love which is the fruit of faith. He adds the reason; namely, that they have learned from God, as he had said earlier. He merely beseeches them to abound all the more, that is, to grow in faith and love, which are never perfect in this life, for they must always grow in them through the Lord Jesus.

[v. 11:] "Take pains…"

As if writing to all, Paul notes that there are some among them, just as they are nearly everywhere today, who, as if religious people and worshippers of God, follow leisure and wish to be nourished from the property of others as if they are due this for their service to God (which they pretend). You see, no one is due support from the work of others except teachers (that is, the ministers of God), as he had said earlier. But Paul speaks those words more clearly in the epistle following (ch. 3: 8–9). Such people became an offence in this way, even to the unbelieving heathen. Therefore he commands them to live by the quiet labor of their hands so that they do not become needy and, under the pretext of poverty and religion, seek to live off the work of others.

[v. 13:] "Furthermore, I do not want you to be ignorant…"

He does not want them to mourn over those who have died in Christ, something which they perhaps were doing. Otherwise, he would not write such things. You see, it would be laughable to the heathen for those who were preaching a resurrection to weep over the dead. In addition, this did not appear to be very Christian, for those who were weeping in this way appeared to have doubts about the resurrection. These are the people Paul is strengthening here as he says: "Just as Christ died and rose again, so also we who die in Christ shall rise again." He also uses this logic in 1 Cor. 15[:12], where he says: "If Christ be preached to have risen from the dead, etc.," where you read more about the resurrection. Thus Paul writes, Phi. 3[:20]: "We are awaiting the Savior from heaven, etc."

[v. 15:] "We say this to you…"

He discloses the mystery in the Word of the Lord, just as the prophets were in the habit of doing, who kept saying: "Thus says the Lord." The mystery is this, to wit, that the Thessalonians perhaps wanted to know if, when Christ came in the judgment, they would be found still alive living the natural life, just as they were doing now, something which we also have in Luke 17[:26], where we read: "Just as in the days of Noah, etc."

((The tale of the fifteen signs before Judgment Day.)) Here that fable about the fifteen signs disappears, in which they teach that all men have died before Judgment Day, so that I do not tell how ridiculously they abuse some passages of Scripture in tales of this ilk. How is that they are not seeing that in the Apostles' Creed where they confess that Christ is going to judge the living and the dead? There we are not permitted to interpret this as the righteous and the unrighteous, because this creed was handed down for common folk to understand simply and without allegory. Furthermore, the Creed reveals or foretells that the living will not go ahead of the dead but that those who have died will be first to rise again and thus at the same time, both the living and the dead (that is, all who belong to Christ) will be snatched up to meet Christ in the air.

Here Paul is speaking about the resurrection of only the righteous, just as he does also in 1 Cor. 15, where he also lays open this mystery, namely, that those who will be found alive will be changed suddenly when they are snatched up (because the natural life cannot possess eternity). What had been their natural body then will become a spiritual body. He says: "Behold, I tell you a mystery, etc." Not only the fact that this is contrary to those words which Paul speaks here, but also contrary to the very order, as well as the bad and awkward coherence of the words and the inappropriate meaning, all argue that the ancient translation is not true. After all, what is: "Not all will be changed in an instant, etc.?"

[v. 16:] "For the Lord Himself…"

Scripture describes the coming of the Lord in this way, as if in wartime some king should come down from heaven to wage war against some rebels and rejoice over his obedient subjects. For this reason, Paul here calls Him "the archangel," as if He were the general, the encouragement,[10] and trumpet of an army (Mat. 24[:29–32]). The sign or banner of the Son of Man in heaven is a great army and majesty. But I take this encouragement and voice of the archangel and the trumpet of God to mean the voice of the Son of God at whose word and power the dead will rise again, and our bodies, now vile, will be conformed to the glory of His body, as Paul writes in Phi. 3[:21]. For Jesus Himself says, John 5[:25]: "The hour is coming in which all who are in their tombs will hear the voice of the Son of God, etc."

CHAPTER 5.

Scripture everywhere says that the day of the Lord will come unexpectedly. He wanted it to be uncertain so that we might be prepared always for its coming (Luke 12[:40]). Just as the day of our death (when the Lord comes for individuals) is uncertain, so that day is uncertain when He will come for all. Just as He finds us in our death, so also He will preserve us until that day, just as you heard earlier [4:14]: "Those who have fallen asleep in Jesus, God will bring along with Jesus."

Because Paul said nothing earlier about the resurrection of the wicked, here he says that death will come upon them suddenly and their grief will never cease, as we read in Pro. 1[:24–33]. Such things will come upon them when they feel especially secure, as the Lord says, Mat. 24[:37]: "As in the days of Noah, etc." This also happened to the greedy, rich man, to whom the Lord said, Luke 12[:20]: "You fool, this night your soul will be sought of you, etc." These things will happen, too, to those who, because they are the children of darkness and night, do not know the light of Christ and,

10   *hortatum*

therefore, fall asleep not awaiting the Lord but trembling in their drunkenness and gluttony, as you see about the wicked servant in Luke 12 and Mat. 24.

Christians, on the other hand, stay watchful and live soberly because they are the children of God and of light, who listen to Rom. 13[:11]: "It is time for us to rise from our sleep, etc." Here he calls being neglectful "sleep" and to be ignorant of the Lord, just as in the parable of the Gospel, something which follows from drunkenness, which we may understand as cares and concerns, as well as the riches and pleasures of this life, as you see in Luke 8[:14]. For gluttony and drunkenness which are now prevailing beyond measure cause people not to foresee that day, as Christ teaches, Luke 21[:34]: "Pay attention to yourselves that you perhaps not become weighed down, etc." The contraries of these he calls "being watchful and sober, etc."

[v. 8:] "After putting on the breastplate, etc."

With reference to these weapons of righteousness, read Eph. 6:12. Here Paul is equipping us with three weapons against the kingdom of darkness: faith, hope, and love. He places faith and love on our breast because, if they are not there, they are not what he calls them. Hope, however, he places on the head because it awaits from God on high what we believe in our heart, etc. In this way, he shows that we must be armed, safe and secure, and says [v. 9]: "For God has not appointed us, etc." The appointment of God is necessary that we not perish. Therefore, let us hope for salvation through Christ, because God has so arranged matters absent our own merits, and that we might entertain no doubts nor be concerned about our salvation. Christ has died for us and killed our death that we might live in and with Him, now that we have denied our own life.

[v. 10:] "…whether we are awake or sleeping…"

He means "always," regardless of what happens to us, whether we live or whether we die. For being awake and sleeping here are posited differently from the way they were stated in the previous chapter, something we know well of itself, although I did not say it. The life of Christians, whether they are asleep or awake, whether they eat or drink, etc., is always the life of Christ in which they do all things to the glory of God (1 Cor. 10:31).

[v. 11:] "Therefore, encourage each other…"

After a general admonition, he is teaching some matters more specially: first, that they edify each other, Eph. 4[:29]: "Put aside every corrupt word, etc."; second, that they respect their rulers with love; that is, that in addition to respect they should also minister to them that they may be at peace with them that, as we read in Heb. 13[:17]: "they may watch over their lives with joy, and not groan." (Lest anyone become puffed up), those have been placed over them who, as Paul says, labor among them, who are in charge of them in the Lord, and who admonish them; that is, as he says elsewhere [1 Titus 5:17], who "labor in the Word." Those are worthy of double honor not because of their title but, as he says, because of their work. The third thing he teaches them is that he wants mutual edification and adds:

[v. 14:] "Comfort the timid…"

The timid are those who are still fearful in many matters, fearing that they are going to be without a body or that they are not going to persist sufficiently in courage through the Gospel when adversities come.

[v. 15:] "See that no one renders evil…"

That is, we are not permitted to drive off violence with violence.

[v. 18:] "For this is the will, etc."

He concludes that such things please God through Christ, so that we not think that we should reject them as human admonitions. Earlier [ch. 4:3] he said: "This is the will of God, even your sanctification."

[v. 19:] "Do not quench the Spirit."

He calls the gifts of the Spirit "the Spirit, through whom the word of wisdom is given to one; to another, the word of knowledge; to another, kinds of languages" (1 Cor. 12[:8]). The person who has such gifts should use them, but (as he says there) for the usefulness of the Church. They should not forbid those gifts to anyone but let each person be carried by his own spirit, provided it be a Christian spirit. They should permit each person to follow his own calling. He speaks in this way in 1 Cor. 14[:39]: "Do not forbid speaking in tongues."

He adds, however: "Do not despise prophecies," that is, interpretations of divine Scripture and declarations of faith. In the same place [1 Cor. 14:3], Paul speaks in this way: "The person who prophesies speaks to people for their edification, exhortation and consolation." Paul prefers this gift of the Holy Spirit ahead of the others and says in the same place [1 Cor. 14:1]: "Pursue love, strive after spiritual things, but rather that you may prophesy, etc." However, that we not take up anything without judgment, he adds: "Prove all things, etc." Christ says: "Beware of false prophets," and, "Pay attention to the leaven, etc." And John says, 1.4:1: "Do not believe every spirit, etc." You see, many who confess Christ deny the power of Christ, that is, that Christ is the Christ. These are the antichrists about whom we read (1 John 2[:18]).

[v. 22:] "Avoid every appearance of evil."

He teaches that they should avoid not only evil but also every appearance of evil, that is, against those offenders who are led by no consideration of little children, that is, of those who have not yet been sufficiently instructed in the faith. Paul writes against those offenders in Rom. 14[:13] and 1 Cor. 8[:9]; and Christ teaches quite terribly against them in Mat. 18[:6] and elsewhere. Here, however, you should remember that offending little children is one thing, but offending the Pharisees is something else. Christ says about this, Mat. 15[:14]: "Leave them alone, etc.," as people who are offended by the word of the Gospel and who are offended in a situation which they cannot avoid without peril of their salvation, etc.

[v. 23:] "May the God of peace sanctify you in all things."
He calls Him "the God of peace" without whom all things are disturbed, for no one achieves peace of conscience unless he believe that God has forgiven him his sins through Christ. It is, however, God alone who gives this faith. Here your eagerness is of no avail. Simply accept what He has offered you, for you cannot bring anything. God, therefore, is the God of peace, just as in Psalm [4:3] He is called "the God of righteousness," etc., that is, the Justifier. Paul says: "May He sanctify you. It is your duty to be saints, but this is not a matter of your efforts. Only pray, etc." Christ says: "Ask, and you will receive, etc."

[v. 23:] "…and whole…"
This means "without corruption." In Greek, this is "ὁλόκληρον - faultless," that is, possessing the entire inheritance, that is, so that you lack nothing. He is explaining what he had said before: "…you wholly." ((In his *Magnificat*, Luther deals with this passage.))

Scripture divides man into three parts, the most important and noblest of which is his spirit, by which he comprehends the incomprehensible by nature if God may have illuminated that, for that is not that other light without which he is in pure darkness and ignorance. Furthermore, these incomprehensible matters are invisible and eternal. This spirit is also the home of faith and the dwelling place of the Word of God.

The second part is the soul which has not been separated from the spirit by *nature*, but by its *work*, which is to give life and growth to the body, and for this reason it has its name.[11] Here the light is reason, which cannot help but err where the spirit has not received illumination from faith, for it is human wisdom and, as Paul calls, "the natural person, which does not perceive the things which are of God" ([1 Cor. 2:14]).

The third part is the body with its parts about whose sanctification he had said earlier was a "blameless spirit," that is, where there is full faith and where the soul exists easily, that is, where the whole life and body will be faultless, but having a spirit which disagrees with God and is seeking a different righteousness (as we read in the Psalm about the unbelieving people: "It does not believe in the God of its spirit." [Psa. 78:8] There is nothing which will not disagree with itself in a person, and he can find true peace of conscience in nothing.

See, then, why Paul demands that God accomplish the sanctification of the whole person, for He is the God of peace. I say: "…of the whole person" so that it cannot accept blame for anything. I am not saying that this means only in the presence of people, but not even at the coming of Christ.

[v. 24:] "He who called us is faithful…"

This is a word of great comfort for afflicted consciences which are still fearful. God cannot help but preserve the faith which He has promised. ((Those who believe the Gospel know that God

---

11   "*anima*." The verb in the preceding clause "to give life" is "*animare*."

has called them.)) He who has called us, that is, who has opened His Gospel for us; that is, who has begun our salvation and will complete it; that is, will complete that which He has begun, just as you have been unable to begin your salvation but were taken up while you were still wicked, as Paul says in Rom. 5[:8]. Thus, you will be unable to complete your salvation, and it would otherwise have perished a long time ago, had it been in your hands and not in the hand of God our Father, through Christ. Paul speaks these words in Phi. 1[:6]: "For it is God who works in us both to will and to do, according to His good will." We who have been called to a knowledge of the Gospel ought to have the certain hope for all these things from God, for He is faithful, just as he says, 1 Cor. 10[:13]: "God is faithful, and He will not suffer, etc."

THE END.

THE ANNOTATIONS OF JOHANNES BUGENHAGEN OF POMERANIA ON THE SECOND EPISTLE OF PAUL TO THE THESSALONIANS.

THEME.

Paul again praises them for being steadfast in the faith and abounding in love, because no adversities were able to turn them away from that intent, as we have seen in 1 Thessalonians. If you remain steadfast in temptations, this is the proof of your faith.

The passages in this epistle are more outstanding, however. The first is in ch. 1, namely, that in the persecution of Christians the just judgment of God is declared that they are considered worthy of the kingdom, while their persecutors are worthy of punishment. Even now, Christians know both these judgments through faith, but they will be revealed at the coming of Christ.

The second is in ch. 2 and concerns not the coming kingdom of the antichrist, but the one which is going to be revealed when the mystery of iniquity which was going on even while Paul was writing these words begins to be detected when that wicked one will be slain in the consciences of people by the Spirit of the mouth of Christ, that is, by the holy Gospel. Nevertheless, it will not perish completely among all until the Lord destroy him with the glory of His coming.

Here Paul inserts the third passage which is worth our memorization; namely, that lying signs must mislead us and effectively deceive us and cause us to stray and slip. That is, those have to believe the lie, who have not received the love of the truth that they are saved. This judgment is all the more horrifying the less people see of it.

The fourth passage is in ch. 3 and concerns the excommunication of those who, under the pretext of religion, seek their support from the labor of others.

CHAPTER 1.

[v. 2:] "…your faith is growing, etc."
Faith alone acts with God and unites us with God. However, the works of faith, that is, of love, serve our neighbor freely without having any reckoning of merit, just as Christ served us. Paul says that their faith is increasing and their love is abounding, because these are always growing (Judge all these words in this way on the basis of the Word of God!), as the Spirit moves us forward. Thus, no one can boast that he has already reached the goal, as he says in his epistle to the Philippians. [ch. 3]

[v. 4:] "…so that we ourselves glory in you in the churches of God…"
The growth of the sheep is the glory of the shepherd. Why, then, is Paul doing this? After all, he says elsewhere [2 Cor. 10:17]: "Let him who glories glory in the Lord." I respond. Paul never glories unless he glories in the Lord. Here he is boasting in the Lord for two reasons. First, he praises the mercy of God and the efficacy of the Holy Spirit in those who have received the Word. Next, he is doing this very thing before the other churches that, by following this godly example they themselves may desire God to carry them forward where the glory of God may be spread still more widely. How will you be able to feel that in these matters Paul is not seeking the glory of God? After all, you are seeing that he is always and endlessly giving thanks to God about them.

[v. 5:] "...proof, etc."

That is, proof from which it is obvious and becomes known whether that judgment of God is just by which He considers us worthy of His kingdom and our persecutors worthy of punishment. "The kingdom of God is now within us," as Christ says in Luke [17:21]. But because we have not yet grasped this, we therefore cannot grasp it sufficiently in this life and we always pray: "May Your kingdom come," about which we spoke in our notes on Colossians. But we do not yet see it, but it will appear when (as he says here) Christ will have come to be glorified not only in His body, but in all His members; that is, in all the saints or believers who belong to His kingdom. You also see this, as we have often said, in Rom. 8 and 1 John 3.

So also the judgment of God has already condemned the wicked who vainly attempt to oppress the truth, as well as those who do not believe the Gospel, just as Christ Himself says in John 3:18: "He who does not believe has already been judged, for he does not believe in the name of the only-begotten Son of God." We do not see this judgment now, but we shall see it when He will be revealed who the wicked now do not believe is going to come; to wit, the Lord Jesus, "from heaven with the angels of His power, with great might or a huge army, and majesty," as we read in Mat. 24[:30–31]. He is going to come "with a burning fire which is going to consume His enemies round about," as we read in Psa. 97[:3] and 50[:7].

Note that those who are suffering for the kingdom of God are worthy of it, not because you think that merit is connected with this (something which Scripture does not uphold and which faith doesn't know), but because God accepts what you are suffering as a worthy matter which He both wishes and is able to compensate, for Paul speaks in this way: "...that you may be considered worthy of the kingdom of God," that is, that you may be considered worthy *by God*.

But you say: "Nevertheless, he says here that God will render punishment and unending destruction to some, and to others a relaxation, that is, a deliverance from all evils, and in addition, eternal glory." I respond. Whenever you see this in Scripture, you see two things which Scripture wants: God commends faith and condemns unbelief. However, we cannot see those things except from their fruits. Because Scripture has been written for us, we cannot see the faith or lack thereof of others except from their works, just as the Savior says: "You will know them by their fruits." [Mat. 7:16]

Therefore, Paul often writes that God will repay to each according to his works. Of course, good works—absent hypocrisy—come from faith; other works, from unbelief. The former, therefore, will receive life from God as their reward; the latter, the wages of death. God gave the former to believers (lest you again think of merits), as Paul says, Phi. 1[:29]: "It has been given to you on behalf of Christ not only to believe in Him but also that you suffer for Him." For He judges them worthy in proportion to His goodness to as many as He illumines. With regard to the latter works, the wicked cannot exist without them, for God judges them unworthy of His grace and sends them off into their stubborn unbelief. But why does He take up the former and abandon the latter? Paul responds to you in Rom. 9[:20], and 11[:34], and says: "O man, who are you to reply to God, etc.?"

[v. 10:] "…in that day."

Martin [Luther] writes: "…because you have believed our testimony to you at this time." In other respects, the following is not an appropriate meaning: "Then Christ will become wonderful among believers because you have now received from us His Word which we have testified to you."

[v. 11:] "…for which we also pray…"

We are also praying that He complete with the power of His Spirit at work within you that calling by which He has called you through the Gospel to the glory of His name and to your glory through that Gospel according to His and Christ's grace." With these words, you see how Paul has removed all merits from us. The calling is God's; the work of growth is God's; the completion of our salvation is God's; and all things come through Christ. (We have also said these things elsewhere as in the epistle to the Philippians.)

CHAPTER 2.

Because Paul had spoken in his previous epistle about the sudden and unexpected coming of the Lord and had said among other things: "Who who shall live and be left at the coming, etc.?"; it happened that many people believed that the day of the Lord would come then while those to whom he had written were still alive. He is beseeching them through the same coming and through the Christian union by which we are now one with Christ and will be gathered to Christ on that day, that they not believe that, as if foolishly persuaded through a spirit, that is, through someone who seemed to have had a revelation about this, or through a sermon or epistle from Paul supposedly. He does not want them to be disturbed and think: "If the Lord is going to come now, how will Scripture be fulfilled about the calling of all nations? How are the things which the Lord preached in the Gospel going to happen before Judgment Day, which the apostles of God had also preached?"

I don't know what other disturbance Paul feared in them, because it is the responsibility of the faithful to await this day, unless he noted at that time that some were still weak. Yet he does indicate quite openly that some deceivers had abused that opinion of people at that time for some reason or other. Otherwise he would not just swear that they not believe this very thing. He therefore says, [v. 3]: "The Lord will not come, unless there first come a falling away, etc."

Next, we must note here in passing that, just as the people then were upset about the sudden coming of the Lord, so also in the last days (which are here now) there are going to come those who are unconcerned and despise as a fairy tale what the prophets and apostles (and, therefore, Christ Himself) had preached about the coming of the Lord. Against these Peter writes (2.3:3ff).

[v. 3:] "…unless there come a falling away…"

Those who are unwilling to accept that Paul wrote these words against the kingdom of the pope (and we see more than enough of this today) should approach here and judge the tree on the basis of its fruit, something of which our Savior advises. This kingdom is so unjust today and has approved for a long time already the saying of unjust things which conflict with the Gospel and has decided to embrace the pomp, pleasures, and riches of the world and to reject the cross of Christ, so that even its defenders in one way or another see in many areas that injustice, as their conscience reproves them. They also add this, namely, that they are filling up their sins and the measure of their iniquity so that they are only persecuting the Gospel and the grace of our Savior, whom the Father has given us as "our righteousness, sanctification, redemption and satisfaction" (1 Cor. 1[:30]). "It pleased the Father (as we read in Col. 1[:13]) that all fullness dwell in Him, and through Him all things are reconciled, whether they be heavenly or earthly things. In Him, you are reconciled through the blood of His cross." Also, we read in Col. 2[:9–10]: "In Him dwells all the fullness of the Godhead bodily, and you are filled in Him who is the head of every principality and power," and who says: "Without Me you can do nothing." [John 15:5] What connection, then, do we have with human tradition as regards our salvation, inasmuch as we have all things in Christ and to whom Christ is everything? Christ is useless to us and we fall from grace if we seek justification in the Law, as we read in Gal. 5[:4]: "You see that justification comes not through the Law of God," for "the Law was not given to justify"—as we read in Gal. 3[:11]—but that through it we may know sin as the transgression of the will of God, as we read in Rom 7[:7].

Nevertheless, they battle for laws which they have thought up by themselves and for human traditions, and they add this to their ungodly unbelief so that they become murderers by killing the confessors of Christ, that is, those who confess and teach that we are justified by faith alone and are saved through the mercy alone of God, absent any human merits; that human traditions thwart salvation; in fact, that there is no salvation when you have faith in traditions, as Christ declares, Mat. 15[:9]: "They worship Me in vain, as they teach the doctrines and commandments of men." Lest they perhaps say: "We command such things that people may fear God," God responds to Isaiah, 29[:13]: "They feared Me because of the commandments and teachings of men."

In this way, they kill either by work or by will so that upon them comes all righteous blood which has been shed from the blood of righteous Abel all the way to the blood of all the martyrs who were slain up to this present day on behalf of the truth of the Gospel. We are saying these things for the sake of those who can still come to their senses, for we ought to desire and pray for salvation for them that God illumine them along with us, who ourselves are also still offending.

The obstinate, however, we must leave to the judgment of God as people who are filthy and still becoming filthy. We advise that for all people who battle against those things which they do not understand. Perhaps God will at some time give them understanding. In both cases, let us permit them to grow, just as Christ wants, until the harvest, for then there will be a separation of the grain and the weeds. Do not judge them before the time when Christ judges.

Believe me; in fact, believe the Gospel, that the grain is the seed of Christ, that is, His Word, which He preached along with His apostles. The weeds are the words and traditions of men which the hostile man, the man of sin and destruction, sowed through the doctrines of demons over sleeping people, that is, people who were not vigilant in their faith, as you read in Mat. 13[:24–30]. You will never cause straw and weeds to become grain which is preserved from eternal fire. Stop trying to do that, therefore, and test the spirits whether they be of God. Furthermore, you will test them not on the basis of traditions nor ancient custom nor on the basis of your own feelings, but on the basis of the Word of God. If the spirits agree with it, they are good. If they disagree, they are evil. Learn from Scripture and its truth to act just as Christ and the apostles acted—not with steel and fire, something which thieves can also do. If, then, you find in someone the fruits described here, you will not give him to me, will you, that I may also call him a wicked tree, that is, the man of sin, the son of perdition, etc.?

First, that which Paul said quite obscurely [v. 7]: "Only let Him who is holding back hold back now until he be taken out of the midst," everyone takes as a reference to the destruction of the Roman Empire, which at that time was in control of the world with its great power under Nero, for that was the fourth kingdom or the fourth beast about which see Dan. 7[:7–8]. Paul had spoken to the Thessalonians more clearly when he was with them, but at that time it did not seem right to him to write them more clearly.

Just as Christ came when the Greek Empire, which was the third, fell completely, so the antichrist (or, as Paul says here, "man of sin") will be revealed when the Roman Empire has been removed, which began to fall under Emperor Heracleus, when those whom we call "Saracens" and "Turks" left the Romans and fell from the faith through the antichrist Mohammed, who used to assert that he was the Paraclete whom Christ had promised in the Gospel—something which that foolish people could have believed. You see, it is necessary that those who do not take up a love for the truth in order to be saved will instead believe a lie. Clearly God blinds their hearts. Mohammed used to boast that he was the interpreter of Scripture and that people should accept nothing from Scripture differently from the way he himself interpreted it, for God had sent him for this purpose.

However, when the Roman Empire had been completely destroyed, Paul foretold that the man of sin would not *come* but would be *revealed*, etc. If you should look at the situation today, that Roman Empire which existed at the time of Paul was removed, and we are all under the rule of the pope, to whom all our kings and rulers are subject and whose mandates they esteem even with their fearful consciences. That pope boasts that he is the lord of the whole world in place of God; that as many as do not obey him are under certain damnation; and that no one is a servant of God unless he is the servant of the pope. He boasts that he is permitted to do this to defend his wealth and to strengthen his power and kingdom.

He also boasts that, if his servants kill and disturb on behalf of his kingdom as many as resist and speak against him, they are the children of God and worthy of eternal life; and that they have power over all things which are of God—over all things sacred and secular. He boasts that all the power of the Holy Spirit which Christ gave by the generosity of God to believers belongs to him as prince and that no one can use it unless he has permitted and approved that by himself or by his officers. He has ratified that he can deliver very many souls from purgatory, because of which his people have removed that one thing which until now they had left to Christ, namely, that very thing for which God appointed Him (as Peter says) as Judge of the living and the dead.

He peddles for money as many times as he wishes the precious blood of both Christ and the martyrs when he boasts that he is distributing the merits of Christ and the martyrs from the treasury entrusted to himself, but he does that for money—something which so many of his bulls and letters bear witness in Germany. Against the Law of God, he approves usury and accepts part of the booty from pillaging as indulgences. He forbids marriage in the very numerous people of his clergymen, as a result of which so many terrible sins have followed that neither the world nor God Himself can bear more.

He causes people to live without marriage and without the labor of their hands and the sweat of their brow, an egregious invention contrary to God and the excommunication of Paul, which you read in 2 The. 3[:8–10]. He prohibits foods which God created for the faithful to eat with thanksgiving. He confirms religious orders and sects, makes offices and schools swear by his decrees, and fills all things with oaths to subject the consciences of people to himself.

He commands the observation of days and months and times when he wants people to fast on some days and to be at rest on other days under threat of the anger of God and of the blessed apostles Peter and Paul. Paul certainly says that he preached the Gospel to such people in vain (Gal. 4[:10–11]).

He posits holiness in vestments, tonsures, oral mutterings and loud roaring, decoration of churches, those unctions, etc. He teaches that we must have faith in the keeping of such things and must repent if we neglect them. If, however, you despise such things or teach that people should hold them in contempt, one hell is not enough for you into which to be thrust; and (to say this again) he himself commands those things which God has not commanded, contrary to Christ, who told the apostles: "Preach the Gospel"; and: "Teach all nations to observe all things which I have commanded you;" and contrary to Paul, who says: "Even if an angel from heaven, etc."

To his servants, the pope gives rich benefits, stipends, magisterial offices, the insignia of doctorates, seraphic sanctity, and copious indulgences, as well as a jubilee year, along with the remission of all sins and promises eternal life.

Those who do not serve him, he deprives of their property, divests them of all honor, drives them out of this world (if this can be done), and judges them worthy of damnation and a curse. All this the pope does even if they have kept all of the commandments of God and despite the fact that faith, according to the Gospel and apostolic doctrine, is alone the worship of God by which we trust in God alone and fear God alone so that no one rules in one's conscience save God alone. The pope has substituted human traditions in place of faith, and teaches that we obtain salvation through them, so that we are afraid to omit them under penalty of mortal sin, under penalty of excommunication already borne or to be borne, and under the penalty of an eternal curse.

Through these things, the pope has bound consciences so tightly that you find people who confess nothing other than that they did not keep Sunday as a day of leisure, although they feared not at all if they were eager to spend Sundays in drinking and eating—not to mention other things. Nevertheless, although the latter are contrary to the Gospel, the former is not. Another thing: they confessed that they did not fast nor abstain from butter on Fridays. Yet here you may find fornicators, adulterers, public thieves, etc., who observe the fasts of the Church (as they call them), and yet fear nothing because of their evil life but even dare to condemn as heresy those who commit those sins, as if fornication, adultery, rapine, murder, etc. are not separations from Christ. With these trifles, therefore, they want it to appear that they are Christians, although the are deceivers and deceived.

Still another thing: one [cleric] confesses that he has neglected the canonic hours; another, that he has neglected crossing himself several times in the Mass; another that he celebrated the Mass without a vestment; another, that he has stumbled over the words in the canon; another, that he has sometimes been inattentive in the words of that most sacred canon. Yet, these people have no fear that they are reading the Gospel of Christ poorly and understand nothing of it. To these Paul says to keep silent if an interpreter is not present. [1 Cor. 14:38]

In the meantime, some of these are usurers, whoremongers, etc., who indeed confess sometimes but do not think about correcting their life, but other trifles which we have mentioned they confess and confess with their hearts that they are going to correct their lives. Because we still see these things, let us not doubt that they have taken that faith in God through Christ from us. Do you see that people fear the traditions and fictions of men more than the commandment of God? Doesn't this pope rule in the conscience of people ahead of God? Isn't he sitting in the temple of God *as* God?

Here where there is no fear, miserable consciences are fearful; and where those consciences have to fear, they fear nothing or do not fear much. In fact, so great a concern of violating a precept of God does not touch the pope himself as much as does a fear of violating his own commandment, something which those reserved cases and bulls of the Supper (not to mention other things) show. Isn't this exalting such things over God? Not even the pope denies that he makes an idol of these idle matters, or places them under the name of God, but he even boasts that he sits in the temple of God. Do you think that it is going to please God that the popes condemn those things which God does not condemn and magnify those which God otherwise ignores and despises and even condemns others?

Such useless ideas are contrary to God and contrary to Christ so that you do not doubt but that those are antichrists who defend such things. Could we not judge that the pseudapostles with whom the apostles had such great warfare were still better than these in their appearance? Those false teachers were doing that to draw those who were justified by faith alone through the grace of our Lord Jesus Christ back into a trust in the works of the Law which God had given to Moses. But the papists with their own laws and with the dreams of men (of which Christ will demand no reckoning from us on that day of judgment, etc.) bind us and want to bind our consciences as if they were bound and restricted to God. This is the ultimate work of Satan.

Imagine now that some antichrist is going to come to burn bodies with fire, harm them with swords, hand them into prisons, etc, and who gives his followers great riches, etc.; tell me, please, what more is he doing than we have already seen in this papist kingdom? What more horrendous activity will he be able to accomplish against the salvation of people than to cast out their reverence for, and trust in, God, cause them to fear his traditions and the fantasies he has thought up and to have confidence and place their hope of salvation again in observing those things? Isn't this taking away all that Christ the Lord has done for us? Isn't this denying that Jesus is the Christ, the Son of God, about whom we read in 1 John 2[:1–2]?

They indeed are not denying Christ if you look only at *names*, but they are certainly taking away His *reality*. They are not permitting Him to be the Justifier in the way the prophets depict Christ, for they attribute righteousness to works, deny that He has the power of God, and teach that He is not sufficient for salvation, as we have said elsewhere.

These, therefore, are the pseudapostles about whom John speaks. Among these are all those today who forbid the preaching of the Gospel of Christ (that is, of the grace of Christ), knowing as they do that, if only those will have been preached (as is necessary), all of their dreams and invented laws will fall out of the conscience of people to the ruin of their tyranny. In the meantime, this is enough about the fruit from which we recognize that the tree is completely different from that about which we read in Psa. 1[:3].

Note again what Christ foretold, that many false prophets and false christs or antichrists (that is, adversaries of Christ whom the apostles call "pseudapostles") are going to come. [Mat. 24:11] They call them "false" because they are not the apostles of Christ, although they wish people to see them as such, just as they boast today that they are bishops and successors of the apostles. We see nothing apostolic in them and they are ignorant of the Word of Christ, which is the mandate for the apostles, for they have nothing in themselves of the Spirit of Christ but seek their own spirits and defend them with injury to the Gospel and the oppression of the confessors of Christ.

Let no one take the prophecy of Christ to mean only those pseudapostles who existed already at the time of the apostles, something which would be foolish, although they are similar to the same who are found with similar and the same fruit. Christ foretold about both the pseudapostles and antichrists (Mat. 24[:11] and Mark 13[:22–23]). About the former, He says: "Many false prophets will arise, and they will mislead many." But about our false prophets now He said then: "If someone will have said to you: 'Lo, here is Christ,' or: 'Lo, there He is,' don't believe, for false christs and false prophets will rise up, and they will give great signs and wonders so that they will lead even the elect into error (if that be possible). Behold, I have foretold this to you."

The report at the time of the apostles was as follows, namely, that the antichrist was going to come at some time. John, therefore writes, 1.2[:18–19]: "My little ones, it is the last hour. As you have heard that the antichrist is coming, now there are many antichrists. From this you know that it is the last hour. They have come forth from us, etc." Thus we often read about many antichrists or false christs or pseudapostles. But here, Paul, as was his habit, discloses to us the coming mystery, to wit, that finally one head of all the antichrists, false christs, false prophets, and false apostles will be revealed, that under him may be contained all the errors and deceits of all those who have deceived the world under the names of "God" and of "Christ," as they transfigure themselves (as Paul writes) into angels of light and schoolmasters of Satan. Why is it, then, that in this chapter he says that the antichrist is going to be revealed, unless he will have hidden himself for some time under the guise of holiness? Otherwise, how would he also be soliciting even the elect to stray, as Christ speaks?

Here don't think that this is some Jew or Gentile in name who is sitting in the temple of God and working signs which are lies! John says [1.2:19]: "They have come forth from us, etc."

You see how these words indicate (as with a pointed finger!) the kingdom of the pope, in which kingdom—although saints sometimes presided over it and were its rulers—elect people who did not accept the truth of the Gospel had to lead. This is the judgment of God. Don't fight it. Christ foretold it; the apostles predicted it. Furthermore, I call it "the kingdom of the pope" from that time when the pope himself ascribed the monarchy to himself and placed his own traditions ahead of the grace of Christ.

The defection or falling away of which Paul speaks is quite well known from 1 Tim. 4[:1]: "Some will depart from the faith, etc." To express the situation well, Paul adds two outstanding examples to indicate who those deserters of the faith are who turn their mind to the spirits of error or deceiving spirits and don't test them through the Word of God as to whether the spirits are of God. Rather, they take up human rather than divine oracles that, having neglected the Gospel, one may say: "I hold with Thomas"; another: "I hold with Scotus, etc." Another says: "That saint created this work; therefore, I will be saved by this work, etc."

They are following the doctrines of demons when they abandon the Word of God, place their confidence in human traditions, and teach people to trust them. It is always the doctrine of demons when people abandon the Word of God and believe in other words which cannot square with the Word of God. You see, in the matter of our salvation, God does not want anything other than His own Word, not to say different from it, even if an angel from heaven speak it, as Paul says, etc.

This doctrine of demons began in Paradise. The Lord said: "You will surely die," but the serpent said: "You certainly will not die." Thus also today the Lord Christ and His Holy Spirit say everywhere that we are justified by faith alone, and we are free of sins. But the spirit of error and the doctrines of demons say: "It is not true that we are justified on the basis of faith alone; instead, do this and you will obtain salvation. Only grant that, if you shall have come to those places, you will have the forgiveness of all your sins. If you do not eat in this way, if you are not clothed nor shaven in this way, etc., you will be condemned." The Lord wants us to believe His Word. The serpent says: "It certainly is not true."

Next, Paul says that the coming demons have not been revealed except to the extent that the faithful can discern them from their fruits. But such things which cannot shape themselves into the angels of light, that is, midday demons, as the psalm calls them, that is, just as Paul says: "...which will speak lies in hypocrisy," [1 Tim. 4:2], will teach under the appearance of great sanctity things of which God is ignorant and which He has not commanded. They will abuse God with fictitious miracles and signs, as we read here, and with lies, to such an extent that they will believe even the deceptions of demons against the commandment of God (Deu. 13[:1–5]). There you see that God has the habit of testing with lying signs whether or not we love Him with all our heart and all our soul.

With this hypocrisy, they will mislead those who do not take up the Gospel of truth to be saved; but they can no longer deceive those who do accept that Gospel, for the light of the Gospel can detect the persona of the midday demon as well as demonic darkness for those, in the same way as the noonday sun strikes human eyes.

We also have the addition that they will have a conscience marked by a hot iron, for they should have been consecrated to God alone. Now, having received an alien brand, they tremble with fear, turn to profane human traditions, and promise themselves salvation if they preserve those traditions. Ultimately they cause themselves in everything they are doing they become uncertain of their salvation because their consciences indeed can never be truly and at rest, except through faith alone in God through Christ.

Finally, however, that I may say what I began, the apostle marked those who will deceive with two outstanding examples that they be unable to hide forever; namely, that they will forbid marriage and abstain from foods, etc. Let these papists listen and come to their senses, and let them pray with us to the heavenly Father that He finally deign to explain to us all every error and unbelief that we may glorify His Word alone in our mind and conscience.

[v. 2:] "…and will be revealed…"

He does not say: "…he will come," that we may know that the "man of sin" will rule and destroy souls before his revelation. He speaks in this way later [v. 7]: "…for the mystery of iniquity is already at work." For, even at that time, he saw both the deceivers and the deceived who were falling away from faith in the grace of God to the works of the Law under the fine guise of holiness. He acts against those in almost all his epistles, and about this he says, Phi. 3[:2]: "Beware of dogs, beware of workers of evil, beware of circumcision," and Acts 20[:29]: "I know that after my departure ravening wolves will enter among you, and they will not spare the flock. Also from you (that is, you Christians) there will spring up men who will speak perverse things to draw away disciples after them." Then he also kept saying: "Hide this midday demon among those who have not received a love for the truth, who wanted to lift up something better than the Gospel." Here, however, Paul is prophesying about the revelation of this error.

Therefore, wee here how insipidly those speak who are trying for so long to defend this error (which militates diametrically against the grace of Christ). See also how those interpret nothing who say that "the mystery of iniquity" here signifies the persecution of Nero all the way to Diocletian and then under Julian the Apostate, who persecuted Christians with skill and cunning, etc. This was not the *mystery* of iniquity but *open* iniquity, of which even the heathen rulers eventually were ashamed.

[v. 3:] "…the man of sin…"

He does nothing else with his traditions than that he causes sin in the conscience of people where sin truly would not exist, were they to understand the truth of God, and they are truly damned, because, as they believe, so they are.

[v. 3:] "…the son of perdition."

He does nothing other than destroy souls as do the pope and his kingdom, which excommunicates, aggravates and aggravates again, forbids, etc. If it sees that these provide no advantage, it calls in the secular arm to destroy not only souls, but also bodies. We complain little about our lost money, but those whom it enriches, magnifies, gifts with indulgences, canonizes, etc.—those, I say, it destroys still more gravely before God, etc.; for their deliriums have reached that point that they believe (or at least want to believe) that they can also excommunicate dead people, lest they leave to God some judgment even about the dead.

[v. 4:] "…who opposes and extols [himself] over all…

That is, antigods or antichrists. "[Mat. 12:30][12]: "He who is not with Me is against Me, and he who does not gather with Me scatters abroad." Paul here explains immediately who his enemy is. He says: "…who is exalted over everything which is called 'God'" or "religion or the worship of God," as Martin says. He wants people to observe his own commandments above the commandments of God. He wants his traditions to have highest priority and to be worshipped by fearful consciences, something God does not want. He does not allow the preaching of the Gospel (that is, the pure grace of Christ), for, if people knew it, those ungodly traditions and episcopal apparitions will completely vanish like smoke from consciences, and people will ridicule the discovered persona of that great god. You see, they will have the worship of the true God—that is, faith, by which alone they worship God scrupulously in spirit and in truth, not with a carnal, feigned, and false worship, that is, with a religion which humans have invented.

I say, they have taken this worship from us and have lifted up for us pure mockery instead of the worship of God in which they worship and enrich not God but themselves. After all, what else do their bells, organs, altars, vestments, chants, anointings, tonsures, etc. want, so that you don't know what they are doing with all these? They cannot be sure in their own conscience that these things are God-pleasing because they do not have a mandate of God to do such things, or at least at least a word that such things do please God. They, however, are ignorant of, hold in contempt, forbid, etc., that which they should do; namely, preach the Gospel. Whether they want to or not, they are forced to hear this from God: "This people honors me with their lips, etc." [Mark 7:6]

[v. 4:] "…so that he sits in the temple of God…"

We know well what "in the temple of God" means in Paul from 1 Cor. 3:16: "Don't you know that you are the temple of God

12 The text of Bugenhagen reads "Luke 11."

and that the Spirit of God dwells in you? If anyone will have violated the temple of God, (which one violates with evil teaching), God will destroy him." The temple of God, which you are, is holy. Therefore he sits in the temple of God who wishes to rule in your conscience where there is room for God alone and where He alone should rule. Luke 12[:5]: "I shall show you whom to fear, etc."; and, 1 Cor. 7[:23]: "You have been redeemed with a price. Don't become the servants of men."

What some people think, therefore, is useless (namely, that the antichrist is going to rebuild the temple of Jerusalem and will sit in it), for we already know that the temple of God is in Paul, as if Paul truly would have called what the antichrist was going to build, "the temple of God." But we ought not dedicate our bodies to St. Francis, St. Dominic, etc., so that we not only have a conscience branded with a hot iron, but also that our body has no marks which separate us from our brothers with some guise of religious scruples. You see, in Christ "there is neither Jew nor Greek, etc." (Gal. 3[:28]). Paul also says, 1 Cor. 6[:19–20]: "Do you not know that your body is the temple of the Holy Spirit, who dwells in us, and which you have from God? You are not your own, for you were purchased at a great price. Now glorify God with your body and your spirit which belong to God." [1 Cor. 6:15:] "Do you not know that your bodies are the members of Christ? Why, then, should I take the members of Christ and make them members of a whore?" If Paul feels this way about physical fornication, how much more true is that about spiritual fornication by which you attribute to your idols what belongs to God? Except for the devil, who has taught you to make factions of your brothers to their harm as if you would be better or more holy than the rest? Let that which the psalmist says in Psa. 73:27 frighten you: "You have destroyed all who have gone whoring from You." Also, God is jealous and wants you to keep faith in Him alone. He does not bear the adulterer, nor did He want uphold the carnal person, even if the latter anoints himself with stibium, as the prophet says. [Mic. 6:15]

[v. 8:] "…whom the Lord Jesus will destroy…"

That you may know that it is not within our own powers that our conscience be delivered from the antichrist, we must call upon Christ here. He is not the secular arm but "the arm of the Lord," as Isaiah calls Him (ch. 53[:1]). Those, then, are acting and feeling foolishly who try to relieve this pest with physical weapons. Nevertheless, we permit the right of the sword against the papists who bring on violence, and this we do in such a way that we do not call it "the defense of the Gospel," which does not allow anyone to defend it, but "the defense of the oppressed."

Paul says: "Christ will destroy His adversary who has taken away the grace of the Gospel, and He will destroy him "with the spirit of His mouth," that is, with the Word of the Spirit which comes forth from His mouth, which He teaches the faithful is in their hearts, that is, with His holy Gospel, just as today. But unfortunately we appear to be (and are) too little thankful for His indescribable grace. Where the pure and only Gospel of Christ is now again being preached, which has been and is being given to us from the mouth of Christ; I say, where that happens, those human fictions and doctrines of demons which have been spoken in hypocrisy as a lie immediately vanish as smoke. In this way, the antichrist in the conscience and heart of the faithful is slain, as we read in Isaiah, 11[:4] about Christ: "And with the Spirit of His lips He will kill the ungodly, and He will strike the earth, that is, the worldly wise, with the Spirit of His mouth."

Thus the Gospel kills the wicked one, and his kingdom is destroyed—but obviously not with the weapons of the flesh. There must be many wicked people, therefore, in whom the work of the Spirit will accomplish nothing and will kill nothing. Instead, the antichristian opinion will continue until Christ's day of judgment, when the glory of His coming will totally erase it. This is the operation of Satan.

[v. 10:] "…in those who are perishing…"

It is comforting that this power and effective error and lying signs will do no harm to those who receive the Gospel with love, that is, who love the Gospel or the truth of God and do not merely hear it outwardly.

[v. 12:] "…that all may be judged who do not believe the truth…."

You see, here the terrible but hidden judgment of God against those who do not believe the truth and who have to be deceived more and can never come to their senses (because they are not afraid of being deceived and love and defend their errors). You see, they have not proved that they have God in their knowledge (Rom. 1[:28]). This is what John cites [12:40] from Isaiah: "He has blinded their eyes, etc." For this reason, we read in John 3[:18]: "He who does not believe has already suffered judgment." These are the judgments of God.

There are some people who not only do not love the truth (against whom Paul speaks so horribly here), but also blaspheme that they could not see nor recognize this truth. Because this is admittedly the sin against the Holy Spirit, it will never be forgiven, as we read in Mark 3[:29], and about which we have spoken elsewhere in the Psalm [28:1]: "My God, may you not be silent to my praise."

[v. 13:] "We should give thanks to God…"

Paul is saying that those who believe the truth are of the elect from eternity, as you see in Eph. 1. He also says that they themselves are not going to be misled. Sheep can wander off temporarily, but the good shepherd does not abandon them. Thus, instructed as we have been by our error, we know what we owe to the light of the Gospel and to our Savior Christ. Furthermore, let us not be thankless.

[v. 13:] "…through sanctification of the Spirit…"

He means internal sanctification, not through the carnal righteousness of works and that hypocrisy of sanctity. What he adds is explanation: "…and belief of the truth"; that is, that we believe only the Word of God and not human doctrines.

[v. 14:] "…to which He called…"

He has chosen from eternity but calls through preaching, Rom 8[:30]: "Whom he predestined, those He also called, etc." Furthermore, Paul says that God called "to the acquiring of the glory of Christ." We are people who know that our own glory, the glory of the flesh and of our works, is confusion and disgrace in the presence of God. Those who recognize some of their own glory in themselves are not worthy of the glory of God. The person who glories should glory in the Lord. Furthermore, we have spoken often about this glory.

[v. 16:] "Now our Lord Jesus Christ and God…"

He prays for growth and perseverance for them through God.

CHAPTER 3.

[v. 1:] "…that the Word of God may run freely…"

This is what the Lord says in Mat. 9[:38]: "Pray the Lord of the harvest…" After all, unless God send them, no one will preach successfully, that is, with the fruit of those who listen, "for how will they preach unless they be sent?" (Rom. 10[:15]). Therefore, let us pray, etc.

[v. 2:] "And that we be delivered from…"

Paul, who had been prepared to die for the Gospel (as we see in Phi. 2[:17]), is not praying this for himself, but for the salvation of those who were still in need of the Word of God, as he writes to the Philippians (ch. 1[:24]). He says: "I must remain in the flesh for your sakes." Furthermore, those are absurd people who fight against not only those things which are of God which they cannot understand but also all reason, for in this way they are blind, etc.

[v. 2:] "…for not all people have faith."

This passage comforts the fearful so that they not be offended by the fact that few people believe, for no one can come to the Father except through Christ (John 6[:44]). Nevertheless, the truth and promise of God remain steadfast, for God cannot be found to be a liar or unfaithful in that so many people are faithless, that is, do not believe in the Word of God and the promise about which I have spoken at the end of 1 Thessalonians, something which Paul expressed in this way in Rom. 3[:3]: "For what is it if some of them have not believed, etc.?"

[v. 3:] "…who will make you firm…"

You see that everywhere in Paul (and, therefore, in all Scripture) that the advancement and steadfastness of our salvation, as well as the beginning thereof, are the responsibility of the Lord, as we have said elsewhere.

[v. 6:] "Now we command you, brother, in the name…"

He calls "disorderly" those who live outside the order of others; that is, who, although others live by the labors of their hands, are willing to live by the labor of the hands of others, for they have found some pretext by which this is owed them by right. He commands us to avoid them, and not only does he command this but even adjures this in the name of our Lord Jesus Christ. Obviously, he has a presentiment of how great a plague such laziness is going to produce for the Christian state. As a result, we call with a perverse name the 'sacred orders'[13] and those ordained into them, whom Paul calls "disorderly." He therefore says about himself [v. 7–8]: "We did not behave ourselves in a disorderly manner among you, nor did we take bread from anyone without paying, etc."

Such people again are going to reduce themselves in rank just as today many are demoting themselves voluntarily, so that here, too, just as in the case of the rest, they are revealing rightly that they seem to have been a deceitful fairy tale to the world. That is, those who were boasting that they alone are in that order or in a sacred or even the most sacred order are demoting themselves from the ranks of Christians. These are so far from Paul's willingness to consider them holy that he even commands us with an oath to avoid them. Such people confirm to us this defection from the faith with their teachings, writings, traditions, and hypocritical behavior about which we spoke before, so that no one will have been able to come to his senses unless God ultimately has mercy, having given us the sacred good news of Christ.

[v. 9:] "…not because we are not permitted this…"

On the basis of evangelical right, no one is owed support from the labor of another except preachers and teachers of the Word of God. Still, Paul was often unwilling to use this freedom lest people appear to consider him an example of that disorderly behavior. He writes more about this subject in 1 Cor. 9, where he was unwilling to employ that right, in 2 Cor. 11[:23ff.], and also in Gal. 6[:14].

---

13   In other words, the monastic orders, which were not ordained by God, and yet lived off the charity of the Church.

[v. 14:] **"But if anyone not believe our word…"**

Note here the Christian or Evangelical excommunication which ought to be made against those who are an offense to the Church of God, and not against the wretched and poor, as now happens at the hands of those who themselves are worthy of excommunication, whom God considers as excommunicated people, who do not accept a love of the truth. See these words of Mat. 18[:17]: "If he not have listened to the Church, he should be to you as a heathen and a publican." Do not understand this as the papists do; namely, that such a person must be thrown into the lowermost hell. ,Rather see here the sound interpretation, for Paul says: "…so that he is filled with shame." (That is, it is better for us to endure the ignominious disgrace of the cross than to be condemned with the glory of the world.)

The result of his shame is that he learns to recognize his error and not to be considered as an enemy because no one is permitted to speak with him, as the papists teach. Rather, admonish him as a brother so that he may come to his senses and become like and equal to your other brothers. Understand what John says (2 John [10]: "Do not greet him.") to be a reference to flatterers and to those who conceal the sins of their brothers, who, as Paul says, share their evil works.

Furthermore, he is speaking there only about those whom we are to avoid, who do not persevere in the teaching of Christ and who do not have the teaching of Christ. There are, as he says, many teachers who have gone out into the world who confess that Jesus has not come in the flesh, as are all those today who teach us other satisfactions and the righteousness of works and do not grant to us that Christ made satisfaction in His own flesh not only for our sins but even for the sins of the whole world, as John says in his first epistle [2:2]; and that we are saved solely by the merit of Christ and not by our own merit. I do not doubt that John is speaking about such people, for at that time there were false apostles. With reference to this, see almost all the writings of the apostles.

[v. 16:] "Now the Lord of peace Himself…"
    We told in the previous epistle why Paul calls Him "the Lord of peace" or "the God of peace."

THE END.

THE ANNOTATIONS OF JOHANNES BUGENHAGEN THE POMERANIAN ON THE FIRST EPISTLE TO TIMOTHY.

THEME.

Paul the apostle is instructing Timothy, that is, the bishop or preacher whom he had ordained for this, as to what he should teach, namely, only faith and love, rejecting fables, useless questions, word-battles, and empty disputations which people start because of their ambitious greed, for these are the plagues of sincere faith in Christ and of love for one's neighbor. He should not admit doctrines of demons in the hypocrisy of those who speak lies, which doctrines Paul foretells are going to rule in the last days.

He instructs these things here and there in this epistle: in ch. 2, about common prayer and what befits women toward their husbands. In ch. 3, he depicts Christian bishops and deacons along with their wives, families, and children. In ch. 5, he prescribes the method of advising individuals and wants the Church to provide truly for widows. He also teaches bishops who are laboring in the Word and doctrine to be worthy of receiving food and clothing, and adds material regarding the judgment of a bishop over against sinners. In ch. 6, he teaches Timothy of what servants and the wealthy should be warned. Furthermore, we said earlier what he is inserting about Christian doctrine.

THE MORE OUTSTANDING PASSAGES.

First, the most necessary passage is the one which explains what Christian doctrine is and what false doctrine is, because of our confidence in the works of the Law, we deny that God is our Justifier or that with empty debate and word-battles and useless questions we do harm to faith as well as love (ch. 1:4 and 6).

The second passage is that the Law was not established for the just but for the unjust person (ch. 3), something which you read in this way in Gal. 5[:18]: "If you are led by the Spirit, you are not under the Law, etc."

The third passage is that blasphemy and insult and persecution against the Gospel of Christ do not harm their perpetrators, for through these they think that they are being obedient to God, provided they later recognize the truth and come to their senses, as Paul says. In the other hand, some people knowingly battle against the truth and blaspheme it. They are committing the unforgivable sin against the Holy Spirit, as we read in the Gospel. Here, the meaning should not destroy us. We must know this passage today (ch. 1).

The fourth passage is that we must pray for everyone, even for kings and those who are in authority that we may live peaceably under them, for God rejects no position, for He leads some from the lowest to the loftiest positions to a knowledge of His Son (ch. 2).

The fifth passage concerns the clothing of women and that they be subject to their husbands in all matters (ch. 2). The sixth concerns the respected office and behavior of bishops and deacons as well as of their wives, children, and family (ch. 4); the seventh, the doctrine of demons. This passage is quite well-known today (ch. 4). The eighth is that godliness is profitable for all things, but physical exercise is of little worth, which is a passage more necessary than it appears (ch. 4). The ninth speaks of widows (ch. 5). The tenth teaches that their hearers owe the necessities of life to teachers (ch. 6). The eleventh speaks about the accusation of, and the judgments against, sinners (ch. 5). The twelfth teaches that neither servants nor the wealthy are aliens from the kingdom of heaven, even in their very servitude and their wealth, provided they follow the things which Paul is advising (ch. 6). Furthermore, he shows with what gentleness we must deal with others (beginning of ch. 5).

CHAPTER 1.

[v. 1:] "Paul, the apostle of Jesus Christ…"

With this inscription, Paul commends his words to Timothy and to all who are going to read the epistle so that we may be certain that this is the Word of God and not the word of man, for in Isaiah, God rejects the doctrines and commandments of men, as does Christ in the Gospel. Also, the Law does not allow anything to be added to it. Therefore Paul says that he is the apostle of Christ and that God has committed to him [Paul] the apostleship, that is, the office of preaching the Gospel. It is as if he were saying: "I am not coming to relate my teachings, but those which God has committed to me."

He calls God "our Savior," because God Himself saves us through Christ. As we read in Eph. 1[:6], He made us His beloved in His beloved Son. He also calls Christ "our hope," because those who do not have Christ live in desperation, as we read in Eph. 4[:19]: "…who in their despair have handed themselves over to shamelessness, etc." Hypocrites, too, suppose that they have hope, but, when temptation comes, they have no hope, for they do not have Christ.

He calls Timothy his "genuine" son, [v. 2] that is, his true son, for he had learned of Christ correctly from the teaching of Paul, who writes that he is Timothy's father because of this. Those who are in the faith are true sons. See the parable of the sower (Luke 8).

Peace of mind and conscience which surpasses all understanding necessarily follows grace and mercy (which is that our sins are forgiven us freely, and we are heirs of the kingdom without any merit), for "eye has not seen nor ear heard, etc." [1 Cor. 2:9] You see, if you do not believe that you have obtained the grace and mercy of God, you will never have peace. I say "obtained," not from your own merits nor from your interest in righteousness, etc., but from God, who loves us so much in His beloved Son that we not only call Him "our Father," but He actually is our Father. As a result, we fear nothing from such great majesty for we are His children on the basis of His mercy. We have also obtained this from our Lord Jesus Christ, under whose dominion and rule the whole army of hell cannot prevail over the children of God and servants of Christ.

You see here that Paul is not only calling Christ "Lord," but also "our Lord," so that you may acknowledge Him as your Protector and your Lord and king in the fact that He is powerful over sin, death, and hell, etc.

[v. 3:] "…that they teach no other doctrine…"

Or, "that they not follow another doctrine," as the old translation has it. He should not teach anything different. Paul wants nothing to be added to the preaching of the Gospel or to faith, regardless of the disguise of godliness under which that is taught, something which the pseudapostles at that time kept trying to do. That's why Paul said in Gal. 1[:8]: "Even if an angel from heaven, etc." Paul obviously had the presentiment that human teachings were going to check the growth of the faith of Christ, as we see has happened. Therefore we must note very carefully here that he is saying that the edification of God comes through faith, for he senses that all the rest of the things which are taught are destruction.

"Edification" is the teaching of salvation; "destruction" is ungodly teaching and the destruction of salvation, as you often see in Paul. Two kinds of people hinder this edification of faith or even destroy it once it has been edified. You see, some people teach that faith is in the works of the Law. Because God gave the Law, it can only be good and necessary. To these, Paul responds that they do not know the good use of the Law. [v. 8] Faith must be taught, for without faith one cannot perform the works of the Law as the Law demands. It is faith which obtains the Spirit, the fulfiller of the Law.

However, where you have faith, you are bound by no Law so that you owe no one anything except that you love your neighbor. (See Rom. 13[:8].) This you will provide not only because you owe it because the Law commands it, but also because you want to, namely, as the Spirit draws your will. This is what he is saying here: "The Law was not made for the just person, but for unjust people who are either punished or killed according to the Law. Thus, there is no need to ask whether the guilty are going to be punished under the new covenant because we are agreed that adulterers, whoremongers, and murderers are not included under the new covenant to which only those who are righteous through faith, that is, believers, belong, "against whom there is no Law."

Next, although they command many things from the Law, they terribly neglect the intention and chief point of the Law, which is, as I have said, love for one's neighbor but not revealed openly as a simulated work but, as it is defined here, "out of a pure heart and good conscience and unfeigned faith." [v. 5] You see that not even alms, however generous they may be, are profitable without faith (for "whatever is not of faith is sin." [Rom. 14:23]). Also, those works which appear to be works of love are not love unless they come from a heart and conscience which an unfeigned faith has purified.

Those people, I say, "have turned away to vain chatter, wishing to be teachers of the Law, but they do not understand what they are saying nor about what they are making claims." [v. 6–7] Indeed, they are presenting commandments and the Law or mandates of behavior, but they are not teaching on the basis of what source you should live in such a way. Today you will find those people who seek nothing in Holy Writ except moral mandates which they next think are similar to heathen commandments such as the prescripts of Aristotle or Seneca. Nevertheless, they do not know what Paul is disputing in the entire Epistle to the Romans or to the Galatians or what Christ wants when He preaches faith (that is, trust in God) everywhere, or what it is that Paul is saying here, namely, that love comes from a pure heart and a good conscience and an unfeigned faith. As Paul says, "they have wandered away from such things and have turned to vain chatter, etc." Up to now, however, we have been speaking about such people.

Others, however, who have learned from Holy Scripture, know that they must not trust works but only the mercy of God and indeed correctly. The curious and superstitious, however, find empty words which Holy Writ does not know and boast of knowledge. Paul speaks against these at the end of this epistle and avoids profane and empty words.

Also, they follow tales; that is, materials which come from outside Holy Writ, many of which are Jewish lies and even many of which our people consider as historical. In addition, they seek unending genealogies; that is, about which you cannot be certain from Holy Writ, which one person reckons in one way and another in another way, and each person prefers his own interpretation. Paul says that these generate questions and doubts, but no edification.

There are also those people, of whom there is a great number, who follow with great pains of spirit nothing except vain questions on the basis of Holy Writ, never hesitating even when they look for a problem where none exists. In the meantime, however, they see as certain as possible sound doctrine and the open Gospel, that is, they see them clearer than light and yet leave the promises of God and Christ on the pages of both Testaments. Such people are in this danger, that they must be afraid that, when they pursue word-battles, they leave behind those words which could edify them and finally begin to doubt the truthfulness of Scripture; and when they follow a shadow as did the dog of Aesop, they lose the truth and the very reality, that is, faith. The case is still worse of those who pursue their own gain through this behavior while some contend that they prefer themselves to others, and others return the favor. Paul speaks about these in ch. 6[:3–4].

[v. 5:] "…from a pure heart…"

Where faith is unfeigned, there is also a pure heart, as Peter says: "…by faith purifying their hearts." [Acts 15:9] Where there is unfeigned faith there is also a good conscience, for who is there who is correctly aware of himself who does not trust God from his whole heart! Next, he speaks of "unfeigned faith," that is, of true faith, against that of which people commonly boast today by which they assent to an evangelical history just as they do to other histories and those which tell the accounts about the Turks, about Alexander, and about Pope Julius, etc. That evangelical history is an opinion about Christ and is an historical faith or rather, a feigned faith rather than that justifying faith which only believers know. As a result, it happens that our people are listening more freely to a fairy tale (which they call "examples") rather than to the text of the Gospel. Whoever has such a faith in the Gospel also considers it not another fairy tale but almost less than those stories.

[v. 12:] "And I thank…"

Paul presents this passage to us lest we despair over any kind of life and any type of sins—provided we come to Christ as did Paul. See here how all things are of God so that we presume nothing here as do those to who think foolishly that they can have an approach to Christ whenever they wish, contrary to what Paul says, [Rom. 9:16]: "…not of one who wishes nor of one who runs, but, etc."

First he says: "...who has enabled me through Christ..."; next: "...who has judged me faithful..."; "...I obtained mercy"; and: "...grace abounded beyond measure"; and: "...Christ came to save sinners, etc." But: "Give the glory not to us, not to us, but to Your name for Your mercy and Your truth" [Psa. 115:1], something which Paul says here in this way: "to the King of ages, etc."

[v. 17:] "...to the King immortal..."

Thus His kingdom is eternal. Invisible as it is, therefore it is not of this world, but spiritual. "...[T]o the only, wise God..."; beside Him and outside Him all things are filled with foolishness so that there is nothing of true wisdom where He does not shed His light and, so to speak, create wisdom. With reference to Christ, it was foretold in Jer. 23[:5]: "And the King will rule, and He will be wise." In Heb. [2:11], we read: "He will sanctify."

[v. 18:] "...according to the prophecies..."

According to those things which I learned from the Spirit of prophecy about this before when I made you bishop, they understand that you are acting according to those things. Moreover, I both here and later in ch. 4, understand the prophecies and doctrines of the Spirit of God or revelation of Scripture which Timothy had received from Paul or from some other source, as we said that prophecy was accepted in our annotations on Isaiah. For this reason, we can read from the Greek: "...according to the prophecies which have preceded up to your time," that is, that you walk according to the doctrine which you have received and which you now have, that you defend the same against those who teach otherwise, that you do this "in faith and with a good conscience" [v. 19], which two we cannot separate.

As Paul says: "Those who have driven away their good conscience," that is, who dare to say one thing and do another which is different from what they know in their heart because of which they appear to be ahead of the rest and on the basis of which they appear superior to the rest by comparison; I say, Paul calls this "blasphemy." [v. 20] He says: "Those who have driven away their good conscience have made shipwreck of their faith"; that is, they have become so imperiled in that which they know deep in their heart that they have finally perished.

[v. 18:] "…this precept…"

Namely, as earlier, that you denounce certain people, etc., and that you commend the grace of God to sinners, just as I have, absent the works of the Law, etc. Or you can relate to this what follows, as soldiers, etc.

[v. 20:] "Hymenaeus and Alexander…"

These knowingly were in the habit of contending against the truth which they knew.

[v. 20:] "…I surrendered to Satan…"

As he had done to the Corinthian who had married his step-mother, about which see our annotations on Philippians. Nevertheless, he is showing that this excommunication of the aforenamed two, as also that other, is useful, when he says: "…that they may learn not to blaspheme." This is not the papist excommunication which we see today.

CHAPTER 2.

((What prayer means.)) Prayer is the desire of the heart to obtain something from God. If this is a true desire, prayer never stops until it receives from God what it desires. This is what Christ says: "Pray always, and do not stop." The person who has no desire prays for nothing despite the fact that he may fill the air with his verbosity; he who has a true desire also will never abstain from his words. As a result, it happens that we call with the general word "prayer" a conversation with God, even when we praise Him with psalms and spiritual songs, that is, which we make in our hearts. As we never cease desiring mercy for ourselves and for our neighbors, so also we desire that the name of the Father be hallowed always that we not appear to be seeking our own. In all things, may your will be done according to God, etc.

Thus Paul is instructing his bishop here that he advise his hearers especially in this: that above all they pray. After all, how shall they understand the Gospel or achieve love for God and their neighbor unless they will have requested from God a good spirit that by this admonition they may learn first of all that all things depend on God when they hear that they must request all things from God?

They should pray for all people, even for their enemies, something which true love demands. They should not exclude from their prayers kings and rulers, although they may be wicked, first, that the peace which we request for them may also come to us and that we many live in peace under them as much as we may through godliness toward God and consideration for our neighbor. Do not take this to mean that godliness and faith are to yield for the sake of the peace of the flesh which pertains to people and that this happens without [damage to] conscience.

Next, this also is acceptable to God that we pray for all without exception, whether they be Jews or Gentiles, servants or rulers. As He is God alone and Lord, absent any exception, so also He wants people, absent any exception, to come to Him. Therefore we should make no exception, not even of wicked kings, for he excepted no one. Thus, He prayed for Nebuchadnezzar, Balthazar, Baruch, etc.

Also, because there is one Mediator between God and man who gave Himself as the Redeemer for all; therefore, we again should exclude no one because we are praying for the salvation of people, etc., for we know that this very thing pleases both God the Father and Christ, whom the Father gave as the Mediator.

[v. 1:] "…deprecations…"

They distinguish in this way that deprecating is to pray that evil be taken away, and entreating is to pray that good come, to complain about those things which harm us, and to give thanks for blessings received, something which the reckonings of the words demand.

[v. 4:] "…who wants all people to be saved…"

"He wants all people to be saved or preserved and come to the knowledge of the truth." [Mark 16:15] He therefore commanded the apostles to preach the Gospel to all creatures. "Many, however, are called, but few are chosen" [Mat. 22:14]; but how does this agree with what Paul says in Rom. 9[:18]: "He has mercy on whom He wants to have mercy, and He hardens whom He wishes to harden."?

I respond. We must not oppose one unclear passage of Scripture to all other clear passages. All Scripture considers the wicked to be condemned and the godly or believers to be saved; the former by the judgment of God, the latter, by His compassion for their hearts. We therefore must understand what Paul is saying here, namely, that God wants all to be saved, etc., as a reference to people of every station, something which the coherence of the text demands. "Pray for all…even for kings, etc.," for this pleases God, who rejects no status of the world because we agree that there have been good kings like David, Hezekiah, etc. "All people," therefore, means people of every station and, in addition, not only Jews, as the

Jews themselves think, but also Gentiles throughout the world. So also Paul says about Christ: "He gave Himself as the ransom for all," [v. 6] (If you don't mind, see the annotations of Melanchthon on Rom. 8.)

[v. 5:] "...one mediator..."

From what source have some people made so many mediators for us without Scripture and without the Word of God? It has not occurred to them that Christ prays and intercedes for us as our Mediator and only Mediator between God and man, something which none of the other saints can be. The saints who are on earth pray for each other mutually, and God hears them—but through Christ, their Mediator, just as He has promised: "If you ask the Father for anything in My name, He will do it, etc." (John 16[:23]).

With reference to the dead saints as regards their praying for you, Scripture and the Word of God have nothing. Rather, Scripture commends to you Christ as our High Priest who has entered into heaven to offer Himself there before the face of the Father on our behalf, as the Epistle to the Hebrews treats in a most dignified way. Christ intervenes for us (Rom. 8[:34]). "We have an Advocate with the Father who is the Propitiation for our sins" (1 John [:1–2]); and "our Propitiation" (Rom. 3[:25]); and "Throne of grace" (Heb. 4[:16]). Furthermore, all Scripture commands and bears witness that we must invoke God alone, and you have no other example in Scripture. Why, then, are you turning aside to those things which you don't know and abandoning that certain thing which Scripture is offering you? Paul says clearly: "There is one God and one Mediator."

[v. 6:] "...to be a testimony in His time."

That is, a testimony that this is the mystery of the redemption of Christ by which all people are redeemed; that is, not only

Jews but Gentiles, too, which is to be revealed to the world at a time which God has ordained, as he writes about this mystery to be revealed (Eph. 3[:3–5] and elsewhere, and here later, ch. 3[:4]). Paul says that God sent him as a teacher to the Gentiles to reveal this mystery. He is, I say, a teacher "in faith" and not in the teachings of the Law, and "in truth," not in the hypocrisy of works. Truth is the faith in which one believes not the doctrines of men (for all people are liars), but the Word of God alone, which is the very truth, etc.

[v. 8:] "I want men to pray…"

Paul continues what he began about prayer. See here that Paul does not require a temple for worship but says: "I want men to pray *everywhere*," that is, wherever they pray, etc. Do not spread here a false charge against Paul that one must pray also in water, along the roads, etc., because he says "everywhere, etc." I could also interpret what I said before, namely, that "He wants all people to be saved" in such a way that "as many as are saved are saved by His will," as we read in John 1[:13]; or "enlightening every person," as "as many as are enlightened are enlightened by God." So also here: "I want men to pray in every place," that is, "wherever they may have prayed." Had I seen that this pertained to the context of prayer as you see in this passage, Scripture reduces these sophist triflings to nothing. Let him who believes believe! The Spirit of God has not conceived these trifles. We must seek the sum of this prior passage (that I may repeat myself again) from its context: Pray for the status or condition of all people, for God rejects no status, and Christ died not only for the Jews but also for the Gentiles in whatever condition they may exist.

Notice that he wants men[1] to pray with godliness, but women to pray with clothing and works which profess godliness so that also with their appearance they appear to be Christians and an

---

1   The Greek reads "ἄνδρας" and the Latin, "*viros*," both meaning "men" and not "people."

example of decency and modesty, lest they turn the hearts of men away, when they come together for public prayer. That Christians had public prayers when they would meet together is the witness of Paul's passage in 1 Cor. 14[:16]: "If you shall have blessed with the Spirit, how will he who supplies the room for an uneducated person say 'Amen' over your benediction?"

((The good works of women.)) The good works of women, however, are not those superstitions of foolish women, many of which they themselves have invented and many of which they have learned from foolish confessors and unlearned preachers. They rather are those which are written below in ch. 5[:2–14], namely, if they shall have reared their children, been hospitable, washed the feet of the saints, served the afflicted and been zealous in every good work. See also Titus 2[:3–4]: "In like manner an old woman, etc."; and 1 Peter 3[:1–6]: "In like manner also you women, etc."

[v. 8:] "…lifting up…"

He is indicating the deportment of those who pray, which is nothing other than lifting the heart to God, as we read in the Psalm [25:1]: "To You, O Lord, have I lifted up my soul," which is what he is saying here: "…lifting up pure hands." The Lord doesn't want to listen to "those whose hands are filled with blood" (Isa. 1[:15]). Hands are not pure unless the heart be pure, and the heart cannot be pure without faith, for, as Peter says, [Acts 15:9]: "…purifying their hearts with faith," which he says here as "without anger and debating."

There are two things which get in the way of hearkening. The first is anger, that is, that you are not forgiving your neighbor who is sinning against you, for you always see this condition added in the Gospel: "If you have forgiven your brother, etc." The second is debating, by which you debate with yourself whether God is going to listen to you. "Here also you will receive nothing" (James 1:7). See also Mark 11[:24]: "Believe and you will receive."

[v. 11:] "Let the woman learn in silence, etc.

That is, she should not speak when people gather together to teach and where they must listen to the Word of God, for men have permission to speak with the teacher. In fact, "if it shall have been revealed to one who is sitting nearby and who was teaching, he should be silent" (1 Cor. 14[:30]). Women, however, should be silent in the Church, as Paul says in the same place, that they not arrogate for themselves power over their husbands against the Law of God [Gen. 3:16], which says: "You will be under the power of your husband." In addition, Adam is the prior in creation, and the woman is the ruin of her husband. Salvation, however, will come through child-bearing. No one regards this as an indubitably good work, although nevertheless the woman may have the word of Paul and, in fact, the Word of God in Paul. In this, therefore, she is obedient to God who says: "In sorrow you will bear children." This is indeed in the work of God, who says: "I shall multiply your seed and your conceptions, etc." He also adds: "If they shall have remained, etc." The Greek verb is in the plural here, but in the old translation we read it not inappropriately in the singular, avoiding the Hebraism. You see, it is a Hebraism: "If they, namely, the women, shall have remained," about which we spoke earlier: "In like manner also, you women, etc." We know well from the prophets that the Hebrews suddenly change number and persons. Those who take this to mean: "If they, that is, the children, shall have remained," they are not seeing how inappropriate this is, as if a woman cannot be saved unless her children also be saved. Thus Paul is saying: "If they, that is, the women, shall have remained in faith and love and holiness, by which they become holier day by day." That is, they grow in faith and love with the addition of chastity, that is, moral integrity which also befits them in the presence of all people.

Note here that women prophesy if they have the Word where there are no men who have the Word, 1 Cor. 11[:5]: "[Every] woman who prays or prophesies, etc." You read in Joel 2[:28]: "Your sons and daughters will prophesy." In Acts 21[:8], you read: "Philip had four virgin daughters who prophesied." Also, Mary sang her *Magnificat*, etc.

CHAPTER 3.

ON BISHOPS AND DEACONS.

At the beginning of the Epistle to the Philippians, I advised that bishops were preachers of the Word whom God had chosen for this work, and that deacons were the ministers of the saints and providers for the poor. Either the people in a city or a bishop, that is, some apostle or preacher who had taught the people there and could not remain there, although the people wished and wanted him to say, chose the deacons.

Moreover, the deacons were selected from the best citizens and each had a wife, children, family and the care of a household, etc., just as consuls are chosen as you are seeing here. For this reason, the offices of the episcopacy and diaconate were not permanent offices as are now imagined regarding an indelible mark. Compare therefore the high offices of our ecclesial officials now and the duties of those in Paul's time, and you will see that our people are ignorant of the apostolic institution.

((The office of the episcopate is not a merit.)) The apostle therefore allows it if there are any who desire to be placed in charge, as he describes here, for they are desiring a good work, not their own glory and advantage, for those are duties and not merits. You see almost the same thing in Paul's Epistle to Titus, so compare that, too, with what we have here. He is describing the sort of people who are not only learned and powerful in the Word and faith of the Gospel of Christ and blameless before God but also against whom not even the faithless have anything to which to object justly or merely to have evil suspicions about, and this not only from his own person but even from his wife, children, household, etc., lest this lead to blasphemy against the good Word of God, etc.

[v. 2:] "…the husband of one wife…"

That is, the bishop is a man who does not have more than one wife, just as now. Some of the Jews and of the recently-converted Gentiles still had plural wives. This restriction is set that bishops not be suspected of indecency. Paul is not saying here that, if death claims his wife, a bishop cannot marry another, as if he then had to give up his household, children and home, which you see here, etc.

[v. 6:] "…not a novice…"

That is, a bishop should not be a recent convert whom temptations have not yet tested, most of such think that they are something although they are nothing. These are arrogant as if strong in faith, and they fall when temptation comes; but they deny that and open their mouth with blasphemies against the Gospel of God.

[v. 9:] "…as they hold the mystery of faith…"

That is, deacons recognize and have within themselves faith which is revealed in their heart and which the world does not see. They have it with a pure conscience, as we advised earlier that faith and a good conscience are connected. That is, they are good and dare not say nor do anything except that which they sense is according to faith. This is what happened in the Acts of the Apostles when they elected deacons or ministers who were filled with the Holy Spirit, as I said in the Epistle to the Philippians.

[v. 13:] "For those who have ministered well…"

That is, as I said earlier, who have served with a pure conscience and without reproach in such a way that no one can bring charges against them. What he adds here about "purchasing a good degree, etc.," however, see that you do not take this to mean ecclesial levels, as they speak today, as if one who had been a good deacon for some time could then receive a promotion to be bishop, because he who performed lesser duties well is worthy of greater ones. It is the same as one who for some time was a good miner could then be promoted to be a cobbler. Our people err in this way who dream only of worldly offices and honors and not of duties, to wit, who minister well. He was a good minister as the result of a gift of the Spirit, and people can also promote him to be a good teacher of the common folk, for that is being a good bishop.

But what if he doesn't have the gift of prophecy, although he may have the mystery of faith with a good conscience, as Paul said earlier, as all true Christians should have? After all, the Spirit apportions out to individuals as He wishes. You will not promote him from being a good deacon into being a good bishop, will you? Simply see here, then, what Christ says: "To everyone who has it will be given," and he who receives the gift from God and uses it to the advantage of the Church will abound, as Paul says: "To each is given the manifestation of the spirit for the usefulness of the Church." [1 Cor. 12:7]

I say, he has this gift; and by this gift of the same Spirit, that grace will increase and abound so that he can provide and benefit still more. This is what he is saying: the persons who have ministered well, that is, who, by receiving this gift of the Holy Spirit so that they can be the chosen ministers of the saints, have used it well for the utility of the Church or of the needy, are acquiring a good grade for themselves. That is, they profit from the gift of God, who increases and enriches them. They go up higher in the same gift so that day by day they can advance more and more than before, because "to everyone who has it will be given, and he will abound."

((He explains the parable of the talents. [Mat. 25])) That parable of the Gospel is well-known which certainly speaks about gifts, where we also have this addition: "It will be taken from him who does not have," that is, even the gift which he had received, just as you see there, for he did not use it for holy gain. Even what he seems to have will be taken away from him; that is, he will become useless because that gift will be taken away. Gradually the faith of his heart will be taken away, and he will become blind because he was unfaithful in the office which had been committed to him.

Here, too, you will be able to make this connection (which pleases me especially and uniquely) in this way: they acquire a good grade for themselves and great freedom in their faith so that they understand a good level in faith so that they who minister well on the basis of their faith grow from faith to faith. That is, those who minister well from a pure conscience receive abundantly a free conscience in all things and confidence in God, and they labor under no anguish of heart and loss of faith. This is as if Paul were saying: "You should choose such people for ministry from whom you may hope daily for greater progress through God."

[v. 15:] "…in the house of God…"

This house has God as its resident. It is the kingdom of heaven, the kingdom of God, the kingdom of Christ, the temple of the Holy Spirit, the support and stay of the truth which the Spirit, as its resident, has founded upon the firm Rock, that is, Christ, who in it teaches every truth, and not even the gates of hell can prevail against it. Outside of it are pure darkness and errors as well as the kingdom of the prince of darkness, etc.

[v. 15:] "…that you may know how, etc."

That is, that you may know the things of which you should take care; for soon in the next chapter Paul is going to speak far differently about our bishops.

[v. 16:] "…great is the mystery of godliness…"

That is, it is a secret, until now hidden from the world, but which the Church of the living God knows, whose ministers are Timothy, Paul, etc. Paul says this to the Corinthians [1.4:1]: "Thus let a person consider us as ministers of Christ and stewards of the mysteries of God." Furthermore, the mystery is this: God was manifested in the flesh which He took on, John 1[:14]: "The Word was made flesh etc… , and we have seen His glory, etc." "He was justified in His Spirit," [v. 16] which does not befit God but the humanity of Christ which certainly was not just of Himself but of God, who alone justifies. Paul therefore is attributing to the true God that Christ is one, God and Man, just as the Son of God is said to have died for our sins. Therefore he is making a correct division; namely, that Christ's manifestation is in His flesh, but His justification is in His Spirit.

He is revealed and preached in the flesh, but He was justified in the Spirit. We believe this only by faith, seeing that God infused righteousness in the Man Christ in such a way that Christ became for us righteousness and sanctification and redemption, as Paul writes in 1 Cor. 1[:30]: "Whom God made wisdom for us, etc." We read in Psa. 45[:7]: "Furthermore, God has anointed You, etc."; and in John 10[:36]: "God has given Him the Spirit not according to measure." The Father loves the Son and gave all things into His hand. This flesh does not profit anything unless, justified, you believe Christ in the Spirit and, therefore, with the righteousness of God through whom we are righteous. This should be enough for our sins and for us to be saved.

Moreover, this is the mystery of God revealed in the flesh of Christ and of the justified. God in the Spirit of Christ revealed to every creature by the deigning of God, for "the angels desire to look into those things which we have through Christ" (1 Peter 1[:12]); and: "Eye has not seen, etc." [1 Cor. 2:9] He was preached to the Gentiles, although the Jews alone seemed to themselves to belong to Him and to the mystery of the kingdom of heaven, as we said in our notes on Eph. 2 and 3.

Furthermore, He was believed in all the world; otherwise, what would it have availed for Him to have been preached? Furthermore, He was taken up in glory that all may glorify the Son as they glorify the Father, that at the name of Jesus every knee should bend, and every tongue confess that Christ is in the glory of God the Father (Phi. 2:10–11). This glory is in all the earth and above all the heavens. "He was made so much higher than the angels" (Heb. 1:4), for He has an eternal and priestly kingdom, etc.

Next, we are certain that the ancient interpreter read it differently in the Greek, just as Ambrose both read and translated it in this way: "…which was manifested, etc." Also, all the things that follow are related to the mystery, but they all go back to the same way of thinking.

CHAPTER 4.

I explained this passage in 2 The. 2:2. I said, however, that these things are the last times, as the ancient translation has it (Isa. 2[:2]).

[v. 3:] "…He created to be received…"

In Gen. 1 and 9, God created food to be received with thanksgiving that they might acknowledge the Father for His blessing. Holy is the person who eats meat and gives thanks, but he who abstains from meat and does not acknowledge his Creator is unworthy of every creature. Read 1 Cor. 10[:29]: "My freedom, therefore, is judged, etc." Read also Rom. 14[:6]. God wanted the nations to acknowledge him for so great a blessing, but there was darkness in the world, as Paul says, Acts 14: "…who were in the first generations, etc."

Why, however, does he say: "…to those who believe," inasmuch as those who don't believe also eat and drink and use creatures? I respond: because God gave His creatures to those who believe, as you see in Gen. 1; that is, before the fall of Adam. After the fall, however, those who don't believe sin in every creature. Titus 1[:15]: "To the pure all things are pure, but to unbelievers nothing is pure, etc." As a result, it happens that, by eating meat on any day at all, believers glorify God. But even by abstaining, the hypocrite and the upright-appearing person sins: first, because they condemn the good creation of God; and next, because they can pretend their thanks but cannot give it because they have rejected the blessing of God. Furthermore, they trust in their own abstinence to the insult of God, whom alone we must trust, etc.

We had been created to be lords of all creatures, but we lost this lordship in Adam. In Christ, however, the Father has returned it to those who believe. For that reason, we read in the Psalm [24:1]: "He is the Lord of the earth, etc." Therefore, every creature of God is useful without sin, provided it not be contrary to the mandate of God.

I am not wasting time on human traditions, for every creature is yours in Christ. Thus, Paul in 1 Cor. 10 cites the testimony of the Psalm. Those righteous-appearing people speak of foods, but we do not believe them. Paul responds: "You are lying." I interpret those believers as those who know this truth of which you are ignorant, namely, that whatever God created is good, and that we must reject nothing if we eat it with thanksgiving.

[v. 5:] "…it is sanctified…"

How is it that the creature of God is good of itself and yet Paul says: "It is sanctified."? I respond. It is good because God created it, but it is unclean to him who abuses it or to him who believes it is unclean for him to use. Therefore, it is sanctified on the basis of the use of the person who uses it, just as he says in 1 Cor. 7[:14]: "The husband is sanctified, etc." There the sanctification has to do with the use of marriage; namely, that a believing woman is permitted to marry an unbelieving man and this without sin—no less without sin than if both were believers. Here the unbelieving person is not holy in himself but is holy in his use of marriage so that the believing spouse uses the unbelieving one as a thing which is good in itself and which God created for this purpose.

So also, food is good in itself. It does not become more holy but is sanctified for use that you may use without sin that food which would not be holy for an unbeliever and for a person who does not give thanks.

Paul says that "it is sanctified by the Word of God," by which we believe that all things are holy for us (as we said above), and through "prayer," by which we pray that God give us such things and we give Him thanks when He has given them (as we said above).

Now you see the foolishness of those who appear to be righteous, who seek their holiness in foods and other creations. Although those things are good by creation, they nevertheless are holy to us, that is, they could not be pure to us without our faith and thanksgiving.

Understand all the things which we have said about the use of foods also as references to the use of marriage, something which you understand quite clearly from the preceding paragraphs. After all, a woman is a good creation of God if you should use her the way God instituted. If you should use her contrary to the institution of

God, as happens in fornication and adultery, she whom God made good is no longer good as far as you are concerned. You, too, are now in the same damnation if you think that you sin by the use of a creature (provided this be done according to God); for you are not only condemning the creature but also the institution of God, etc.

[v. 6:] "...you will be a good minister."
Now the doctrines of demons say: "You are a heretic."

[v. 8:] "...godliness is good for all things..."
In Scripture, "godliness" (from which the godly are so called) is the honor of God. You honor God if you believe Him, if you trust Him, if you fear, praise, and love Him, knowing that all things are yours, namely, that in God alone is your salvation; that nothing—absolutely no human righteousness—can deliver you from sins or save you, but only the grace of God through Christ Jesus, our Lord. Contrariwise, where these things are not present, there is ungodliness, despite the fact that all things may appear very holy because the lust of the eyes has deceived your senses.

Therefore, you should exercise yourself for godliness, not because you are striving to prepare yourself for such things with your energies—something which cannot occur, for Timothy already had them. When, however, you endlessly beseech God for these things, knowing as you do that those who hunger and thirst for righteousness are blessed, then you are endlessly and zealously pursuing your calling.

This godliness is also useful for all things, for it is the salvation of others, too, and a certain salvation—but certain through the Word of God. For "it has the promises of the present and the coming life," and both promises save, provided you believe them, for, if you believe the Word of God, you are thereby justified. As God promised many earthly blessings to the godly, as we read in the Law of Moses; so also he says to us: "…all these things will be added unto you." [Mat. 6:33] After all, of what importance is it to advise about the promises of the life to come?

Furthermore, physical exercise does not have such promises. Nevertheless, it does have some usefulness; namely, when you do not consider it as a substitute for godliness but as a servant of godliness. You exercise your body with watches, fasts, abstinence, and hardships lest it become hardened against the Spirit and hinders godliness rather than serves it, as Christ admonishes [Luke 21:34]: "Pay attention to yourselves that your body not become overburdened with gluttony and drunkenness." You see, physical exercise is something you can do or avoid as you decide, as is necessary for your body. But if it can happen as a result of physical exercise or external work that you believe that you are justified thereby, now physical exercise does not have any usefulness but it is also ungodly and condemns you, for you are ascribing what belongs to God to your own works and are worshipping the works of your hands.

All the works of righteous-appearing people, therefore, are lying here and in addition cannot be done in the faith of salvation, for they do not have the promises of God. The orders of all the sects, therefore, are far from salvation. As Paul shuts the mouths of those who contradict him, he adds [v. 9]: "This is a faithful saying, etc." Today almost everyone has doubts about this, and many even blaspheme this truth, but Paul wants what he is approving in all ways to be indubitable so that the whole world holds those things in contempt, although all the wise people and those little saints may be conspiring among themselves against us. Let us, however, not be separated violently from this truth.

Those gainsayers are placing their hope in physical exercise and ceremonies and their trust in dead things which can be of no benefit to themselves. But we are teaching that such things are ungodliness and have our hope fixed on the living God. For that reason, the world cannot help but hate us.

May these words strengthen the hearts of those who have learned recently that it is the only godliness which God respects, and to such people we especially commend this passage.

[v. 6:] "...Nourished in the word..."

He is saying two things, namely, that the person who wants to teach well must have received the word of faith.

[v. 7:] "[Avoid] profane and anile ..."

Even a child knows that we call that which is not sacred "profane." Therefore, whatever is not from Holy Scripture is a profane old wives' tale, although the hypocrite and the world may consider that very thing as great wisdom. The Christian person will by no means place in his heart that which he holds in contempt. If he does, he is not a Christian, etc.

[v. 10:] "...who is the Savior of all, etc."

We are certain that Paul is saying this about temporal salvation, otherwise he would not have said "especially of those who believe," that is, "he saves those who are far more worthy," as we read in the psalm: "O Lord, You preserve people and beasts." [Psa. 36:6] Therefore, let the heathen and the hypocrites learn that they must not trust in creatures nor in their own works—because of which they suffer wretched torture and perish, so far are they from obtaining salvation. Moreover, let them trust in Him alone from whom they receive their physical blessings—something which they cannot deny.

[v. 11:] "Command..."

If you listen to Paul here, you will be a heretic today!

[12: "No one [should despise] your youth..."

That is, live and perform the duty committed to you in such a way that you cannot be an object of contempt, something which he explains quickly, saying: "...but be an example of believers, etc."

[v. 13:] "...until I come, etc."

He does not want Timothy to become neglectful of his pastoral office, which he here calls "the gift." [v. 14] Two things are required for this gift: prophecy and calling. Without these two, no one should presume to be a pastor or bishop. Prophecy is the gift that you be able to teach powerfully the things of the faith. If you have that gift, wait until you be called either by God or by people, just as all the prophets and apostle were called. At the time of the apostles, calling was done by the laying on of hands on the head of the person called, by which sign people acknowledged that he was called and received. Thus, they were not apostles (so that our apostles do not arrogate this for themselves) but other disciples gathered from the apostles who chose the seven deacons, prayed for them and laid their hands upon them in the sight of the apostles. Thus, with this sign, they showed the apostles and the rest of the crowd that they wanted and chose such men as their ministers.

Also, Paul laid his hands on Timothy, who had learned Holy Scripture from his boyhood and was learned in the faith, as the apostle says in 2 Timothy [3:15]. But he not only laid his hands upon him, as you see here, for what is translated here as "by the authority of the priesthood" is not in the Greek, but "μετὰ ἐπιθέσεως, etc. – with the laying on of the hands of the presbytery," as if you should say in the Latin: "of the senate," that is, "of the elders."

You are seeing that Timothy was elected by the consensus of others. Take what he says later: "Lay hands on no one quickly" to mean the same thing, as well as what he writes to Titus [1:5]: "Establish elders throughout the cities, etc."

The laying on of hands was a familiar thing to the Hebrews when they would commend something to God. Thus Jacob laid his hands on the two sons of Joseph (Gen. 48[:20]). Thus they would place hands on the head of a sacrifice about to be killed (Lev. 1[:4]). In this way, Christ laid His hands upon the little children. [Mat. 19:14] With reference to believers, Christ said: "Lay your hands upon the sick, and they will become well." [Mark 16:18]

Because this was an external sign, they could either omit it or perform it, because it was not instituted nor mandated. It was merely the sign of election. The things which were instituted, like the fact that a bishop was to be without accusation, apt to teach, etc., we neglect and despise, and we make much of empty signs. Yes, I am saying "empty," where the reality is not present. Besides, we fill everything with external signs and invent the sort of things of which Christ and the apostles were ignorant.

[v. 16:] "Practice these things…"

As earlier he reminds Timothy of his office: "Practice these things," that is: "Persist in them."

CHAPTER 5.

[v. 1:] "Do not rebuke an older man, etc."

This is not fawning flattery, for he later says in this same chapter [v:20]: "Rebuke sinners in the presence of all, that others also maybe fearful." This is Christian modesty with all people and is especially necessary for a Christian teacher. In this way, even our words breathe love. But here he adds [v. 2]: "…with all purity," so that the charming name of young ladies is not only pure among us but is also above suspicion among themselves and others. We must provide good things not only before God but also before people (Rom. 12[:17]).

[v. 3:] "Honor widows…"
This passage concerns widows who are destitute of every assistance. The Church would take them up to feed them, and the deacons would provide for them from the goods collected from the Church for the poor. The Church would receive them, not because of some vow (which the Church never knew), but because of their poverty. He calls these "true" widows who were deprived not only of a husband, but also of children or friends (who could have fed them), or of goods. Paul commands us to honor these widows not with words or gestures but with actual things, just as we are commanded to honor our parents. Later [v. 17] he says: "Elders…are worthy of double honor, etc."

Please see how diligently Paul is careful not to set a snare and not let those very widows fall into the snare of the devil, for the Church was taking them up to be fed and not that they might pursue leisure in the labors of others and begin to fall from the faith of Christ with their shameless behavior. See, too, how well Paul knows this kind, about which he says [v. 6]: "She who is involved in pleasures is living by the flesh but she is dead to God." That is, she has renounced her faith.

But where are those who praise virginity and widowhood, who do nothing else but thrust them into snares with their crazy praises while being ignorant of what they are affirming? Paul is careful of setting those snares against virginity and widowhood, just as he also says in 1 Cor. 7[:2]: "Because of fornication each should have his own wife"; and, here [v. 14]: "I want the younger widows to marry, have children, etc." In this way, they will follow not Jerome but God, who created them for these purposes, knowing as they do that such activities please God and that through them they are serving their neighbor; that is, their husband, children, and household. For the rest of the things on this passage, see the end of my booklet on vows.

With reference to widows, there is less danger today. Still, Paul writes about them alone that we must feed them but not bind them to a vow. The doctrines of demons, however, set endless snares for almost every age and both genders.

[v. 4:] "But if some widow…"

We should feed those widows who are sixty years old or who are truly widows and abandoned. If they are not desolate but have children and grandchildren, they should have control over their own household in a godly way, that is, in the Lord and in the teaching of faith. They should repay their parents and grandparents. That is, they should serve the younger ones who belong to them (whom they call their children and grandchildren), just as their parents and grandparents served them. If they are unwilling to do this, they have renounced the faith and are worse than unbelievers. After all, what faith do those have who don't want what God wants and who reject those whom God has given them? If they don't serve them, they cannot serve anyone! Tell me, what love would those who neglect and despise their own kin show to strangers? Faith cannot exist where its fruits are not revealed not only to strangers, but even to those to whom nature has inclined.

[v. 5:] "Next, she who is truly a widow…"

He is describing who is truly a widow as a woman who is desolate and entertains a chaste hope of eating. If, however, she is quite young, she should marry and not be welcomed to be fed. We should hand her over to a husband to be fed lest she later become wanton against Christ. Who today, however, hands over a poor woman to a husband? That is a happy arrangement, but we have not preserved it. It has degenerated to the infectious destruction of both sexes.

[v. 10:] "…in the testimony of people, etc."

He does not take up all widows who are sixty years old, although they may be desolate, but those whom the testimony of people have approved. This he does that they not later become an offense to Christians among the heathen. They should be blameless, that is, without accusation before people.

[v. 12:] "…their first faith."

That is, their faith in Christ; otherwise, he would not have said: "They began to be wanton against Christ." Next, these not only are an offense to Christians but also become contradictory in the homes of others, even of heathen, when they are looking for a husband. (See my booklet on vows.) This is what he is adding here; namely, "that they not give an adversary an opportunity" to have a handle for cursing the teaching of the Gospel. Paul is showing quite clearly that he means faith in Christ and not a vow, as we see from what follows [v. 15]: "Some have already turned aside and have followed Satan."

[v. 16:] "But if some faithful person…"

Even now monks are boasting that they have abandoned their own resources and are living off the benefits of the Church. The clergy, however, are keeping their own resources and living by the sweat of the poverty-stricken. Paul doesn't want the Church to be burdened with widows whom their friends can support.

Up to this point Paul has been speaking about widows, etc. The precept of love demands that we assist those who are truly widows. The rest of the things which Paul arranges about widows here are good for being careful of the many snares we find in widows. But do not take these words as if Paul is prescribing a law for you, because the spiritual man could also change some of these and observe other practices according to place and persons, should it appear expedient.

Furthermore, he is writing about these that this is honorable and acceptable before God. But you—see to it that you do not despise these matters! Be careful of snares! Be careful of offenses! Paul was not ignorant of the wiles of Satan.

[v. 17:] "…the elders who rule well…"

The elders who rule the rest of the multitude in the city and who do that well are due double honor: first, that we defer to their authority and obey them with reverence, for they are ruling well, that is, they are arranging all things according to the judgment of the spirit which they have, and doing that without neglect. The other is that we provide with the necessities from the treasury of the Church for those who are unable to have a care for their own resources because of their occupation and zeal for governing and caring for the things which are healthful for the flock. Because we owe these things to those who rule well (that is, who rule in the Lord), we also owe them especially to those who labor in the Word and in doctrine, that is, those who are evangelists or teachers (Mat. 10:9–11, 1 Cor. 9:9–15, and Gal. 6:9–10).

[v. 19:] "Against an elder…"

Those who rule readily incur the hatred of the disobedient. Therefore we should not listen readily to those who make accusations against such people, both because accusers are suspect and because they cause a greater scandal if those who are ruling have been marked with an accusation or are suspect. But if it has been revealed to the Church that they have sinned or are sinning, or if it has been proved against them by two or three witnesses according to the Law (Deu. 19[:15]), then the bishop (that is, a teacher of the Gospel) or apostle who has been entrusted with that duty should rebuke them in the presence of all, that, while this be winked at, their error not appear to be approved or not to be an error and find imitators thereof.

Therefore, it is not necessary to ask how this squares with the words of Christ, Mat. 18[:15]: "Correct him between you and him." For this is said to the Church. Therefore elders who sin must receive correction before the Church, if they have been thus found guilty. Furthermore, there is greater danger if those who are rulers sin than other brothers. Notice, then, that the text demands the consequence that you take what the text says, namely, "those who sin" to mean elders (that is, presbyters). If, on the other hand, you wish to understand this as a reference to any sinner at all, nevertheless it is necessary that you understand this as a reference to manifest crimes or about those convicted thereof according to the Gospel.

[v. 21:] "I entreat you before God, etc."

God, Christ, and the elect angels see our affairs. Let us, therefore, execute those duties which have been committed to us as if in their very sight. Paul says: "…that you serve these duties without prejudice but with sound counsel and diligent inquiry through witnesses, etc. Do nothing according to the inclination of your heart, that is, by carnal judgment and favor over against a person, or in hatred. That is, see to it that you do not pass sentence quickly according to a sudden feeling, for the Law of God says about judges, Deu. 16[:18–19]: "Let them judge the people with just judgment," and not turn aside to either party. Let them not respect persons nor receive gifts, for gifts blind the eyes of the wise and change the words of the upright. Pursue justly that which is just.

[v. 22:] "[Lay] hands quickly, etc."

That is, suddenly, that you not commit the duty of bishop to anyone. Rather, test him first to see if he be the sort of man as I depicted above.

[v. 22:] "Do not share others' sins."

If some people act unjustly, if some do not carry out justly that which is just; then see that you do not agree with this, that you do not wink your eye at it, that you not keep silent about it; but do see to it that you speak against it, etc. In this way, if you should accomplish nothing else, nevertheless you would deliver your conscience. That is, you will accomplish what Paul adds: "Keep yourself pure."

[v. 23:] "After this do not drink water…"

As a result, you have it that we can keep, change, interrupt, or skip physical exercises which we use according to the reckoning of our body so that we preserve it, and that it not perish, etc.

[v. 24:] "The sins of some people…"

Because Paul had said: "Do not share the sins of others"; Timothy was fearful that this was too superstitious, and might ask: "What if I don't know the sins of others, that is, of those with whom I share things?" Paul responds: "The day will teach this. Therefore the things which I have said, that you not be rash in your judgments; conceal things which will not be revealed, but in the meantime judge nothing. Consider these as good things about which no one has bad feelings, which provide no one with the opportunity to sin. This will be of no danger to your conscience or to your office." I believe that this is the true meaning which the context requires here, so that you do not take that to mean the final judgment of Christ, but human judgment in this life which he had committed to Timothy earlier.

Paul speaks in this way [v. 24]: "Some sins precede to the judgment," that is, they don't need judgment that you should judge or pass sentence on them because they have already been judged. "The sins of some, however, follow after," that is, they will become known later, and you will recognize them from their fruits. So, too, "good works are manifest before," that is, before they receive judgment or before sentence is passed upon them. Those things, however, which behave differently, that is, which people perform in secret and badly or which people peddle as good works through their hypocrisy, cannot be hidden. That is, they will come forth in their own time.

At that time, the Church will have to judge them as evil when it becomes known that they are evil. That Christ had Judas as His disciple did not stain Christ, for the rest did not know that he was a devil and a betrayer. In the meantime, Judas did not teach badly, he did not neglect his office, he offended no one, etc. This is what you read about the manifest fruits of the flesh and of the Spirit, Gal. 5[:15–22].

CHAPTER 6.

[v. 1:] "whoever are servants under the yoke…"

In 1 Cor. 7[:24], we read: "Each brother should remain before God in the calling to which he was called." He says "before God" that you not believe that you must remain in some shameful condition when you come to the faith. Understand therefore about these means: all external means besides the ones he forbids are indifferent. Thus it is of no importance whether one is Christian or a Jew, whether he be a Gentile by flesh, or a servant or a master or male or female, cobbler or consul, hayseed or prince, etc.

Therefore servants do not neglect their duty because they have become Christians, for God has given them this condition so that they spend their life in it, unless a better opportunity even for physical freedom shall have offered itself, without injuring their master or with the will of the master. Let them serve, therefore, with a good conscience even if their masters are heathen, because it pleases God that the grace of the Gospel not be blasphemed. Rather, such servants and such people will receive commendation if it makes their masters Christians. You see, then, they are servants who are serving not so much masters as brothers, about which they also rejoice that they have such masters who are unable to demand shameful activities. With reference to this passage, see 1 Peter [2:8–9] and often elsewhere in Paul.

[v. 2:] "Teach these things, etc."

He is repeating all the things he had said, for (as he advised in the beginning,) he wants Timothy to avoid those who teach differently, that is, as he says, who do not come with the sound words of Christ and of doctrine which pertain only to godliness. Here you see that all who teach differently are heretics and to be excommunicated. You also see that all the Pauline epistles are nothing else than the words of Christ and the teaching which looks only to godliness. For how would he teach anything else which he himself forbids on the basis of the curse of excommunication?

Notice here how ugly he depicts that class of teachers which teaches differently, namely, that they are puffed-up people, ignorant, not of sound mind, inclined to useless questions and debates about genealogies, Judaic fairy tales, separated souls, choruses of angels, feigned revelations, and human traditions—all things which Scripture does not know and from which are born envies, while each person strives to place himself first in his own wisdom.

In sum, Paul is saying that these are people who have been deprived of the truth (that is, of faith in Christ), who attempt all things, whose concern is their own gain. In the meantime, however, they call godliness, that is the glory and worship of God, their gain. Here you are seeing sophist theologians and the papist kingdom, about which subjects he will speak again at the end of the epistle [6:20–21]: "O Timothy, etc." There he commands such teachers to be excommunicated and the teaching avoided because they have empty and invented words which Scripture does not know. To Scripture they oppose their own wisdom (which does not deserve the title "wisdom" but "senseless ignorance"). When they profess it, they have strayed from the true target of faith.

They themselves consider free will as grace, reason as faith, opinions as the judgment of the Spirit, the doctrines of men as sacred doctrine. They speak of nothing else but the primacy of Peter, acquired faith, formalities, elicited action, the relations of reason in the case of sins, etc When they debate as if very learned people about any matter at all, they oppose themselves and their wisdom to those whose opinions differ. But Paul is saying that they are far from faith and are not Christians, but are boasting that they are very wise uprooters of heretical corruption. He says: "Separate yourself from people who are of this ilk."

[v. 6:] "Moreover, [godliness] is gain, etc."

What does it matter that false knowledge and human doctrine mislead the world as if profitable—although godliness has true and great gain and is content with its own lot? Oh, brief and very sweet statement, which, when believed, creates in both lives blessed people who are at peace in their minds! But those who have no concern for godliness, who are unwilling to be content with their lot but want to enrich themselves, that is, the will they owe to God they consecrate to mammon and fall into temptation and a snare, etc., because they begin to act against conscience and lose faith, just as you see in the Gospel about the seed which falls among thorns— and this in order to achieve profit.

Furthermore, pay attention to what Paul is saying, namely, that those who want to become wealthy are not content with their lot. He is not saying: "Those who *are* rich," for riches are means which we can use spiritually in the right way. This is what he is saying later: "Those who are rich, etc." [v. 17], where he is describing what it means to use it correctly if you have wealth.

[v. 10:] "…with many hardships."

Because this happens to all who abandon their concern for God according to the Gospel: "Don't be anxious, etc." [Mat. 6:24]; what do you suppose is going to happen to those who, contrary to conscience and godliness, dare to seek their own gain?

[v. 11:] "You, O man of God…"

This does not pertain to him who wants to serve mammon.

[v. 11:] "pursue righteousness, etc."

We are dealing with God through these: "Pursue love, godliness, gentleness." We are also dealing with our neighbor through these. These are the riches of Christians about which Christ says: "First seek the kingdom, etc." [Mat. 6:33]

[v. 12:] "Fight the good fight of faith…"

Be steadfast in the faith, yield to neither adversities nor adversaries so that you do or omit those things which are contrary to the reckoning of your faith, that is, against that which you think you have learned. Lay hold onto eternal life, so that you despise this life on behalf of the truth, and lest because of your love for this life you commit something against the faith or yield to your adversaries in some matter. Paul is saying: "You have been called to this." The Christian person is called to the death of this life and to the death of whatever of us is from Adam. His sanctification is not perfected until all things perish. Lay hold to as much of eternal life as departs from this life for him who is baptized with the Spirit and with fire. This is mortification to life. When then you are called to life, be sure that this very thing cannot happen without death. Christ is not glorified without the cross; so also the Christian will not be glorified without his cross.

[v. 12:] "…you have professed a good profession…"

Namely, in Baptism, at which only Christians are present that they may know that this is a brother who is receiving Baptism and whose confession those standing nearby as witnesses hear—unless you should wish to understand here Timothy undertaking the profession of teaching the people and the office of bishop in the presence of many witnesses, that is, in the presence of Christian people.

[v. 13:] "I command you before God, etc."

In this epistle, you see with what great concern Paul commends to Timothy the things which belong to the duty of a bishop. He commands and adjures him through all the sacred things of Christians, just as you often see, but something which he doesn't do in other epistles; namely, showing upon whom all things in this situation depend. But if one does not have godly concern and abandons the teaching of godliness, all the things which are Christian perish, as we see has happened.

As a result, he here is commanding before God, who gives life to all things and before Christ, who did not depart from His profession when He was sentenced to death, that Timothy have a very firm grip on the life to which he was called and on the profession which he had professed, and that he do this even when death and hell are present. That is, he orders him to keep the commandment which he had received, to be spotless before God, and blameless before people to the end. This is especially important for a bishop: that he perform those duties for which a bishop is responsible, for which he certainly needs not a small spirit. It is also necessary that he continually demand this from God. If he does not, he will accomplish nothing.

[v. 14:] "...until the appearing..."

True Christians put aside all things that, prepared and vigilant as they are, they can meet Christ when He comes in judgment and know that they then are going to be glorified, just as the parable about the five wise virgins has it. [Mat. 25:10] You read this everywhere in the New Testament, especially in the discourses of Jesus, our Savior, and in the Pauline epistles. On this day, all who have gone through this life are being preserved to be raised again and yet those who have departed as we shall have done are preserved. Then, too, all who have been reprobates will be condemned and, at the same time, all the elect will be glorified.

[v. 16:] "...and who alone has immortality..."

Therefore you will have sought in vain elsewhere if you are immortal; for, just as He alone *has* life, so He alone *is* life itself. Furthermore, I have spoken about our immortal and blessed God earlier in ch. 1[:17].

[v. 16:] "the inaccessible Light..."

That is, the Light incomprehensible to people, something which he explains saying: "...which no one has seen, etc." (See our notes on John 1 and Isa. 6.) From what source, then, do we come to know God, without whom we cannot be blessed? I respond: "Read 1 John 4, and you will find the answer."

[v. 20:] "...the deposit..."

That which has been entrusted to you, namely, your teaching and office.

THE END.

THE ANNOTATIONS OF JOHANNES BUGENHAGEN OF POMERANIA ON THE SECOND EPISTLE TO TIMOTHY.

THEME.

In this second epistle, because Paul now knew that he was going to be slain, he urges Timothy that, just as he had begun, he would go on to carry out his duty, so that, strong in the spirit of God as he was, he fearlessly and without embarrassment would teach the things which are of faith and love just as he had learned from Paul himself and from Holy Writ, so that he may endure steadfastly until death, after the example of Paul.

You see, many people were already teaching otherwise; many, offended as they were by the shame of the cross, were giving up. Many people who earlier had seemed to favor it were even persecuting the teaching of the Gospel. Already then those had begun to spring up whom Paul had foretold were going to multiply in the last days. Those, under the guise of great godliness, knew how to conceal the very things which the Gospel of Christ did not permit, just as we saw in the previous epistle, and they were speaking only the things which wicked ears listened to gladly.

For all these reasons, Paul urges the bishop to be watchful, for, while people were sleeping, the enemies were sowing weeds (Mat. 13[:25]), that is, the doctrines of demons in the hypocrisy of those who speak lies.

THE MORE OUTSTANDING PASSAGES IN THIS EPISTLE.

The first is that God through Christ gave us the grace of the Gospel before the creation of the world, but He has now revealed that [1:9–10]: "...who has saved us, etc." This point of predestination was treated more clearly in Eph. 1[:5ff.] and 3[:8ff].

Second, he who is be the energetic soldier of Christ [2:3] is either any Christian or especially a bishop, someone who has undoubtedly received the Spirit, that is, who has come to know the grace of the Gospel, who does not blush with reference to the Gospel, or has been offended when temptation came (as Phygellus and Hermogenes), and who embraced nothing except sound doctrine (ch. 1[:13]). "You therefore should not be ashamed, etc." "Hold fast the form, etc." [2:13] He is certain that this reward of his still remains (that is, the glory after the cross), after the example of Christ. "Remember Jesus Christ, etc." [2:8] In fact, Paul himself presents himself as an example of faith, 1[:12]: "I know...and am sure, etc."; ch. 2[:9]: "in which I am afflicted with evils, etc."; and ch. 4[:6]: "...or I am already being offered, etc." Those are the things that come to this soldier, if he be a bishop, and thus he goes forth into battle, ch. 4[:1]: "I therefore charge you, etc.," because, as he says in ch. 1[:7]: "God has not given us the spirit of fear, but of boldness, faith, love, and sobriety."

Third, he tells what sound doctrine is, namely, the form of the saving words about faith and love ("which you heard from me in faith and love," [1:13]), just as Paul teaches them and just as is everywhere in Holy Writ, ch. 1[:13]: "Hold fast the form, etc"; ch. 2[:2]: "Commit these words to faithful people, etc."; ch. 2[:15]: "Study to show yourself, etc."; [3:10]: "You have followed my teaching, etc."; [3:14]: "Persist in those things which you have learned, etc."

Therefore, sound doctrine is whatever is of faith and love according to the form of sound or salutary words and comes to us in Holy Writ. Thus Paul is commanding that we avoid whatever is opposed to sound doctrine; namely, profane vanities of words (as he said in his preceding epistle), contentious and quarrelsome debates, foolish and stupid questions, and those things which he mentions in ch. 2; and, in addition, the doctrines of hypocrites which they teach for gain and not for the truth and glory of God. That, you see, is shameful adulation and pure insanity which move from the truth to the fairy tales of people of corrupt minds and from whom the truth has been removed, as he said in the preceding epistle. "Continue in these things" (ch. 3[:14]). "Moreover, know that, etc." (ch. 3[:1]); "For the time will come, etc." (ch. 4[:3]).

Thus you are seeing with what great care Paul has described in these two letters the energetic soldier and sound doctrine. The senselessness of those who are corrupt and reprobate of mind concerning the faith, who resist the truth or sound doctrine, as do especially those in the last days who will foster under the guise of godliness doctrine which is opposed to that of our Lord Jesus Christ. Paul foretells in ch. 3 that they are not going to be concealed to the end but will become obvious to all before the end of the world. This prophecy of Paul began to receive fulfillment twice in our times, unless some blind heart still not see this very thing. Thanks be to Christ. Amen.

The fourth concerns vessels of wrath and vessels of mercy ch. 2[:20]: "Furthermore, in a great house, etc." See this passage in Rom. 9[:21].

The fifth concerns those who come to their senses, who had earlier resisted the truth, ch. 2[:25]: "…instructing those, etc.," the point which we made third in the prior epistle.

The sixth is that, although the faithless do not believe, God nevertheless remains faithful, and his promises remain true, ch. 2[:13]: "If we do not believe, etc.," a point which he also made in Rom. 3[:3]: "Will their unbelief, etc.?"

Seventh, we have noted an outstanding passage in this epistle in a few words; namely, that only those are misled by unsound doctrines who must be misled, and only those perish who have to perish, ch. 2[:18–19]: "They overthrow the faith of some, but the foundation of God stands firm, having this seal: 'The Lord knows those who are His'; and let all who call upon the name of Christ depart from iniquity." Christ speaks in this way in John 17[:12]: "None of these perishes except the son of perdition"; in Mat. 24[:24]: "...so that even the elect will be misled into error, if that can happen"; and in John 10[:27–28]: "My sheep hear My voice, and I know them and they follow Me. I give them eternal life, and they will never perish. No one will snatch them from My hand." They can go astray for a time, but Christ the Shepherd leads them back in His own time, as we read in the Gospel parable. You see, He knows His sheep even in the midst of their falling away, because He has marked His sheep.

In the meantime, therefore, while we are ignorant of the judgments of God, we must preach even to the ungodly, for they must be charged and warned. We must also pray for them even with our weeping, and we must try all things through Christ that they may regain their senses from the snares of the devil, just as we read here and just as Paul did for his Jewish friends, as you see in Rom. 9[:3–5]. When we see them perish without hope, there is nothing which we can bemoan more, certain as we are of the judgment of God, for nothing has left us, nothing of ours has perished except what was lost to us already before. Yet we must say this: "You are upright, O Lord, and your judgment is correct."

[CHAPTER 1.]

[v. 1:] "Paul, an apostle..."

As far as this inscription is concerned, we have spoken generally about it in the previous epistles, except that he says here "according to the promise," or, "according to the promise of life in Christ Jesus." With these words, he is signifying that he is not the preacher of an earthly kingdom. You will hear here that all who want to live a godly life in Christ Jesus will suffer persecution. He is not saying that he is the preacher of the Mosaic Law which promised the life of this world to those who do the Law, saying: "If you will have done this, you will dwell in your own land, you will have all things in abundance, you will rejoice in peace, your enemies will become your subjects. If, on the other hand, you will not have done the Law, you will suffer stoning, you will be killed, you will be cast out of your lands, you will become scattered throughout the whole world." (See Deu. 28.)

He is saying that he is the apostle or preacher according to the promise of life or according to the life to be promised to believers, not in the world, not in the works of the Law, nor in any human glory, but in Christ Jesus. This is a truly spiritual and godly life through which all things which belong to this creation die, so that finally, after we have mortified our members, Christ alone dwells in us as He lived in Paul, who said: "I live, yet not I, but Christ, who lives in me." [Gal. 2:20] Only believers know this life. The flesh cannot even recognize or dream of it, for outside it, it sees nothing except the cross and death. For that reason Paul says, 2 Cor. 4[:16]: "But although he who is outside, etc."

[v. 3:] "...whom I serve from my ancestors..."

It is entirely unimportant for your salvation whether you may have had godly or ungodly parents or grandparents, just as the wickedness of his father Ahaz did not get in the way of the Hezekiah, and just as the godliness of his father Hezekiah did not get in the way of the very wicked Manasseh. How did it get in the way of believing Gentiles that their forefathers worshipped demons? After all, the children of God are born of God, not of blood, not of the will of the flesh or of a man. The necessity of the Spirit has nothing to do with the flesh. Of what advantage would the faith of their parents have been for Paul or Timothy if the latter themselves would not have believed in God? Nevertheless, it is a great grace to be instructed from boyhood in the right faith of one's parents. But to whom this has not been given, he nonetheless has, provided he come to Christ. I do not think that Paul here is saying that this pertains to the fact that a bishop is blameless so that even the unbelief of his forefathers could have been brought against him. Otherwise, none of the bishops could have been a bishop. The bad reputation of parents is something which may hinder a person from being chosen to a bishopric but nevertheless not in such a way as the disgrace of his own home does; that is, of his household, of his wife or children, as I said in my notes on the previous epistle. In order to advise Timothy of the correct faith, Paul here says that which isn't a fact, namely, that he is not describing what Timothy ought to be, as is quite clear.

[v. 3:] "…in a pure conscience…"

The conscience is not pure when in no area you are aware that you have either wanted to do or actually did anything different from the way you were feeling, in which conscience you must not trust. You see, the heart is still only human, and the intention is only human, however good or very good it may appear to you, unless the spirit of faith rectify the conscience. For he acts wickedly who trusts in his own thoughts, as we read in Pro. 12[:5] and 28[:26]: "He who trusts in his heart is a fool"; and Paul says, 1 Cor. 4[:3–4]: "I do not judge myself, for I am not aware of anything against me, but my justification does not lie in this, for the one who judges me is the Lord." See this in Paul, namely, that he used to serve God according to the Law, as he says in Gal. 1[:14]: "I was a greater imitator of the paternal traditions"; and in Phi. 3[:6]: "I spent my life without complaint according to the righteousness which is in the Law." He was not aware of anything, but he was not seeing Christ in the Law and the Prophets. Therefore, it was necessary that he stumble against the stone of offense and the rock of scandal, that is, against Christ, as he himself said in 1 Tim. 1[:5].

See where 'good consciences' and 'godly intentions,' as people call them, lead you when you have followed them! The Word of God does not control them so that no one stumbles anymore against the Gospel of Christ, when those little plaster saints who have arrogated for themselves an opinion of sanctity without the Word of God and the Spirit, etc. Thus Paul is not glorying here about a good conscience, but about God, because God has always led him as He wished until now, and because he now worships God truly as Him whom he always thought he was worshipping as far as his conscience was concerned. You see, we must not overlook what he says, [v. 3]: "I thank God, etc."; so that you know that not even this very thing is what we are asking of ourselves. We must first receive the enlightening of the Spirit of faith before we ask; otherwise, for what would we ask except that we be certain that God will listen to us because of His promises? Paul thus thanks God for giving him the mind to pray always for Timothy.

[v. 4:] "desiring to see you…"

Namely, because the saints also desire to see each other according to the flesh, as we said elsewhere; and, what it means to pray day and night. [v. 3]

[v. 6:] "…that you arouse the gift of God, etc."

That is, those who were present and I charged you that you take care of the duty of the bishop not neglectfully, as we said in the first epistle. For "God has not given us Christians the spirit of fear" that someone not be afraid at the sight of his enemies or be ashamed and offended in the cross, but "He has given us the spirit of power" to stand firm, too, at the sight of death and hell and all temptation, and the spirit of love by which we love not only our friends but even our enemies, so that we dare give up our life for them if the situation demands. He has also given us the spirit of temperance by which we not only take care not to burden ourselves with gluttony and drunkenness but also that we be of sound mind and not wise beyond our needs but only according to sound doctrine, so that we not sleep with drunkards, but keep watch for every assault of Satan. These three; to wit, power, love, and self-discipline, he opposes to timidity or fearfulness of the spirit. Paul then is saying: "You have obtained the power of God; there is nothing left for you to fear—not your own cross nor mine, etc." For why are we who have received eternal life through the Gospel fearful at death?

[v. 11:] "…to which I have been appointed…"

He is boasting of his calling, not only that we may know that this is the Word of God which he is preaching as was his habit, but also much more for the sake of Timothy, as if he should be saying: "This has been entrusted to you just as it was to me. We have the same Spirit; so then, be quick! Bear up for the sake of the Gospel, as I am doing!" We said this earlier in the section on passages.

[v. 14:] "…whom I have believed…"

Obviously, through Christ. That is, that which I believe and hope I am going to receive, namely, the redemption of this body through the resurrection and eternal life, when God will be all in all, as he says later [4:8]: "There is laid up for me a crown of righteousness, etc." "Then the righteous will shine like the sun in the kingdom of the Father." [Mat. 13:47] "Then each will receive according to his works." [Mat. 16:27] The faithful who have done good works will receive eternal life; those who are faithless and who are workers of iniquity, eternal fire. Christians have everything for which they hope in both lives entrusted and deposited in the hand of God, and for this reason they know and believe that they are receiving them all.

[v. 15:] "You know this…"

These are examples of those who in time of temptation fall away and, again, of those who persist when temptation has come, as Onesiphorus and his household. Good works are the testimony of our faith, but only temptation and persecution test the steadfastness and reality of our faith.

CHAPTER 2.

What we saw in the first epistle he does in all ways that he might urge Bishop Timothy, still a young man, to take care of the office committed to him; that is, that he teach the things which he had learned from Paul, and commend those very things to others also, who were suitable to be taught them. Here he strengthens himself through the grace of Christ that he give way to no hardships, that no threats terrify him, that he not care for other matters and abandon the Word. After all, he does not lack corporal support to which an eternal crown is also owed, about which he speaks often in this epistle. That he may affirm this, he employs three similes: of a soldier, of an athlete, and of a farmer. In addition, he adds the example of Christ, who was glorified through the cross, which example Paul himself says, he is imitating in his chains. Aren't these powerful persuasions?

[v. 4:] "No one who serves as a soldier involves himself with the matters of this life," namely, to seek his victuals, etc.

[In v. 4,] "God" does not appear in the text, something which we have been reading in the ancient translation, so that we have only a simple simile: "Just as a soldier cares for nothing except his military service, so also you have taken up the responsibility of a bishop. Leave other matters behind you and take care of it. You will not lack a salary in its own time, etc." One who fights legitimately will not lack his crown; that is, it must be that one who performs the work of a farmer will not lack the fruit thereof, etc.

[v. 9:] "…but the Word of God is not bound."

Phi. 1:22: "I want them to know, etc." I am indeed bound in chains, but the Word, as I have preached it, has free course, as we read in the Psalm: "His word runs swiftly"; and in 2 The. 3[:1] he wants us to pray that the Word of the Lord have free course.

[v. 10:] "On this account I am suffering all things…"

This passage explains what we read in Col. 1:24: "I am rejoicing now over my afflictions on your behalf, etc."

[v. 13:] "If we do not believe, He remains faithful, etc."

Those who do not believe make God a liar. Behold how great their blasphemy is! But God, who is truth itself, cannot be made a liar, for He cannot deny Himself. That is, that He who is the truth be made a liar cannot happen, for then God would no longer be God. This statement is especially comforting to troubled consciences. God has made a promise, and He is not a liar because unbelievers do not receive the promise. For believers receive what God does not owe unbelievers. We have the same passage in Rom. 3[:3]: "What if some of them do not believe, etc.?"

[v. 14:] "…testifying before the Lord…"

That is, in the sight of the Lord, that even those who have

been adjured may be seen. Paul knew how great a departure from the faith would occur because of word battles. Therefore he wants those who are of the one faith also to speak about their faith with the same words. Furthermore, he had said before [v. 13]: "Hold fast the form, etc." That is, very many disagreements had developed first from profane words (that is, from words which Scripture doesn't know), when those words were taken into sacred doctrine. For that reason, those disagreements have taken over wretchedly not only people's books, but also their hearts.

[v. 15:] "Study, etc."

He is writing in this way to a justified person that you not draw this over to someone else, for you heard earlier [v. 1]: "Strengthen yourself through the grace which is in Christ Jesus." He says: "Show yourself to be a workman who is not forced to blush before God because of the service you neglected so that you rightly divide and tear apart the bread of the divine Word which has been committed to you and this in proportion to the grasp and condition of individuals. Do this in such a way that you spread about to all the bread, that is, the word of truth, not by the wind of human traditions." Mat. 24[:45]: "Who do you think is the faithful and wise servant, etc.?"

[v. 17:] "…as the disease of cancer…"

Just as the disease of cancer gradually takes over more of the body, so also those empty words finally extinguish the whole of faith if one accept them as sacred. As witnesses, we cite the Scotists and Thomists, etc. Such are the inventors of new teachings, like Hymenaeus and Philetus, who began to assert that we must not hope for another resurrection after the resurrection had already been completed in Christ. In this way, those will be pleased who trust in their own inclinations outside of Scripture and think that they are handling sacred matters with their empty and profane words.

[v. 19:] "[The foundation of God] nevertheless is solid, etc."

You could have said: "This is an anticipation." You see, how do they overturn the faith of some when true faith cannot be overturned? We read about true faith that "the gates of hell cannot prevail against it." Paul responds: "True faith is not overturned, etc.," as we see above in the section on important passages.

[v. 20:] "But in a great house…"

Here again is an anticipation. Why does God permit others to mislead the wicked and others to be misled? Why does He not dignify them with His grace? Paul responds with a simile about household equipment and utensils in the house of a wealthy person, as we read in Rom. 9[:21] about the vessels of the potter, which read, etc.

[v. 21:] "If someone purge himself, etc."

That is, if he will not have consented to their unfaithfulness and ungodly persuasions, he will be a vessel, that is, a tool of God, etc. He is hinting at all tools with the word "vessels" in the Hebrew custom.

[v. 21:] "…sanctified…"

He explains what "sanctified" means and says: "…accommodated to the use of the master and prepared for every good work." You see, "sanctified" means in the Hebrew fashion something which has been set apart for the master and prepared for his use. Jer. 1[5]: "Before you came forth from the womb, I sanctified you," which he explains in this way: "I gave you as a prophet to the nations," clearly, "when you were still in your mother's womb." Gal. 1[:15]: "…who separated me from my mother's womb."

[v. 22:] "…youthful…"

"…that you not have anything even in appearance because of which your adversaries may accuse you."

[v. 22:] "…with these…"

This is a circumlocution. That is, "with believers." He says: "…[that call upon the Lord] out of a pure heart," that you not think that this is something different, like a muttering of the mouth without faith. This is not even an invocation, not to mention purity of heart. Those invoke God out of a pure heart who believe the promises of God and do not doubt that they are going to receive whatever they may have prayed for, etc.

[v. 23:] "…foolish…"

The questions are foolish because through such they harm righteousness, faith, love and peace.

[v. 23:] "…with gentleness…"

Not with flattery or pretense, as Paul writes about himself, 1 The. 2[:5]: "We were never, etc." (See above in the seventh place in the important passages.)

CHAPTER 3.

We have spoken earlier in the previous epistle about the last times, and elsewhere he speaks of perilous times, because under the guise of godliness they will conceal all things which Paul is speaking of here, and this to destroy souls, as has already happened. For their folly is now being betrayed to the world, as we said earlier.

[v. 2:] "…lovers of themselves…"

That is, people who are seeking their own advantages and not seeking the things of Christ, just as follows: "greedy, boasters, arrogant."

[v. 2:] "…cursers…"

"Or blasphemers," just as today those seem to be quite saintly. They are blaspheming not only against those who confess the truth but also against the Gospel of Christ.

[v. 2:] "…disobedient to their parents…"

As are those who teach that obedience to the prior or to the guardian is far preferable to obedience to parents. This surely is contrary to the commandment of God. They have the doctrines of demons. All these sins are the controlling factors within them now and necessarily control those who do not have the Gospel of Christ in their heart. They are "ingrates," namely, to both God and people. They are "ungodly," without faith and without the Spirit. They "lack affection," namely, affection toward people.

[v. 3:] "[Breakers] of some truce…"

That is, they are liars who do not keep covenants, just as they also rejoice to deceive. Some keep pacts and promises until they receive no advantage therefrom. But, when they get a whiff of profit or see an inconvenience, they abandon their promise. They are "calumniators," that is, people who make false charges; "intemperate," that is, given over to sexual sins and adulteries. Those who forbid marriage are especially these, as we said earlier. They are "savage," that is, without mercy and kindness.

[v. 3:] "…neglectful of good people…"

That is, they have no concern for those who are good. These narrowly are those who with their false hearts care for nothing, whether that be something just or unjust. They are "traitors," that is, people who don't keep secrets and, in addition, hand over into death people who feel correctly about the Gospel over against human traditions. Those traitors think that they are offering their obedience to God in doing so. They are "precipitous in judgment," that is, judging anything at all according to their head. They have no judgment of the spirit, according to those words: "The spiritual person passes judgment on all things, but the natural person does not perceive those things which are of the Spirit of God." [1 Cor. 2:15] They are "puffed up," that is, people who do not yield to the judgment of those who have correct feelings.

[v. 4:] "…lovers of pleasures, etc."
That is, they seek their own advantages, as we said above.

[v. 5:] "…having a form, etc."
They cover up all these things with an appearance of godliness which does not exist within them, as Christ said to the Pharisees: "…outside are white-washed tombs" (Mat. 23:27).

[v. 5:] "…and turn away from these."
You see that those have already begun to arise who Paul foretells are going to multiply in the last times.

[v. 6:] "For of these are those, etc."
But today we are not unaware of such people for, because they do not dare or are unable to contradict the manifest truth of the Gospel, they secretly pour out their poisons in secret conferences and secret confessions and in private homes, saying: "Why do you believe heresy? Why don't you believe what your parents believed?" Those saints from the worship and invocation of whom Paul is now calling them away offer such great benefits, for all things

perish when their Masses are finished.

The wicked people [whom Paul has been describing] do these things with little old ladies, whose consciences are over-burdened and who are led by various desires, that is, who are now experiencing superstitiously that very thing as they always keep learning from wicked and superstitiously-learned schoolmasters. Such women bend to every wind of doctrine and never arrive at a knowledge of the truth. This is the same thing that happens to all (something which we have experienced) who have followed them from the path of superstition and human traditions to heavy consciences which need unburdening and do not embrace the Gospel of Christ which frees them from all this. "Jannes" and "Jambres" are the names of magicians of the Pharaoh, but their names are not expressed in our books. Read Exo. 7.

[v. 10:] "But you, etc."

In sum, this is: "Imitate my teaching and example in setting forth the Gospel. In addition, you know Holy Scripture, which has all these teachings and which the man of God needs for his salvation."

[v. 12:] "All who wish to live godly…"

He makes an exception of no one here. The cross is the testing of faith. Necessarily present with faith, therefore, is love as well as patience. Just as these give way to good in the godly, so they give way ultimately to damnation to persecutors and deceivers who resist the truth under any guise, regardless of what they may have done. They advance into a worse condition, that is, they always increase their damnation and blindness.

[v. 15:] "…the Holy Scriptures…"

If these things are true, why are you troubling yourself with human doctrines and traditions?

CHAPTER 4.

Paul is again charging Timothy that in every way he take the opportunity from any source and at anytime to go on to carry out whatever is part of his duty; that is, that he preach earnestly in season and out of season. Whoever interprets his preaching is unimportant, for the Word of God has not been bound to persons or places and not even to times, however one may judge it.

There is always a need for the Word, that we may believe and remain steadfast in temptations, because we are always waiting for the coming of Christ at whatever time of night He may come. Reprove those who are sinning, threaten the judgment of God upon those who are hard-hearted, exhort the godly to go forward and others to return to their heart.

You see here that Paul is commanding the preaching of Law and Gospel. The Law terrifies, the Gospel comforts. Paul says: "Do these with all "μακροθυμίᾳ" - that is, with longsuffering by which to endure patiently, and do not cease from your teaching. If they do not believe immediately and even if they resist, they perhaps will believe later," as we read in ch. 2[:25–26].

[v. 5:] "…tolerating afflictions, etc."

Next, he warns, and not in vain, the bishop to be watchful for, as he says, [v. 3]: "The time will come when they will not sustain sound doctrine, etc.," as we said earlier that this was a foolish people. They threw out good preachers and sought the kind who pleased itching ears. Isaiah describes them in this way, ch. 30[:9–10]: "This is a people who provoke one to anger, etc."

[v. 6:] "For I myself am now being sacrificed, etc."

Here is another reason why Timothy should be watchful, for, as Paul says: "I shall no longer be able to be present for this business, for, now that I have finished my ministry, I am about to be sacrificed to God through death." Paul foreknew this now through the Spirit by which he is at the same time prescribing to Timothy and all bishops their aim of steadfastness and faith; to wit, that they be like him and carry out the duty entrusted to them until the end of their lives, as we have said above.

[v. 7:] "I have fought a good fight…"

He is not boasting about himself but about his gifts from God, who had comforted him that he might complete all these matters, just as he says elsewhere: "I can do all things in Him who comforts me." [Phi. 4:13] What he adds, however, namely, "which has been laid up, etc.," is nothing for you to think foolishly here pertains to human merit, for he is saying about it that it has been laid up for him and which God is going to render to him, not that which is due to his merits. You see, Paul was God's child and heir, not a mercenary servant who does not remain in the home forever. Paul had received all things from God; namely, that he was converted from ungodliness to Christ, he was made an apostle, he carried out his ministry exceptionally well, etc. These are the very gifts which God will crown. Our merits are the merits of God, and our rewards are the rewards of God and, again, all our possessions are the possessions of God, because as many of us as love the coming of Christ are the children of God. The ungodly certainly do not love his coming, for they would wish that He never come, etc.

[v. 9:] "See to it…"

He is writing some friendly words.

[v. 14:] "Alexander, the coppersmith…"

He is describing two classes of those who appear to favor the Gospel but are being tested in temptation. For some resist and begin to attack the word of truth, like Alexander. We must be careful of these as wolves. They will find their reward before the just Judge. Others pretend human weakness and do not dare confess what they believe. That very thing will not be counted against them, for they eventually will be strong through Christ, although they are still weak. Of their number were those who abandoned Paul as soon as he stood before Nero. Nevertheless, this tragic evil gave way to the greater glory of Christ and the Gospel by preserving him whom all abandoned so that the preaching of the Gospel was completed among the nations through him. Paul is now glorying about Christ and says that he cannot perish, being in the hand of God as he is: "And He will snatch me, etc.," [v. 17].

THE END.

THE ANNOTATIONS OF JOHANNES BUGENHAGEN OF POMERANIA ON THE EPISTLE OF PAUL TO TITUS.

THEME.

Paul is instructing a bishop who must teach his people, as he did in the epistles to Timothy. In the meantime, he commends in an excellent way and in detail throughout the epistle the freedom of the Gospel which is in Christ Jesus, our Lord. He does not remain silent as to what fruits the faith of the Gospel produces in individual people toward their neighbors regardless of the condition or status of their life.

THE MORE OUTSTANDING POINTS IN THIS EPISTLE.

The first is that God has promised His elect the grace of the Gospel from eternity (something which is a matter of predestination) but which has now been revealed in the last times through Christ by the preaching of the Gospel. Ch. 1 contains the inscription. In ch. 2, grace appeared; and in ch. 3, goodness. (This point occurs in Ephesians and also elsewhere often in Paul.)

Second, he tells what sort of man is a teacher or bishop and what sort of teaching his should be, as in the previous epistles to Timothy.

Third is a very important point about the soundness of faith or about Christian liberty contrary to the superstitions and traditions opposing the truth which people have invented who say that they are Christians and attribute to works the confidence which they owe God. "They therefore are denying with their deeds what they are confessing with their mouth" (ch. 1[:16]).

The fourth is that Christians should show with their good works what is necessary, and with their temperate lives good faith, and adorn with those the teaching of our Savior before the world to embarrass our adversary who has nothing to justly charge against us. This Paul does from the beginning of ch. 2 to the end of the epistle.

The fifth is that we must excommunicate a heretic, that is, one who teaches and thinks contrary to the word of truth (or, as Paul calls it, "sound" teaching) and this we must do through the Law which Christ has prescribed to us, Mat. 18[:15–17]: "If he shall have trespassed, etc." At the end of the epistle, he says that man is the instigator of sects.

CHAPTER 1.

[v. 1:] "Paul, a servant of God and apostle of Jesus Christ…"

Leaving the notes, let us see what this very rich inscription of this epistle has which commends the grace of God in such a way that he wants us to be absolutely certain of it. For what good is it to hear, write, and read many things about grace, if we still doubt whether they all pertain to us? Therefore, he says that God cannot lie about that which He has promised, for, as He cannot be deceived; so also, he cannot deceive, something which he says to Timothy in this way: "God cannot deny Himself." [2. 2:13] He says, [v. 2]: "…before eternal times," that we may be absolutely certain that He not only loved us when we became His friends, as he says (Rom. 5[:8–10]), but even when we did not yet exist. With reference to this point of predestination, see Eph. 1[:4ff.]. That I not mention other matters, you see here what Paul is saying in Rom. 11[:35]: "Who has first given to Him, and he shall be repaid," so that those teachers of merits are completely confounded? After all, what did we earn before the creation of the world?

But the blinded hear and see these matters everywhere in Scripture, and they do not understand, according to the judgment of God (Isa. 6[:10]). Although this grace is eternal (because nothing new is eternal with God), nevertheless it now has been revealed, clearly at the time which the Father has predestined. We should look for no reason why He did this other than His good pleasure or good will, as we see in Eph. 1[:5]. As Paul says, that grace was revealed not through just any preaching at all (for he condemns the pseudapostles and preachers of superstitions and human traditions), but through the preaching such as was entrusted to Paul through the divine call of our Savior in whom he boasts of his calling. He is in the habit of doing this so that we may be certain that he is teaching not his word, but the Word of Christ. All his epistles bear witness to what sort the preaching of Paul is.

Other preachings (which are not according to the doctrine of our Lord Jesus Christ) not only obscure but obliterate this grace, as has happened, so far was it from being revealed. After all, why would He reveal grace to those who in the matter of salvation, as they falsely think, know how to place faith or not place faith in works alone? In addition, you see in this passage how foolishly those err who describe the grace of God (about which Scripture speaks and through which we are saved) as a 'disposition' or 'quality' in a person, although it is a favor in God who is benevolent to us as His children. For where, I ask, was that grace in us when the world had not yet received its creation? After all, you see Paul saying this here: "…who made us His beloved in His beloved Son before the creation of the world."

See about "grace" and "gift" in the *Loci* of Philip [Melanchthon].

[v. 1:] "…according to the faith of God's elect…"

Now let us also see those words which we skipped earlier in this inscription: "Paul, a servant of God and apostle of Jesus Christ, etc." It will be more clear if we read not "*iuxta* - according to" but "*ad* - for"; that is: "an apostle of Jesus *for* the faith of God's elect, to wit, an apostle or preacher sent for this; namely, to preach the faith of God's elect—not that each person may *imagine* a faith for himself as they trust in the thoughts of their own heart, but that I may preach the faith which those whom God has chosen *have*. This faith is not in some *thing* nor does it seek salvation in some *work*, nor trust therein. Rather, it despairs of all such things and hopes in God alone through Christ for grace and eternal life, something which he explains, saying: "…for the knowledge of the truth, etc."; that is, an apostle for the knowledge of the truth. That is, through me let the truth be recognized. This does not mean any knowledge such as are that the sum of two and two is four and that man is a rational, living creature, but that the truth is acknowledged which is according to godliness, which pertains to the fact that we learn to trust in God and take care of our neighbor as well as the things which have to do with faith and love, as we said earlier in our notes on 2 Timothy.

Paul is saying that this godliness "is in the hope of eternal life," [v. 2]. That is, it does not respect glory nor merits. What it hopes for is not what it has merited, but what God has promised; namely, eternal life, for we also have this addition: "…which God has promised." Godliness has no respect for this life nor for all the things which are visible in which godliness must be afflicted and all things mortified. Rather, it looks to eternal life and to those things which are not seen (2 Cor. 4[:18]).

[v. 4:] "To Titus, my true son…"

That is, this Titus is my true son because he has learned from me the faith which he and I now have in common.

[v. 5:] "For his reason…also establish in every town…"
Paul is showing what sort of elders or preachers of the Word of God who were to be in charge of the people Titus should appoint, so that in all matters the Word of God would be prepared and promoted. We have just spoken in 2 Timothy of those things which are pertinent here.

[v. 6:] "…blameless…"
That is, without accusation according to the judgment of the world; otherwise, no one is without accusation in the sight of God.

[v. 6:] "… of riotous living…"
That is, of drunkenness or gluttony, to which he opposes sobriety.

[v. 6:] "…unruly;"
That is, disobedient people, who listen to no good persuasions."

[v. 7:] "…not a striker…"
This a Greek word signifying one who strikes with his tongue, as if to say: "…not a snarling person," that is, one who rages against someone out of envy (2 Tim. 2[:24]). ((He wants us to be modest that we not oppose the Word of God against them.)) Our people who do not willingly listen to evangelical chastising relate such things to the fact that a preacher must say pleasing things, against what we said in 2 Tim. 4[:3]. In the meantime, however, they are not seeing what follows here [v. 123]: "Rebuke them sharply."

[v. 8:] "...temperate;"

That is, chaste (*keusch* in German). You see that he attributes temperance and chastity also to him who has one wife. ((Chastity in the case of a virgin is never praised in Scripture.)) Thus, they do not perceive the teachings in the hypocrisy of those who speak lies.

[v. 9:] "...as he holds fast his, etc."

He who is of sure words speaks according to his teaching, that is, who is suitable for teaching that he does not permit himself to be torn away by any occasion or contradiction or persuasion. That is, he should hold on to the Word firmly that he may teach the people. He says: "...that he may be able, etc.," that is: "That you build with one hand and hold your sword in the other," as you read in Nehemiah. He who does not have those two or that power of the Word should not be a bishop, that is, a preacher. You read about Christ, Mat. 7[:28]: "The crowds were amazed by His teaching, for He was teaching them as do those who have power, not as their scribes" and Pharisees. That is, He was speaking not a cold word or in the persuasive words of human wisdom, but He was speaking the Word which was effective in the hearts of people so that they were convinced that His teaching came from God.

[v. 10:] "For there are many unruly people, etc."

He is speaking about the false prophets about whom we have spoken often before.

[v. 11:] "...who [subvert] whole houses..."

2 Tim. 3[:6]: "...who sneak into houses, etc." That is, they enter secretly and don't want to be seen.

[v. 12:] "Someone has said..."

((He is not citing this in favor of godliness because this quotation teaches nothing.)) He is citing a line of the Greek poet Epimenides against the Cretans. Our false prophets have nothing else in their mouths when they teach save Aristotle and whatever is heathen. They do not think that Paul can prove that they are false when they teach, however, because he is citing a heathen. They think that this pertains to sound doctrine and that it is confirmed on the basis of this heathen source. But Paul is teaching nothing from this source as far as salvation is concerned and is indicating that this is something against the Cretans on the basis of the testimony of the false prophets.

Next, he is indicating that in the writings of the heathen there is a lie, when he says [v. 13]: "This testimony is true, etc." They are "slow bellies," that is, they are nothing else but bellies who do all things for the sake of the belly.

[v. 13:] "…sound in the faith;"

There are those who have the faith of God's elect, as we said above, who undertake nothing for the righteousness of God except Christ. Others attribute righteousness to dress, food, drink, days, fasts, prayers, ceremonies, and other works. They are denying God with these activities which lift them up before God when they trust such things and attribute to them the righteousness which they owe to God alone. In the meantime, they nevertheless say that God is a kindly-disposed Father, and that they must be saved solely on the basis of the mercy of God.

See, then, that you understand what Paul is saying [v. 16]: "They profess that they know God but deny Him with their actions." He says this not only about gross sinners, fornicators, adulterers, drunkards, etc., who mislead no one from the faith with these activities, but much more and, in fact, *only* about those who subvert homes with Judaic fables and the teachings of men who do not uphold the truth, as he explains clearly in 1 Tim. 3[:5–6]: "They have the guise of godliness but deny the power thereof, for those who sneak into households are of these, etc."

[v. 15:] "All things are pure, etc."

This is an outstanding passage against the teachings and traditions of men. The faithful person whose only concern is the commandments of God uses every creature of God which God has created for human use, and this not only without sin, but even with the increase of holiness and faith. When using them, he gives thanks and magnifies God from a pure heart, acknowledging Him as a godly Father and Giver (1 Tim. 4[:4–5]).

On the other hand, for the ungodly whose hearts faith has not purified—that is, for the faithless—all creatures are impure because those people are themselves impure in mind and conscience. Because their life is sin, the use of every creature cannot help but be sinful for them, for who of you can deal with the world with unclean hands? As the Law has it, Luke 22:6: "Whatever an unclean person has touched will be unclean."

The faithless person can use no creatures correctly, for they were created only for the faithful to use, something which we can show easily from the book of Genesis. Paul confirms this in 1 Timothy [4:4–5]. Therefore, it follows that they sin in all their works. If these works appear to be good, they are pure hypocrisy, for whatever is not of faith is sin. A bad tree cannot produce good fruit. Paul says that they are hateful to God. Those are unwilling to acquiesce to the truth which condemns their hypocrisy and human traditions, and they are suitable for no good work because they are bad trees.

CHAPTER 2.

These words cohere with the preceding ones. Some people teach Judaic fables, the traditions of men and their hallucinations to their own destruction and to that of others. As for you, teach sound doctrine, about which we have spoken often before. Here, however, you see that the sound doctrine of Christ has been accommodated to every sex, age, and condition when it is truly sound and whole, that is, when a spiritual person handles it who is powerful in the Word and when human doctrines are not mixed into divine ones. Were we to see in our people those things which Paul here is commanding Titus to teach, we certainly would see the face of the Church in the glory of the holy Gospel. Now, however, nowhere does this teaching exist; as a result, nowhere is there integrity [or wholeness] of life. Rather, of what sort the people are, of that sort is their bishop.

There is no Church of Christ of which the Word of Christ is not in control. We are following our judgments and not those of God, and we shall therefore perish. That these statements are still pertinent, you also see elsewhere often in Paul. Behold, those people speak Pharisaic righteousnesses and the traditions of men; "but as for you, speak the things which will befit sound doctrine." [2:1]

[v. 2:] "…sound in faith,"
These are the people who do not mix that faith in God through Christ with the superstitions, doctrines, and traditions of men in their hearts and who do not yield to strange doctrines. To old men, however, Paul commands this, not only because they are naturally superstitious, but also that they may teach the rest soundness of faith.

[v. 2:] "sound in love,"
These are people who love even their enemies and who pray for those who persecute them.

[v. 2:] "sound in patience."

These are people who endure to the end in every temptation, giving way to no adversities.

[v. 3:] "...that they may teach good things."

See here that a woman teaches, but she teaches adolescent women. I have said elsewhere that a woman may teach both old and young women.

[v. 4:] "...to become modest,"

This is because it used to happen often at that time that a heathen man would marry a Christian woman. With her chaste behavior, she might also attract her husband to the Word of Christ.

[v. 6:] "...that the young men be sober."

Among us, people perish from gluttony and drunkenness not only in their hearts, but also in their bodies. Gluttony and drunkenness overburden our bodies so that we are not watchful for that day of Christ and the appearance of the glory of our great God. The Lord bears witness in Luke [21:34]: "Take heed that your hearts, etc." See to what evils those things lead which we in the meantime make of little concern.

[v. 7:] "Show yourself as the pattern..."

1 Peter. 5: "..having become the pattern for the flock among the people,etc."

[v. 7:] "...in doctrine integrity and respectability."

We must connect those in this way and read between the lines: "Show the Word," or "Keep the Word," or something similar. He adds [v. 8:] "Sound speech," that is, "complete," just as he said "sound doctrine" earlier. That should be "blameless" speech, that is, which no one can charge with being false, not even from Scripture, and against which no one can raise an objection that you are not living what you teach. The two preceding marks, therefore, explain the final two. What he said, namely, "wholeness in doctrine" he calls here "sound speech"; and what he called "gravity" or "respectability"; he here calls "blameless speech," so that no one understand here that hypocritical appearance of respectability which peddles itself only to humans.

[v. 8:] "…he may be embarrassed…"
Thus, see 1 Peter 2 and 3.

[v. 11:] "…has appeared…"
See the points that pertain to this in the *postilla* of Dr. Martin [Luther] for Christmas Eve.

[v. 11:] "…to all people."
That is, to both Jews and Gentiles, as well as males and females, young and old, masters and servants, about whom he had spoken. Therefore it is necessary that all people receive instruction so that they all may live worthily to God, just as follows: "…that having denied, etc."; that is, that having mortified all things which have to do with Adam, we may live a new and spiritual life according to Christ, and this in the present age, without respecting those things which are now perishing for us and which we are mortifying in this life, but awaiting those things which are not seen and which are going to happen at the coming of the Lord.

Here, however, you say: "How can I deny myself that I may live worthily to God, that I may abound in good works that all those things be fulfilled, inasmuch as these are not within the power of a human? Therefore you find correctly in Christ what you do not have within yourself, provided you have that through faith, something which Paul takes care of here in this way, [v. 14]: "He who gave Himself, etc."

[v. 15:] "Let no one despise you."

That is, live and teach in such a way that no one may have the right to hold you in contempt that no one here may take this to mean that anyone who despises him must be avenged immediately, contrary to the Gospel.

CHAPTER 3.

We must obey princes, powers, and rulers in all things which are not contrary to God; that is, in all things in which you do not sin against a healthy conscience, although those powerful people sin greatly when they demand certain things, for instance, as Jeremiah wanted the Jews to submit themselves willingly to the king of the Chaldeans. You see, at times God is pleased to punish our sins through such matters. When we endure burdensome tyranny patiently, we have a better situation, for God is present with us everywhere, as the examples of the ancients teach us. Thus, Christians obey the Turks without sin. If good rulers exist anywhere, they are worthy of double honor. But if they are evil, we must still obey them, unless they command us to do something contrary to God. Here we must say: "We must obey God rather than people." [Acts 5:29] Paul thus adds [3:1] that they should be prepared for every good work, etc.

[v. 2:] "Speak [no] evil…"

He means either about rulers or about other people.

[v. 2:] "…quarrelsome…"

That is, don't be contentious either against your rulers or against others; that is, especially against those who in this way want to appear evangelical and yet argue against anyone at all without humanity or gentleness and constantly pour out whatever they have in their heart, and those feelings which either accomplish nothing for the business of Christ or are the sort of things from which we must not begin. This they do in the face of people to whom the Gospel has not yet been preached. They are accomplishing nothing except offending such people and later are blaspheming the teaching of the Gospel, etc. Why do we who ourselves were foolish, disobedient, and erring—but who now have been delivered through Christ by the goodness of God and not on the basis of our own righteousness—not suffer along with such weak sinners? Why aren't we dealing with them just as we used to want them to deal with us? Why don't we hope that the same grace will come to them when God might have wanted? Of what are we boasting as if we have not received it, etc.? These are the things which Paul is saying here up to that passage: "This is a faithful saying, etc.," [v. 8]. Read about this in the *postilla* of Dr. Martin [Luther] for Christmas Eve.

[v. 3:] "...foolish..."
That is, faithless, who do not acknowledge...

[v. 3:] "...disobedient..."
That is, to the Word of God.
These are the sort of people we have been, but we have been delivered by the goodness of God. Why are we not hoping that others, too, are going to be delivered by the grace of God?

[v. 5:] "...through the washing of regeneration..."
See that you don't consider water alone. He is speaking about the Baptism of the Spirit and of fire, about which I spoke in

my annotations on Isa. 4 and elsewhere, through which Baptism we are born again and the new person comes forth.

[v. 6:] "…which he poured out on us abundantly…"

This He did so that we who have Christ be lacking in no grace. The person who does not have the Spirit of Christ is not a Christian. He gives His Spirit abundantly when through His Spirit He reveals all truth; that is, everything which pertains to our salvation. Furthermore, He gives the rest of the gifts of the Spirit both to our brothers and to us for our use, as he says to the Corinthians [1.12:7]: "To each is given the manifestation, etc." He "pours" this out through the Word. He is alluding to Baptism, because we are in the habit of pouring things which are liquid.

[v. 8:] "This is a faithful saying…"

Obviously, He is who I have said He is.

[v. 8:] "…to [devote yourselves] to good works…"

That is, that they may go ahead for others by the example of light. See here in Paul what good works he wants; namely, those which one does from faith. He says: "…that those who believe in God provide good works." He wants the sort of good works which are honorable and useful to people and, just as he says later [v. 14], "which are valuable for the necessary uses," such as the works of the papists are not. Rather, these should be works of love for one's neighbor, works for which the faith which flourishes in the heart enlivens by its own nature and produces voluntarily, for it knows that the things which it does for a neighbor according to the Word of God pleases God. A good tree cannot be fruitless but will give its fruit in its own time.

[v. 9:] "…foolish questions…"

See in 1 Tim. [6:2], where he says: "Teach useful things," such as faith and love and patience. But reject the things which have to do with quarrels, even if they appear to be from Holy Writ. We should gladly ignore the things which clearly are unprofitable. We do harm to faith and love with quarreling.

[v. 10:] "…an instigator of sects…"

That is, a person who follows other ways and teaches people to follow those ways, rather than sound doctrine and that unique righteousness of faith and is unwilling to come to his senses after receiving a warning from the sound words of Christ. Judge him according to the Gospel (Mat. 18) until he should come to his senses and be ashamed, and "not as an enemy, etc." (2 The. 3[:15]).

You have here the heretics, that is, those who despise the Word of God, who create sects, and keep themselves apart as if they were better than others. Even after receiving the warnings of God, they are unwilling to come to their senses. These must be cast out of the Church and considered as non-Christians and as heathen publicans, such as are all who have abandoned the Gospel and have found more perfect ways outside every Word of God. Today, as these people repay an egregious favor, they call "heretics" those who cling to the Gospel and try to kill them so that the blood of Christ and of all the upright people whom they have killed falls upon them. May God open the hearts of them all! Amen.

THE END.

THE ANNOTATIONES OF JOHANNES BUGENHAGEN OF POMERANIA ON THE EPISTLE TO PHILEMON.

THEME.

Here you see a wonderful example of love in Paul, who commends with very great enthusiasm a fugitive slave, as Onesimus himself appears to be. Although Paul could now with all authority urge Philemon [to return Onesimus], nevertheless he surrenders his right and urges him with Christian entreaties and persuasions to return him so that he compels Philemon to look not upon his own interests, but to those of love. You see, in this way we empty ourselves for our brothers just as Christ emptied Himself for us. (See Phi. 2[:30].)

[v. 1:] "Paul…"

You see how many arguments true love finds in favor of a brother. I believe that Paul was not going to write these on behalf of himself in a similar case. There are those who here commend Paul for his modesty and humanity, and rightly so. From what source these flow, however, we must especially note. After all, the faith which was living in his heart could not produce these in an external work that you might know that true faith is not a matter of good works. Furthermore, Scripture calls good works the offices of charity shown to a neighbor, and these flow from a single work which is the sum of all works, namely, "the work of God which is in Christ Jesus" (John 6[:29]).

[v. 1:] "…a prisoner…"

Here he is no longer writing the titles of his apostolate to persuade that his preaching came from God. Here he forgets his own authority and mentions that he is merely a brother, as if to say: "I am now performing the duty not of an apostle or teacher but of a Christian man."

First, he gets to the heart of the matter as powerfully as he can and says that he is a prisoner. In this way, Philemon should not despise the entreaty of him who is being held in chains because of the Gospel, as he says later [v. 9]: "Moreover, I am now also a prisoner of Jesus Christ."

He also calls himself a prisoner so that Philemon will not despise him when he prays for him "whom he begot in his bonds" [v. 10] for Christ. Paul is also praying for the man who served him while he was a prisoner, something which Philemon himself would have done, had he been present. That's how far Philemon was from having to disdain what the slave had done. In fact, he had to rejoice that this benefit had come to Paul through this slave, just as Paul says all these things later.

Next, Paul calls himself a prisoner so that the Christian Philemon will not add an affliction to Paul's affliction, if he does not listen to Paul and despises Paul with great energy as he entreated now no longer for a slave but for his brother, something which he says later [v. 20]: "Refresh my bowels in the Lord."

He then adds Timothy [v. 1], so that he not appear to be praying for this by himself and that the entreaty of two may be stronger.

Furthermore, he makes Philemon his helper and partner in this inscription in case Philemon does not wish what Paul himself wants. After all, why would different spirits agree among themselves, for he speaks in this way later [v. 17]: "If then you consider me your partner, accept him, as you would accept me."?

For these reasons, he inscribes this epistle not only to Philemon but also to Aphia, as the latter's wife, I think, and to the bishop Archippus and to the entire Church which is in the house of Philemon, so that, if the entreaty will have less power from one person, it will become stronger if perhaps many pray along. What will a Christian be able to deny to Christians when they ask for something in a Christian way and ask for that which the Christian himself ought not have been asked according to the Gospel?

[v. 1:] "…a prisoner of Jesus Christ…"
Although by the counsel of the devil Paul was a prisoner of Nero and was condemned to death, nevertheless he gives this glory to God that he ascribes no power to either the devil or the world. You see, he is not writing that he is the prisoner of Caesar but a prisoner of Jesus Christ for the sake of whose Gospel he had been taken captive and without whose will he could not have been imprisoned, etc. ((The saints know that all things are in the hand of God.))

[v. 5:] "…love and faith…"
Assign individual things to individual people: faith, to the Lord Jesus; love, to all the saints, that is, to those who believe; for Scripture calls those who believe "saints," who are involved with us in the world and who need our mutual assistance.

[v. 6:] "…that the sharing of your faith…"
That is, "that your common faith," that is, that faith which you and we have, "may become effective in the acknowledging of every good thing which is in you in Christ Jesus"; that is, that this faith may grow and advance so that you recognize every good thing which happens to you through Christ. I think this is the same idea which Paul often writes, as in Eph. 1[:17], where he says:"…that the

God of our Lord Jesus Christ and the Father of glory grant you the Spirit of wisdom." See there and elsewhere that you may know the things which the Father has given you through Christ.

[v. 7:] "For we have joy…"

Thus we must connect what came before, to wit: "I thank God." Why? That the sharing of faith, etc. Again, "I give thanks because we have great joy, etc." Christian love should pray endlessly for the illumination of others, and rejoice over progress in that area.

[v. 7:] "…because the bowels, etc."

That is, because you have been a great comfort to the needy saints in offering them the necessities.

[v. 8:] "Therefore…"

(Until now he has been mollifying Philemon not with flattery but with Christian truth. Now he is attacking the real business [of the epistle].) That is, because from your faith you are doing so well for all the saints, it cannot happen that you would reject my command if I were to command that which you acknowledge you should do. Furthermore, I am not commanding but rather I am asking for the sake of love, because, as I say, I am unwilling to use my authority, for I am Paul, an old man—and a prisoner of Jesus Christ, in addition. This is as if he were saying: "My very submission should move you to also give up your right [with regard to Onesimus]."

[v. 10:] "Moreover, I am beseeching you on behalf of my son…"

He does not say: "…on behalf of my slave," that Philemon may appear to accept not so much a slave as Paul himself. What happens to his son, a father judges has happened to himself. He says: "…whom I fathered in my chains," that you may know that he is dearer to me for the reason that I fathered him in perilous straits. It is the same with women who love those children more to whom they have given birth with greater pain and peril.

[v. 11:] "Formerly…"

He is arguing from utility. Before he was faithless to you, neglecting his work and perhaps even had stolen something. Now his faith does not allow such behavior. Paul adds, however, that he is increasing his worth and is very useful to you and to me. He is also alluding to the name of the slave, for "Onesimus" to the Greeks means "useful." This is as if Paul were saying: "Up to this time we have been calling him 'Onesimus' incorrectly," etc.

[v. 12:] "…my bowels."

Earlier [v. 10] he had called him "my son." that you may see on what basis Paul wants Philemon to take up himself [Paul] in Onesimus.

[v. 13:] "Whom I, etc."

He says: "By sending back your slave, I am showing greater respect for your advantage than for my own. In fact, that is not even my own advantage."

[v. 14:] "…not as if out of necessity…"

That some people bring up free will from here is foolish, as if sending Onesimus was necessary for this, that Philemon might have free will in returning him. The sense is rather that good works have to come from a free heart. I say "heart" meaning through the spirit of faith, without which spirit whatever you do is sin. God requires the heart not the work, for "whatever is not of faith is sin." [Rom. 14:23]

[v. 15:] "For on that account…"

He also proves that the flight of the slave had been useful, for on the occasion of his flight Onesimus heard the Gospel at Rome and became a believer. In this way, all things, even bad ones, work together for good for the elect, as God works miraculously in this way. This God does in such a way that human reason and human judgment can by no means understand where God is leading.

[v. 18:] "If he has harmed you in any way…"

That is, "if he has cost you some loss or has stolen something." Paul is anticipating everything so that Philemon will not deny what Paul is going to ask for.

[v. 19:] "…I shall repay it."

"I shall repay," that is, "I shall on his behalf pay you what he owes, and you have my signature on this. This is not that I am saying: 'It's no big thing if I make my own the debt of your slave which I am now ascribing to myself or that I am not compelled to pay or render to you what you may have given me. After all, you not only owe me this in one way or another but also owe yourself just as much.'" Here Paul is hinting not only that a Christian owes a Christian everything that he is, but also that Philemon had been converted as a result of his [Paul's] preaching, etc.

[v. 20:] "Yea, brother…"

This is the "yea" of one affirming something, as if he were saying: "Certainly!," as in Mat. 11[:26]: "Even so, Father…"

[v. 20:] "…let me have joy from you in the Lord."

"Cause me to rejoice about you in the Lord"; that is, "I am rejoicing that I may rejoice over a Christian." This is what follows: "Refresh, etc." That is: "Be a comfort to me." He adds: "through" or "in the Lord." to signify that he is asking nothing more than not only what is he permitted through the Lord, but even what he ought to do through the Lord.

[v. 20:] "Refresh…"
That is, be a comfort to me, etc."

[v. 21:] "…you remain steadfast…"
Tell me, which of all speakers could have used more effective persuasions and arguments in this case?

THE END.

THE ANNOTATIONS OF JOHANNES BUGENHAGEN OF POMERANIA ON THE EPISTLE TO THE HEBREWS.

ON THE AUTHOR OF THIS EPISTLE.

That Paul did not write this epistle is clear from ch. 2[:1–4], where [the author] says that he had learned the Gospel of Christ from the preaching of others and from seeing miracles, something which Paul energetically denies in Gal. 1[:12].

THEME AND MORE OUTSTANDING POINTS OF THIS EPISTLE.

Because he wrote to the Hebrews, to whom—after God—nothing was more holy than Moses and whatever was part of the Law; therefore, that those of Hebrews who had been converted to Christ would not fall away from Christ to Moses (which would be a terrible blasphemy against God) because of the persecutions which they were suffering at the hands of their own Jews, they again hear from Holy Scripture that Christ is far superior not only to Moses, but also to the angels from whom He received the Law. This is despite the fact that for our sakes for a brief time He became in His suffering "a little lower than the angels," according to the Psalm [8:5]: "You made Him, etc."

Therefore the author is inferring here that, if people could not neglect the things which were given through the angels or Moses without the vengeance of God, how much less unavenged will it be if someone has despised the words of Christ, even after we have been forewarned through the Psalm [95:7]: "If you will have heard His voice today, etc." Here the author, having given the occasion, is indicating that Sabbath of the Christians (ch. 4).

Furthermore, they are hearing that by no means should they compare the priesthood of the ancient Law and its sacrifices and the rest of its sacred rites to the priesthood of Christ, to his sacrifice on the cross which He offered once, and to the invisible altar and temple, and, therefore, that those former things—already revealed as figures—have now ceased in the reality of the latter ones. The author deals with this material about the priesthood of Christ in a very dignified way from Scripture with great comfort to our consciences from ch. 7 to ch. 11. Next, in ch. 11, he gives an outstanding commendation of faith on the basis of the examples of Scripture. Then, all the way to the end, he encourages Christian patience and behavior.

BY WHAT PLAN OR ON WHAT OCCASION THIS EPISTLE WAS WRITTEN.

The reason why the author wrote the epistle we detect from his words, for he feared for the Hebrews that, had they been overcome by temptations and afflictions or poverty, they would slip back into unbelief. For this reason, he admonishes, ch. 10[:32]: "Remember, etc."; and ch. 12[:3]: "Consider again, etc." To this pertain also those passages in which the author appears to deny repentance to those who fall away [12:4] after knowing the truth. The first passage is in ch. 6[:4]: "Is is impossible for those, etc." and the second, in ch. 10[:26]: "…only willingly, etc." We shall look at these passages in their own place and learn from the actual text what they have, etc.

In the THEME above we told by what plan or on what occasion the author begins with the glory of Christ. In the meantime, he remains silent about Moses and the things which are related to the Law so that he does not immediately at the opening of the doors offend the ears of the Hebrews. However, he does use Scripture which the Jews cannot hold in contempt and with which he proves that Christ (whether you consider His divinity or His humanity) is superior to all created things, even angels, because He has names which have nothing to do with angels.

CHAPTER 1.

[v. 1:] "Formerly God [spoke] at various times and in many ways…"

God has always spoken to His people through His Word. Therefore we are not preaching a new God now, but the same true God who at that time spoke through the prophets and fathers; but now on a much higher level, He speaks to us through His Son, who is the Lord not only of the fathers and prophets, but also of all people. "At various times," that is, at different times; and "in many ways," that is, now with clear words, now with figures and other revelations. "In the last days," that is, after which we should not wait for another sending of the Word, all the way to the end of the world. "In these days," that is, during the time in which we now live. He says this that the Jews not say that those final days have not yet arrived, and therefore we must still await the Messiah. I have said that these are the last Christian times (*Annotations on Isa. 2* and elsewhere).

[v. 2:] "…has spoken to us through His Son…"

According to His divinity, Christ is by nature the Son of God; according to His humanity, He is by adoption the Son of

God. This adoption was completed at His resurrection, just as ours will be completed, as we read in Rom. 8[:23]. Therefore He Himself is called "the firstfruit of many brothers" and, in the same place, "the firstborn of the dead" (Col. 1[:18] and Rev. 1[:5]). In Acts 13[:23], Paul therefore also cites about the resurrection: "Today have I begotten You," which has never been said to any of the angels, although we are in the habit of interpreting this as a reference to the divinity of Christ. (Concerning this subject, see the *postilla* of Dr. Martin [Luther].)

To be sure, what follows [in v. 2] (namely: "…whom He established as heir of all things") pertains to the humanity of Christ, just as he makes clear in the following verses from the Psalm [8:6]: "You have subjected all things beneath His feet." Christ Himself also said, Mat. 28[:18]: "All power has been given to Me, etc." Here it follows that all—as many as are in Christ—are heirs of all through Christ: heirs of God and coheirs with Christ. You see, in the following chapter [v. 11], he makes Christ our brother—not the brother of angels, whom he here calls "the servants" of Christ. This is our indescribable dignity, provided we believe, for faith glorifies us in such a way.

But to His divinity belongs the fact that it is said: "Who does not see that He also made the ages?" (You read this in Gen. 1, John 1, and Col. 1.) From this, it again follows that no one in the kingdom of Christ can perish because God Almighty has created all things. From what we said before, it will not be necessary that you create two sons, for God and Man are one Person in Christ but are two only in name. Therefore it is necessary in Scripture that you discern wisely the things which pertain to the divinity of Christ and those which pertain to His humanity.

[v. 3:] "because He is the brightness of glory…"

In His divinity, He is called "the Son" as a Person different from the Father. God is the glory, His Son is the brightness of His glory; in fact, He is the glory of the glory of the Father, like the Father in all things, not of a different substance but of both the same substance and of the same name, and something which is added, "the expressed image," not of the face, but of the substance of the Father. Therefore Christ is the omnipotence of the Father, the wisdom of the Father, the righteousness of the Father, etc. He was indeed begotten of the Father but only the natural God as Father and, thus, one God with the Father.

It follows [v. 3]: "He controls," or rather, "He upholds all things with the word of His power," that is, by Himself who is the Word and by whom all things are made and preserved and arranged, as he says [John 5:12]: "My Father is now working, and I am working." What advantage would it be that He created all things, unless He also preserved and controlled all things? In Christ therefore is the whole of divinity, and all the glory of God is His.

In Christ we acknowledge our Father, because He is the brightness, glory, and image of the substance of the Father. We acknowledge Him through His Word, provided His Spirit will have taught us. In the face of Christ, we now see the glory of God, but we do not see it in the face of Moses, as we read in 2 Cor. 3:13: "Through himself, etc." This is the great esteem of such great majesty (which we have already described) in that He emptied Himself and served us in our sins so that He washed them away and became obedient to the Father, etc. (Phi. 2[:8]).

[v. 3:] "He sat down at the right hand of majesty…"
This is something he also said to the Philippians [2:9] in this way: "God therefore has also highly exalted Him…" Be careful here that you not think along with the wicked that Christ took away sins just one time and then handed over other sins for our satisfactions to take away, for that is to deny Christ and all the things which we read here, etc.: "So much the better, etc." For He was cast

down lower than the angels, because He washed away our sins (Isa. 53), as we shall see later. But now up to the end of the chapter he is showing from Scripture that Christ has a name far more excellent than the angels, just as Paul says [Phi. 2:9]: "He gave Him a name which is above every name."

[v. 5:] "You are My Son."

This is clear in the Psalm [102:13] and in the Book of Kings we read clearly also: "After you will have slept, etc." See the *postilla* of Dr. Martin [Luther]: "And now again, that is, in His second coming, He introduces, etc." In Acts 1, here is Jesus, who was taken up. Here was the Lord of the angels and the true God, whom the angels worshipped.

[v. 7:] "…who created His angels spirits…"

That is, He made them spiritual creatures. He also makes them "a flame of fire," that is, of a fiery nature and swiftness. But God is not saying to them: "You are My Son," and "the throne of God, etc." In fact, these [angels] worship His Son.

[v. 8:] "Your throne, O God, is forever."

Here God or the prophet is calling Him "God." Only according to His humanity is He said to have been anointed by the Holy Spirit, but "ahead of His fellows," [v. 9] that He Himself might be "the firstborn among many brothers." [Rom. 8:29]

[v. 10:] "In the beginning O Lord, You [laid] the foundations of the earth." [Psa. 102:25]

These words are said to that God about whom we also read in the same Psalm [v. 20]: "…who in His assumed flesh looked down from His lofty, holy place to loose the children of death."

[v. 14:] "Are they not all ministering spirits, etc.?"

The angels who are ordered to worship Christ are so far from being preferred to Christ or from being equal to Christ that they are also the servants and ministers of us who are in Christ.

CHAPTER 2.

[v. 2:] "If the Word which the angels had spoken, etc."

From the things we have said before we argue as follows: if the Law which was given through the angels just as Stephen also says (Acts 7[:53]), people could not hold it in contempt without the vengeance of God. All the less will anyone who has despised the Word sent to us through the Son (to whom not even the angels can be compared) escape the vengeance of God, etc. This is something which Moses himself also foretold in this way in the words of God about Christ, Deu. 18[:19]: "I shall be the avenger of him who has been unwilling to listen to the words of him who speaks in My name." It is to this that Christ appears to have looked back when He said in John [5:45]: "The one who is accusing us is Moses, in whom you hoped, etc."

[v. 1:] "…lest at any time we drift away."

This may happen, obviously, when we are unable to hold onto the words of life which have been sent us through the Son and drift away, wavering here and there, "moved as we are by every wind of doctrine" (Eph. 4[:14]).

[v. 3:] "…in us by those who had heard."

The author is indicating that he had learned the Gospel from others who preached and performed miracles, as we said above [2:1], and through the distributions of the Holy Spirit (1 Cor. 12[:11]), "…dividing to individuals as He wishes."

[v. 5:] "For He did not subject to the angels…"

He is showing with another proof that Christ is far superior to the angels; namely, as I say, Christ according to His humanity, on the basis of Psa. 7. On the basis of this passage, he, at the same time, is busy with what the Hebrews might have been able to raise as an objection: "For we have seen Him despised and the least of men, etc." (Isa. 53[:3]). He says that this happened for the brief time of His passion for our sake. For He was soon crowned with glory and honor and appointed over all things.

[v. 5:] "…the world to come…"

He means the kingdom of God which the prophets foretold was going to come and which would be far more suitable than all the kingdoms of the world, just as Isaiah calls Him "the Father of the age to come." Because the kingdom of Christ is spiritual, all creatures have been subjected in spirit to Christ and to those who are in Christ. For all people are serving us to our salvation, even sheep, oxen, and fishes as well as sin, death, and hell. The reason that you do not see that all things have been subjected to Christ is that the flesh does not see these things which have to do with the spiritual kingdom of Christ, which consists in faith and hope. You will see what you have been waiting for when the Father will place all the enemies of Christ under His feet.

[v. 7:] "You have made Him a little lower…"

This "a little lower" is a reference to the time of His passion or, if you prefer, to the time of the mortality of Christ. (Read also 1 Cor. 15.)

[v. 10:] "For it befit Him because of whom all things exist…"

This is what Christ said: "It was necessary for Christ to suffer and rise again and in this way to enter into His glory," not only because Scripture had foretold this, but also because otherwise He could not have been like us. Scripture calls Him "our brother" in whom we are more excellent than the angels. From this it follows that the things [of the Law] which were handed down through the angels were again abolished. Also, heaven forbid that the angels or prophets be placed ahead of Christ! The result is that even the mortal human beings who are in Christ have something because of which they may glory above the angels, etc.

Obviously, it befit Him to be God the Father, for, because of Him exist all things; that is, He created all things because of His goodness alone, for He had no other reason. Through Him are all things, because without Him they would not exist. Understand here that the author is speaking about God the Father, the Son, and the Holy Spirit, for the things which He is saying about Christ he is saying about His humanity. I say, it befit Him as one who has many children. That is, He had brought the believers into glory, and this once and for all to the end of the world according to His predestination. He had led them, however, through the disgrace of the world and in no other way.

Tell me, why did that befit Him? Namely, that no other way would glorify their ruler and leader, Christ, because He sanctifies believers with His blood, and those who believe are sanctified. They are all from one, namely, from Adam, flesh and blood according to their body, and yet at the same time are sharers of His body. Our Father, therefore, is Christ.

[v. 14:] "…that through death He might destroy Him who … of death…"

See here Christian freedom that resulted from Christ's abrogation of the Law under which people used to serve the fear of death. Despite this, they remained uncertain of conscience because they never could have satisfied the Law. Thus they not only used to fear the death of the body, but also eternal death, just as we also have experienced when we have the foolish desire to receive justification through our works. This is what Peter says in Acts [15:10]: "Neither we nor our fathers could have borne the burden of the Law." But the author is connecting the power of death and the power of the Law, for, as we read in 1 Cor. 15[:56]: "The sting of death is sin, but the strength of sin is the Law." Paul writes about the abrogation of the Law in Eph. 2 and often elsewhere. See the *Loci* of Philip Melanchthon as well as John 1[:31]: "Now is the judgment of the world."

[v. 16:] "…He took on the seed of Abraham."

Obviously when He wished to become united with the same creature by nature, etc., "that he might be merciful," that is, taught as He was by experience, that He might faithfully take care of His priesthood before His Father on behalf of our infirmities, sins, and temptations. But see more about these matters in the following verses and in ch. 8.

CHAPTER 3.

[v. 1:] "…consider the Apostle, the High Priest of our confession…"

Thus, because we are certain that Christ was sent to us in the flesh to be our Apostle, Teacher, and High Priest, the Mediator between God and man, just as He says later [8:6]; let us consider Him that we not turn away from His voice and His teaching and that through unbelief we do not enter into the kingdom of heaven, which is that holy Sabbath. This is the same as those formerly perished in the wilderness who could not have entered into the promised land because of their unbelief (Num. 14[:22–23]).

This is the sum of the entire chapter: we must have no fear that this Apostle and High Priest is not faithful to Him whom He has sent and has appointed with an oath as High Priest, that is, that we must not be afraid of Him as if He is doing anything which God had not sent Him to do, as He speaks in John 12[:42ff]. You see, as Moses was doing all things and teaching all things according to the Word of God, as we often read in his Law, so also Christ said and did. Here He is of far greater glory beyond that of Moses, for, although both were faithful to God who was sending them so that they were concerned about nothing else in the house of God (that is, in the church of the believers which God had entrusted to them); nevertheless, Moses was merely a servant, but He [Christ] is also the Son. Moses was part of the house of God, but Christ was the Lord and Heir of the house and, in fact, the Builder and Creator of the same house. Here the author is openly extolling Christ over Moses, something which he did in a more concealed way at first, so that he next may show that the rest of the things which were handed down in Scripture through Moses were completed in Christ, and that Moses was not longer required as the high priest of the Law when we welcomed the Son as Heir and eternal Priest.

[v. 7:] "Today, if you will have heard His voice…"
    The preaching of Moses will endure until Christ comes; but what advantage was it to hear one in whom you did not believe? There is a prophecy in the Psalm, therefore, when people will again hear the voice of God through Christ, that we, similarly unbelieving, not perish.

[v. 12:] "See to it, brothers, that there not be in anyone, etc."
    Those who already know the truth do not need to learn every day but only to be admonished that they not fall away from Him whom they know, etc. Also, note carefully that in this epistle

the author calls sin "unbelief" alone, just as Christ does in the Gospel, saying: "The Holy Spirit reproves the world of sin, etc." [John 1:8] In Him are all those who are not delivered through the grace of Christ, etc. The beginning of substance, etc.; that is, of that which is of Christ, that is, of those things which look to the faith of Christ.

CHAPTER 4.

This chapter coheres with the preceding ones and, from an opportunity taken from the Psalm, shows a different Sabbath of believers from that which is of the seventh day. [95:11] The wicked used to celebrate the latter outwardly every seventh day. The former only the godly knew from the beginning of the world, a Sabbath into which the unbelieving have never entered, for they are unable to come in. You see, when only the best are seen, they seek to be justified by their own works—something which is diametrically opposed to the Sabbath of God. But the godly enter into this Sabbath and they cease their own abominable works, just as God ceased from all His works, so that they may take up the Word by which they were re-created and became a new creature. Then they know that they are celebrating this effectively as every will of His and not of their own, just as God promised His Word by which He created all things.

Next they know that its power and efficacy with which creatures were endowed in creation are acting in the creatures, something which is to cease, and yet they are always working, just as Christ says: "My Father is working and I am working." [John 5:17] Thus those who truly believe (that is, who cling to God alone and trust in nothing of this world, in no human righteousness or merits) have this Sabbath which God has sanctified, which goes on endlessly and is eternal, about which see Isa. 58. "The Lord your

God will give you rest forever, etc." If you will have turned your foot away from the Sabbath, etc. That is, the feast and the Sabbath will be unending. It is, however, the sentence of God and something to be feared, namely, that those unbelievers who have always tempted God have been forbidden by the oath of God to enter into His rest. That is, they have been blinded by His irrevocable sentence that at that time they are unable to come to their senses.

[v. 3:] "…although the works…"

We cannot take what is said about rest here to mean the Sabbath of the seventh day, for everyone knows that this was said about the promised land. Furthermore, who does not see that we are being warned by David not about the Sabbath of the seventh day, nor about the promised land, lest we harden our hearts to the voice of the Lord, just as those people did; and lest, in like manner, we do not enter into the rest of God, just as those people did. For when David was writing, he was already in that promised land.

You see three rests here, so to speak: rest from your labors on the seventh day, rest from adversaries in the promised land, and rest in the kingdom of heaven which is the rest of true believers and true rest which will receive completion in the final resurrection. In the meantime, this flesh is bothersome and urges us to fight, just as at that time the rest of the nations in the promised land were greatly stirring up that people to battles.

[v. 12:] "For the Word of the Lord is alive…"

This is the reason for the preceding words so that we do not perish because of a similar example of unbelief, as did they. People generally and commonly cite these words as a reference to the grace of the Word of God, but they certainly are most dreadful, as those have experienced who have been unable to enter into the promised rest (Num. 14), where we read that the people lived in excessive luxury. The condemned will feel in eternity this punishment of the Word of God as He passes judgment on them. The saints feel it, too, abandoned as they have been temporarily in their horror of the judgments of God. These are those voices in the Psalms [38:3]: "There is no soundness in my flesh because of Your wrath, etc."; [22:14]: "All my bones have been pulled out of joint, etc." Here the conscience, overcome as it is, feels the judgment of the Word of God and eternal damnation upon itself. When one's spirit has no plan but all things are filled with desperation, his bones must tremble, his body perish, all the powers of his body and soul grow weak and are separated from each other, because it is a dreadful thing to fall into the hands of the living God.

The godly Father, however, does not abandon his children in this very dreadful inferno. Here again are those words of thanksgiving about deliverance [Psa. 6:10]: "Let all my enemies be ashamed and deeply upset, etc."; and: "You have saved me from those going down into the lake, etc." The Word of God (namely, that which He speaks against the unbelievers against whom He has sworn that they will not enter into His rest) is a living, not a dead, letter, and it is effective, that is, it accomplishes what it swears. Therefore we must not argue against it, but fear it, because of the judgments of God. In this way, this letter is often frightening.

[v. 14:] "Having a great high priest…"

Because the author had started to speak about the priesthood of Christ, given the opportunity, in the meantime he has been interpreting the words of the Psalm [95:7]: "If you will have heard His voice today, etc." Now he returns to his subject and says: "Having therefore, etc." Thus we begin correctly from this passage. However, in the beginning, he advises that, because he described earlier the very great majesty and excellence of Christ, we not flee from Him because of our awareness of our weakness and sins, because

He Himself was tempted and made less than the angels for a short time, as he said before, "that He might become merciful, etc."

The humbling of Christ, therefore, created for us a trust in His coming because we know that He was cast down for our sake. However, His power creates a confidence in persevering, obviously because no one can snatch us from His hands, etc. "He has entered into, etc." (See ch. 6 and 8.) He is alluding to the entry of the priest into the holy of holies once a year not without blood.

[v. 16:] **"Let us therefore come confidently to, etc."**

With this single statement he interprets for us what that ancient propitiation signified. So also Paul calls Christ our "propitiation" (Rom. 3[:25]).

CHAPTER 5.

[v. 1:] **"...to offer gifts and sacrificial victims."**

According to the Law, it was once the duty of the high priest to mediate between God and man, something which he did with teaching and prayer. Next, sacrifice also had to do with prayer. But he had to do that mediation with figures of flesh until Christ, the true High Priest, came. At the former time, they would anoint the priests with carnal oil. The priests indeed would teach, but they did not receive the Spirit by which they understood and kept all things. They would pray, but they were not heard for their own sake. They would make sacrifices for sins, but they would not sacrifice themselves, for they were sinners.

Furthermore, carnal priests would perform the sacrifices, but God nevertheless chose them to do this, and they would make carnal sacrifices not according to their inventions, but according to the command of God, as we see in the Law of Moses. Also, those priests not only were weak but they were also mortal, and their priesthood expired with their life.

But Jesus was anointed with the Holy Spirit. God the Father swore an oath and made Him Priest and High Priest forever. With His own Word, He put His Spirit into the hearts of believers because the Father listened to Him because of His reverence when He was sacrificing His sacrifice once on the cross, that is, when He sacrificed Himself, which sanctifies us eternally.

He does not need to pray because of His sins, but He is always present on our behalf before the face of His Father through His blood, which He shed once for us when He entered into the holy of holies as "a sacrificial victim worthy of God in the fragrance of sweetness," as the Law said. [Phi. 4:18] Thus you see that the author is saying here nothing about high priests and priests (as they are called today) but is showing that the carnal priesthood according to the Law was a figure of the eternal priesthood which was completed in Christ, just as that carnal kingdom was completed in Christ, for then both became spiritual and now were no longer external and visible.

But that the priesthood of Christ was not going to be external was revealed in the priesthood of Melchizedek, about whom the Holy Spirit speaks in this way in David [Psa. 110:4]: "The Lord has sworn and will not repent, etc.," about which there will be more later. We have no greater consolation than in the Priesthood of Christ. He is that Priest and that King who reconciles us to God. He makes and keeps us safe. He justifies and saves, etc.

[v. 4:] "Let no one usurp this honor for himself…"

Even though they were born Levites (that is, men of the priestly class), they should not come to the high priesthood or priesthood unless they have been chosen, etc.

[v. 7:] "...who in the days of His flesh, when, etc."

In His mortal flesh, Christ always prayed for us when He always desired and thirsted for our salvation. But He prayed especially in the sacrifice of the cross: "Father, forgive them, because they don't know what they are doing." This is not to mention His other desires [on our behalf].

[v. 12:] "...when by reason of time you had to be..."

When the author was about to speak of the priesthood of Melchizedek from Scripture to the Hebrews who knew Scripture, he seriously reproves those who for a long time had heard Christ from Scripture that they had to be schoolmasters for others. Nevertheless, they are still stuck on its easiest points, although they do believe in Christ, and they are incapable of grasping the more difficult ones, as is that which the author is stating about the priesthood of Christ.

Also, this rebuke applies especially to our priests who are surprised when we speak about the Priesthood of Christ according to Scripture otherwise than they were dreaming up to now and who nevertheless chant and say three times a day: "The Lord has sworn and He will not repent..." He digresses from this rebuke, and in ch. 7 returns to the priesthood of Melchizedek.

CHAPTER 6.

[v. 1:] "Let us therefore leave the simple teaching which begins in Christ..."

These words go together with the preceding ones. Therefore, we are leaving the primary rudiments in which little children receive their first instruction and as were sufficiently instilled in us. Now let us recognize and learn loftier teachings and those which are the stuff of full-grown men, and do this in the faith of Christ (Eph. 4[:11ff.]).

[v. 3:] "…if God permit."

The rudiments are to teach and have regard only for the external Sacraments as well as some voluntary observances according to the ritual which the apostles had observed, as was the laying on of hands, without which the Holy Spirit could then be given and was being given and is always being given to Christians. Those rudiments also include teaching us to say: "I believe in God the Father, etc."; to teach you to abstain from fornication, false witness, etc., and to say the Lord's Prayer. These alone are the sort of things which our men teach where they are the best, namely, the perfection of faith and how rich it is to be in God, as those who don't know and are unable to teach in this way.

Therefore the people err along with them, when they never truly come to their senses and always are stuck in the same mudhole. Still, they invent a repentance from dead works once a year for themselves. Thus they are wrong and are not Christians until God has mercy on them and opens for them the way of salvation that they may learn not to cling to external works in vain like little children, but to hope for salvation through Christ Jesus in God alone. We must call forth such people to better things, as you see here. We shall hear another judgment about those who truly knew Christ and later blasphemed His grace, which is terrible wickedness.

[v. 4:] "For it cannot happen…"

Daily and continually, we call upon the mercy of God not only because of our temptations, but also because of our sins, as the Lord commands. Therefore, we shall not deny that Christian repentance which all Scripture declares with words and examples, even though an angel from heaven may preach a different Gospel so that this is not a concern for you in this author, if you cannot understand other than that he denies repentance. After all, you have the divine Word to which any human word at all must give way. It is strange because this author, whoever he may have been, very carefully proves everything from Holy Writ but only this statement he does not prove in which he appears to deny pardon for slips after one's first conversion to Christ. However, from what source does he prove it inasmuch as it is completely different from Scripture, unless you understand this as a reference to the sin against the Holy Spirit, as we shall say?

Nevertheless, this passage about the Priesthood of Christ which he handles here from Scripture in a very dignified way shows clearly that the author is not denying repentance and the forgiveness of sins of those in whom human frailty causes one to slip, while the foundation of Christ still stands firm. Otherwise, after the first promise, the Priesthood of Christ will be useless; but the author himself says [4:16]: "Let us approach the throne of grace confidently, etc."; also, in ch. 7[:25]: "…whence also the Savior can approach God forever through Himself, always living to intervene for us"; and ch. 9[:24]: "…that He may now appear before the face of God on our behalf"; and ch. 12[:1]: "Let us set aside every burden and our inherent sin." These things, we are sure, he is not saying to those who have not yet experienced conversion, for he is writing to Christians who have converted from Judaism to Christ, as he says clearly in ch. 3[:1]: "Holy brothers, sharers of the heavenly calling, etc.," not to mention other passages.

Therefore, he is not denying pardon now, and this clearly from Scripture and here and there elsewhere in this epistle, as we indicated earlier. He may appear to be denying penitence, without adding Scripture and in this way is making us uncertain as to what his wish is. Therefore, we must interpret this from clearer Scripture and, if possible, from the words even of this author, just as we must do everywhere in the case of the more obscure passages of Scripture.

In his epistle [1.5:16–17], John posits two sins, one which is not to death, the other which is to death. If a brother may have sinned, he wants us to pray for the former, but not for the latter. With reference to the former, he also says this [1.2:1–2]: "My little children I am writing these things to you that you not sin, but if someone may have sinned, we have an Advocate before the Father, Jesus Christ, the Righteous. He is the Propitiation for our sins, and not only for ours but also for those of the whole world." In the former instance, isn't John speaking the same thing as this author of ours, except that John makes Christ an Advocate, while our author makes Him a Priest? Paul uses a single word and calls Him "the Mediator."

Christ calls the sin unto death "blasphemy against the Holy Spirit, which will never receive forgiveness" (Mark 3[:29]), about which sin we must also understand the things which our author says here. We shall see this in the words of the author if we shall have first indicated that in the world that sin is.

Moreover, that sin occurs when you see the open truth of God so that you are overcome within yourself in your heart and conscience, as the real situation holds and cannot be otherwise. Yet, you dare wickedly to speak and contend contrariwise that this is not true, that it is not from God, that it is perverse, and that it comes from the devil. Because of such a terrible blasphemy, aren't you afraid of the sword of the Lord brandished against you, as if you are permitted even to sin willingly against God?

You see this from Mark 3[:22ff.] where the scribes were attributing the obvious work of God to Beelzebub, contrary to conscience. For this reason, after the Evangelist wrote the words of Christ, who said that blasphemy against the Holy Spirit is never forgiven, he added, [v. 30]: "…because they said: 'He has an unclean spirit.'" But if Christ said these words about others who were wicked and unwilling to accept the truth but kept attacking it, although it was so obvious that it could not be denied; why accuse this author of ours for condemning those who, enlightened as they were not only with external words and miracles but also in their heart, have tasted the heavenly gift after receiving the Holy Spirit, and who have tasted the good Word of God and the power and efficacy of the kingdom of God? But they slip away from all these and blaspheme the grace which they had acknowledged because of the great testimony of the Holy Spirit.

He says that falling away from Christ is a sin, just as he calls unbelief a sin, if you should examine correctly ch. 3 and 4. Christ says in John [16:8]: "The Holy Spirit will reprove the world because it does not believe in Me." Furthermore, he adds "intentionally" that he not make them guilty of this sin: "…if it perhaps may happen to some that they deny God, as happened to Peter."

But he is signifying that those among the godly confess those things which they know are true, but among the wicked they blaspheme the things which they know are true and shamefully live with the others, contrary to conscience. In this way, they are considering their own situations and are mocking both people and God, using that hope that they can repent as many times as they may have wished. That's the way they think, but they are wrong. This is what it means to crucify the Son of God again and to consider Him a joke, just as he says here [v. 7]: "For the earth which has often drunk in the rain of the Word of God coming from heaven," Isa. 35, "grew from faith to faith, bearing the fruit of faith and confession and was blessed by God."

But that which made fun of the work of God raining and working those things, is producing nothing other than blasphemies instead of a confession, has been condemned and is close to the curse, that is, to this dreadful sentence to be burned. Take a very careful look at the words of ch. 10[:26], so that you may see clearly that the author feels what he has said. He speaks in this way: "For if you will have sinned intentionally after receiving a knowledge of the truth, no sacrifice has been left for sins." After all, you have denied the Priesthood of Christ and His sacrifice for sins which is satisfactory for ever. You have denied and blasphemed them along with the wicked, and this you have done intentionally. You therefore no longer have a sacrifice by which to become reconciled to God, because there is no sacrifice beside that unique one.

If, however, it were the case that you, as a very great sinner, did now have a sacrifice in Christ, you would not be beloved of God because of the beloved Christ, that is, because of this High Priest, who always stands firm before the face of the Father on our behalf to intervene for us. He says: "You no longer have a sacrifice left except a dreadful one, etc. Because you have denied and blasphemed the Savior intentionally, you will not be able to have Him except as your Judge." He also says: "…because fire is going to consume the adversaries, namely, of Christ and of God." Take from this that he is speaking about those who are blasphemers of the Gospel and of the Christian truth, and not to mean those who are in Christ, although they are sinners. After all, what person is there on earth who is not a sinner?

Furthermore, the words which follow in this sentence are quite clear. He says: "The person who has trampled upon the Son of God and the blood of the covenant by which our High Priest has entered into the holy of holies had a profane program through which he had been sanctified before, that is, set apart for God, and insulted the Spirit of grace, that is, he blasphemed against the Holy Spirit." These are frightful words. Let those see and be careful who intentionally dare whatever they wish against conscience with that hope by which they think that they can make satisfaction through some works. That, however, is a pure and real mockery of God.

Because I cannot help but understand how easily the tender and weak consciences of some people are harmed and driven into despair, I say that those who return to God from the depths of their heart have the certain testimony that they will never be subject to this sentence, even when they appear to fall under it, so long as God is saving them. For those who may have fallen under it will never be able to come to their senses; for they will be blinded either by their obvious malice or by their imagined righteousness, just as we have seen the Jews to have perished.

[v. 9:] "**Furthermore, we have persuaded ourselves, etc.**"

He eases the warning and rebuke lest they interpret from his words that they are damned. However, they should understand that he is warning them that in their security they not cast away Christ.

[v. 10:] "**…to forget your work…**"

See to it that you not confirm human merit from these words, for he adds clearly "…the work and labor you have undertaken out of love." You see, then, that the works are works of faith. And again: "…which love you have showed to His name." He is also showing that works bear witness of internal faith.

[v. 11:] "**…to the full assurance of faith …**"

Note carefully that our good works are testimonies of our faith not only to others, but also to ourselves. From them, we are certifying that we have faith and hope until our trust is perfected and we learn to hope in God. See these points in 2 Peter 1[:8 and 10]: "When these things are in you and abound… Exert yourselves to make your calling and election sure."

[v. 13:] "**For God promised Abraham…**"

Because the author had warned that through faith and the cross, which accompany each other, we receive the inheritance of the promise, that is, of the Gospel which He promised also to the patriarchs and not just to us; he takes the opportunity to speak about the promises of God which God also confirmed with His oath so that we not entertain doubts that we would receive them.

[v. 14:] "...unless blessing I shall have blessed you..."

This is a great oath which God takes through His silence, in which we must hear between the lines: "Let me not be who I am," that is, "let me not be God," just as we say: "Let me die," or: "Let me despair," or the like.

[v. 18:] "...through two immutable things..."

There are two immutable things in God: a promise and an oath. He who is the truth cannot deny Himself, either when entering, that is, leading us into the eternal kingdom of God, or rather, which anchor does not get stuck in the mud but is fixed in heaven where Christ is. But he is alluding however to the entry of the high priest within the veil, about which we shall speak later.

CHAPTER 7.

[v. 1:] "For this was Melchizedek, King of Salem..."

After so long a digression, he is returning to the priesthood of Melchizedek, about whom you read in Gen. 14[:18-20]. According to his order, Christ in the Psalm [110:4] takes an oath and promises that He will be the High Priest or Priest forever. With wonderful arguments, the author is placing the priesthood of Melchizedek ahead of the priesthood of the Law or of gentleness which was according to the order of Aaron. He also chooses correctly the figure which the Holy Spirit indicates in the Psalm for Christ according to His name, office, dignity, and life. This he does on the basis of the history which was written into the figure of Christ by the care of the Holy Spirit so that Melchizedek appears to have had neither a beginning nor an end, although nevertheless no one doubts that he was a mortal human being.

[v. 2:] "…who by interpretation was first…"
Until now, he has been speaking history. Now he indicating from history the figure and, from the figure, Christ, etc.

[v. 2:] "…the King of righteousness…"
He is calling Christ not only "righteous" but also "the King of righteousness," to whose kingdom righteousness looks, for it is through that by which all believers are justified. You see, if He is the King of righteousness, then His kingdom is the kingdom of righteousness, just as, on the other hand, the kingdom of the prince of the world is the kingdom of iniquity.

[v. 2:] "…the King of peace."
He is that because peace of conscience immediately follows justification and follows it as much as you can believe. Therefore, you are seeing the things that are in the kingdom of Christ; namely, grace and peace. It is wonderful that, when he is about to describe the Priest, he also makes Him the King. Formerly, God had ordained Him to be the true King before kings existed in Israel so that His kingdom and priesthood might be joined together. Also, although there were judges, nevertheless those judges were obedient to His priesthood, too. As a result, it angered God when they demanded that the king be under Samuel. That external unction of both the king and the priest was completed in Christ.

[v. 3:] "Of unknown father and unknown mother…"

This is because such things are not written in Scripture so that the figure represent more fully the divinity of Christ and the eternity of His kingdom. It is also because you do not read that He died, nor that His priesthood was established nor ended; and yet, He was the Priest of the most high God and the King of Salem [or Peace].

[v. 4:] "But consider how great this man was…"

Abraham gave Melchizedek tithes from all the spoils of war. Therefore Abraham acknowledged him as his superior even by divine right as well as the priest of God both after they began giving tithes to the priests in the name of God according to the Law and before the laws of tithes are read to have been given, which tithes were given to God, as Jacob said: "I shall offer you tithes and sacrifices of peace." Also, Melchizedek, as the priest of God, blessed Abraham, as the account reads. Therefore Melchizedek acknowledged that because of his office he was superior to Abraham.

From these points, it follows that, if the prince of that clan to whom God had promised a blessing and of whose father all the Jews boast, is inferior to Melchizedek; the entire clan of Abraham according to the flesh all the way to Christ is inferior to Melchizedek. Thus not even Levi, to whom the priesthood neverethless was owed, is excepted from being inferior. Although Levi may not be greater than his brothers by nature or in merit, nevertheless he is greater according to the Law of God and, according to the Law, he received tithes from his brothers as his inferiors. Furthermore, Levi was still going to come forth from the loins of Abraham and was already in the flesh of Abraham when Abraham gave tithes and in Abraham was receiving the blessing from Melchizedek, who alone according to the Law had the right to receive tithes and to bless the people.

From all these facts, you see that the dignity of Melchizedek is placed ahead of that of Abraham and of his entire clan, and that the priesthood of Levi was far inferior. Furthermore, because this priesthood was among mortal humans, that also signified that at some time it would perish and be abolished. We do not read that Melchizedek died, nor that his priesthood was removed. This priesthood did not exist before Melchizedek, nor was another substituted for it after Melchizedek. Rather, he alone was the priest and remains that forever. In him, we see Christ as the only and the eternal Priest.

[v. 11:] "Accordingly, if perfection came through the Levitic priesthood…"

He is making clear that the Levitic priesthood was imperfect, for the eternal priesthood in the Son of God had to be substituted in its stead, which priesthood in Christ cannot be a priesthood according to the Law. After all, Christ is of Judah, not of Levi, and, according to the Law, no one of Judah could have been a priest. Furthermore, it was written that an eternal Priest was going to come, and such priests the Law could not establish.

From this, it follows that, if the carnal priesthood has been abrogated, the carnal Law which was received through that priesthood has also been abrogated. Just as the carnal and temporary priesthood has been changed into a spiritual and eternal one, so also the carnal and temporary Law has been changed into a spiritual and eternal one. The priesthood and that Law made clear their own imperfection because it was necessary to substitute some priests for others constantly because priests would die, endlessly repeat the works of the Law, and repeat their annual sacrifices and even their daily ones, because the Law brought no one to perfection. Otherwise, they would have ceased making sacrifices, as we read later in ch. 10[:2].

Therefore the Lord God instituted that priesthood, but He did not do that with an oath because He was going to abolish that one again along with everything which belonged to it. However, the Father instituted the priesthood of Christ with an oath because it is eternal and cannot even be changed. In the figure, those priests would often sanctify the people with their carnal sacrifices, but here Christ did that once with His offering on the cross and truly sanctified His people, that is, believers, forever. But tell me, please, when those sinners were made perfect? Jesus, the High Priest without sin and immortal before God, sanctifies once and without any sin and grants us the Spirit, who is the Law of life in our hearts forever. At that time, the Law would only command and condemn; therefore it was unbearable. Now the Spirit of Christ accomplishes in believers those things which are of the Law, not by mandate, but by will.

This is so far from seeking the spiritual person from the Law that all the things whichever are against the Law of God in themselves are so burdensome that that spiritual person still feels them because of the age of the flesh. Although those contrary things are sins in the sight of God, nevertheless they are not counted because of the Spirit, who fights against them and condemns them and because of our Priest, who endlessly intervenes.

Only those who have the Spirit of God understand this abrogation of the Law, as Paul says [2 Cor. 3:17]: "Where the Spirit of the Lord is, there freedom is." All the rest of the people are still under the Law and condemnation.

[v. 26:] "For it befit such a One to be High Priest for us…."

The priesthood, the Law, sacrifices, the temple, the altar, sanctification, anointing, and all the spiritual things which were done in Christ are no longer external, for the priesthood of Christ is in heaven in the presence of the Father and not upon the earth (as we shall see in ch. 8), just as His kingdom is not of this world.

CHAPTER 8.

[v. 1:] "We have such an High Priest who sat at the right hand…"
To the figure of the high priest of the Law, the author brings forth from what he has said Christ, the ruling High Priest and Administrator in the holy of holies and the tabernacle not made with hand, having an eternal sacrifice once offered, as we shall see in the verses following. God is not dwelling in man-made churches today, but the kingdom of heaven is an invisible kingdom on earth, an eternal kingdom through Christ, its Priest and King. He administers it in His Spirit invisibly and not of the elements of this world. These are the tabernacles of God, the tabernacles of assurance and security, the eternal tabernacles about which they often sing in the Psalms and Prophets.

[v. 4:] "If He were on earth…"
That is, if He were an earthly priest and were administering external matters, He would not even be a priest because He is not of the tribe of Levi. According to the Law, therefore, He could not have offered the sacrifices which those priests offered temporarily and through which priesthood they served not real things but only the shadow or model and figures of heavenly things. That is, they served the figures of spiritual things of which Christ is High Priest and Administrator, as Moses showed (Exo. 25). He saw the spiritual tabernacle, the figure of which he built, until that which is spiritual should be produced for all through the Word of the Gospel.

[v. 6:] "Now He has obtained this more excellent priesthood…"
The Priesthood of Christ is far more worthy than the old priesthood, for the latter would intercede with figures before God

on behalf of people under the old covenant. The former, on the other hand, intercedes with the very truth, that is, through Christ Himself, and His invisible and eternal sacrifice is now under the new covenant. The people were unable to keep the old covenant which those priests had, so far was that old covenant from justifying. The new covenant in which Christ has given the justifying Spirit, who remains with us forever. The former covenant was written on stone tablets and was the letter. The latter is written in hearts and is spirit and life, which the author shows from Jeremiah. [31:31–35]

CHAPTER 9.

[v. 2:] "…the lamp stand and table and the show bread…"
We read about these in Exo. 25 and in the following verses. The tabernacle of God which Moses had built was divided. The first part was the entrance of the tabernacle, and this he calls "the first veil," for he says that the holy of holies came after the second veil, because the first part of the tabernacle was called only "the holy place," or in the plural, "the holies."

Because this author does seem to have been well-versed in Jewish affairs so that he does appear to have been a Hebrew, it is clear that he places in the holy of holies a gold censer, although we read that there were more gold censers, but not in the holy of holies, into which the chief priest would enter once a year with the gold censer. It is also clear that he also places in the holy of holies the gold urn with the manna as well as the rod of Aaron, which we read were preserved in the tabernacle to be eternal reminders to the people in the presence of the Lord. Of what would these have warned the people, had they been in the holy of holies into which they were nether to enter nor look?

You read about the manna in Exo. 16, and about the rod

of Aaron in Num. 17. But you do not read that the gold urn with the manna and the rod of Aaron were in the ark. In fact, you read something different, for Moses, by order of the Lord, placed nothing in the ark except the stone tablets (Exo. 25 and 40). We read clearly in 1 Kings 8:9: "There was nothing in the ark except the two tables of stone which Moses had placed in it, etc." But here there is no danger when the author says about these that he was going to sit upon them. He deals in a very sacred manner with what the two tabernacles or the one divided into two sections signified.

The tabernacle in which God dwells among people, as we read in the Law and later from Solomon and finally through Jeremiah, is the very hearts of people, as Paul says. [1 Cor. 3:17:] "The temple of God, which you are, is holy." But at that time a double tabernacle or two parts of one tabernacle was built. The other part was open and exposed to the eyes of people. The priests used to enter it daily in the figure of the ancient Law, the ancient priesthood and of that people when the worship was God was performed in the elements of this world and with visible things, but nevertheless according to the Word of God, as a figure of things to come. Therefore the objects which were visible there signified invisible things. The lamp stand was the light of the Word of God; the table, Holy Scripture; the show bread, the food of the Word of God; the gold censer, the prayers and desires of the godly; the manna in the gold urn, the Word of God in the perfect and very fine heart; the rod of Aaron, God's election to the office of teaching which the greenness of the mind, the leaves of eloquence and the very sweet fruit in the teacher and those who listen to him follow. Those things have not been difficult to interpret on the basis of Scripture.

However, the second part of the tabernacle was hidden in darkness, removed from the eyes of people and into which no one would enter except the high priest once a year when he had to make expiation for the sins of all people (Lev. 16). This was a figure of

Christ, through whom alone we are given access to the Father and receive expiation from our sins in His blood, which He offered once. As a result, the objects which at that time had been hidden from the sight of that people now have been revealed through the Gospel, as Christ Himself said [Luke 10:24]: "Many kings and prophets have desired to see and hear what you, etc."

That second part is also a figure of the kingdom of heaven, not having the righteousness of the flesh, not serving God in the elements of this world, but worshipping God in spirit and in truth. Here, then, all things were hidden although in the figure, and they used to signify externally invisible things. Here was the ark of the Lord, that is, the dwelling place of God in which the tables of the Law were being preserved and which carnal eyes were not permitted to see. They signified the Law of God written in the secret places of the heart according to the prophecy of Jeremiah, as we saw earlier. This was no longer the letter but the spirit. This was wonderfully rehearsed when the earlier tablets were made by Moses. After the second were read and before the first were enough of the letter, they were preserved in the ark where the Lord is dwelling to signify the spiritual Law of God hidden in hearts through the Spirit of Christ.

Therefore this is the Church of the living God, not gold, lest it arrogate something for itself, but gilded, that is, outstanding inside and out for its divine glow and for the riches of God. It is also excellent for its golden crown, that is, for the royal dignity of Christ and His eternal priesthood. It is made of wood which doesn't rot because the living Spirit of God can never be corrupted.

On the other hand, the mercy seat which covers the ark is of the purest gold, for it signifies Christ, the Propitiator (Rom. 3[:25] and Heb. 4[:16]), by whom we are reconciled to God. The Cherubim are also of gold, because they signify the Word of God, which is gold in itself in the two Testaments, divine to us because of its mystery which is of choice silver. The preaching of the Word is silver, while faith is gold and precious stones. The Cherubim with their faces turned toward each other look down upon the mercy seat, for the two Testaments agree on Christ.

Although all things have a figure, God alone has no figure but wishes to be known only by faith in His Word, for He promises that He is going to dwell in His tabernacle, just as He promises that He is going to sit later between the Cherubim above the mercy seat, and there is going to listen to those who call upon Him; and that because no figure was seen but only believed. Therefore, all those things were also given that people might believe that God was present there where all things were happening according to the Word of God and which are now happening in our Sacraments. Furthermore, pay careful attention to the fact that, although all things were occurring according to the Law in the front part of the tabernacle, nevertheless in the unseen part, that is, in the holy of holies, the high priest was seeking and invoking God as well as listening to Him.

The fathers, you see, were saved not by the works of the Law but by the same faith by which we are saved, for they looked upon the grace which was going to be revealed at some time. Those who do not have respect for the faith of the Word of God have become hypocrites through the works of the Law. That which belongs to God alone, that is justification, they are attributing to works.

Also note carefully that, when the expiation took place once a year at the hands of the high priest, he entered the holy of holies through the blood and thyme of prayer, as a figure of the expiation which happened through Christ one time, when He entered through His blood into the holy of holies which was not made by hand, that is, which is invisible to the flesh. All the people were ordered to stand outside with the priests, who were in the habit of making daily sacrifices in the temple. You see, no one is admitted to this expiation except Christ. The enthusiasms, merits, and judgments of men here are nothing, for the priests of the Law, who otherwise were in the habit of sacrificing, and all the people and all their sacred rituals are here expiated through the greatest High Priest.

[v. 7:] "...for the [sins of] ignorance of the people."

Other things still remained which God had not yet made public. You see, there had not yet been time because that people were still living in the night and darkness of figures. Nevertheless, they were living according to the Word of God which saved them through the grace which they were not seeing but for which they were waiting along with faithful Abraham.

[v. 11:] "But Christ, the High Priest of good things to come..."

Those "good things to come" are invisible and eternal, as we read in Isaiah: "...the Father of the age to come," and earlier here. Moreover, He said that they were coming to the whole world.

[v. 12:] "...by His own blood He entered the holy place once..."

Because redemption is eternal, there formerly was a temporal expiation. Therefore it was repeated each year. But this happened only once in the figure of the expiation of Christ, which occurred just one time. Repetition used to indicate imperfection. Because the sacrifice of Christ absolved all things once and was perfect, therefore it cannot be repeated. Otherwise He who was the Expiator of the first sin of the world to the final sin of the world would have to have died often since the beginning of the world, as we read later. Those people should have seen this who want to sacrifice Christ every day on the altar where He committed no sacrifice, that is, suicide, for us. Rather, a commemoration of that sacrifice once made through Christ Himself has been entrusted to us as often as we ourselves eat and drink His body and blood but not as often as we have entrusted these things to others, as we foolishly err today. However, the institution of Christ in this Sacrament is clear in this matter. Why are we exposing what Christ instituted as some joke?

[v. 13:] "For if the blood of bulls…"

See Num. 19:9, where you also read about the carnal expiation because of purely carnal uncleanness, just as we read elsewhere, [v. 12]: "Through the blood of goats and calves…"

[v. 16:] "For where there is a testament…"

With reference to a will, it is clear that the death of the testator confirms it. At that time, the death of brute animals would confirm it. The old and carnal could not have been the true and eternal as is the new will, for, after it had been created, the Testator died and confirmed it with His own blood. We read in Exo. 24 [:5–8] that the Law and people of the Law were expiated through the blood of goats and calves.

[v. 17:] "As long as the will remains, all people…"

The author is showing that the death of Christ expiates believers indefinitely up to the judgment. First, He comes to us with our sins which He has carried; second, He will come without sin in glory to all who love His coming.

CHAPTER 10.

[v. 1:] "For the Law has a shadow of things to come…"

The author is making clear the imperfection of the Law, as he did earlier when there was only a shadow of coming affairs, and when the affairs themselves were not seen as present.

[v. 2:] "…because they now would have had no…"

Do Christians therefore now have no awareness of sins? This is truly so, but blessed is the person who understands. Paul, who always connects grace and peace in his epistles, says [Rom. 5:1]: "Justified as we are by faith, we have peace…" It is good to know that our merits and righteousness do not save us, but when shall we finally know that our sins do not condemn us? This would be, and truly is, the Christian freedom of consciences which is impossible for those to know who conclude among themselves from this declaration that they now can sin freely. That is something they should not infer from these words to the insult of their Deliverer, Christ, even if they were to have a tiny spark of faith. In fact, they should be shocked because of their astonishment at such great generosity and love of their kind Father toward His children.

If they look within themselves, Christians are not ignorant of the fact that they are sinners and condemned, for they have no righteousness within themselves, but by faith they are mindful of Christ, whom God made for us righteousness, wisdom, sanctification, satisfaction, etc. Here all sins vanish even from the conscience of a person, provided he has correct faith which cannot judge that the righteousness of Christ is not perfect. Here all things are possible for the believer. Now there is no condemnation for those who are in Christ Jesus, for they do not walk according to the flesh. Desiring this out of faith, they always pray: "Father, forgive us our debts, etc." As we have said elsewhere, the righteousness of works can never reach this freedom.

Let us do here the will of God as we believe in Him whom He sent, as he shows here from Psa. 40[:6]. We are sanctified through this will alone through the satisfaction of the body of Christ which He offered once, and we are sanctified forever so that we have no awareness of our sin when that offering is ours. Furthermore, that offering is ours when we believe that it is perfect for the sins of the whole world from its beginning. This is what God said in Jeremiah [31:34:]: "I shall remember no more their sins and iniquities."

Next, the author concludes [v. 18]: "Where there is forgiveness of sins, there in no more an offering for sin." Where, then, is that papist satisfaction? All the points that follow look to this.

[v. 19:] "Therefore, brothers, when, etc."

Those words make clear that we are priests and high priests in Christ, etc.

[v. 32:] "Moreover, recall to memory…"

He softens his words, as he did earlier in ch. 6, and advises them not to fall away from the offered hope because of which many people have suffered.

[v. 36:] "…that when you have done God's will…"

We have spoken about this before. He is also saying here that confidence has a great repayment of reward. He is not saying "works of the Law" or "good works," for they are the signs and fruits of faith. Rather, he has connected the cross to faith and therefore says: "You need to be patient." These words kept making sufficiently clear what he said earlier about falling away from faith.

CHAPTER 11.

[v. 1:] "Moreover, faith is the substance of those things, etc."

He is making clear with very fine examples that we are saved by faith. Those, then, who do not have faith or who have fallen away from faith cannot be saved. (See this [topic] in the *loci* of Philip [Melanchthon].) Also, you have here a full definition when you have both parts, for he repeats this statement twice as if to say:

"Faith is the certain possession of those things which are not seen and for which you are hoping."

[v. 6:] "...for he who comes to God..."
There is indeed a level of faith, namely, to believe that God exists. But this is not enough unless you also believe that He is *your* God, that is, your Savior. Contrariwise, the wicked person says in his heart: "There is no God."

[v. 13:] "...strangers and pilgrims..."
This is what David confessed in Psa. 39[:12]: "I am a stranger and sojourner before You, as were all my fathers."

[v. 16:] "God is not embarrassed..."
In Scripture, God calls Himself: "The God of Abraham, the God of Isaac, and the God of Jacob." With these titles, He is commending faith to us, namely, the faith that He is the God of believers.

[v. 19:] "...whence [He accepted] also him..."
Understand this not only as the resurrection of bodies but also deliverance as often we are brought back from the terror of death and hell into life by the consolation of the Spirit.

[v. 21:] "...and worshipped [leaning on] the top of his staff..."
Jerome reads: "Israel turned to the head of his couch and worshipped the Lord." You see here that, as faith existed in the fathers, so also did the cross.

[v. 37:] "...they wandered about in sheepskins and goatskins..."
As did Elijah and the hundred prophets whom Obadiah killed (1 Kings 18[:40]).

[v. 40:] "…that they…[not] be made perfect."
We ourselves are sanctified by the same offering of Christ, and, at the same time, we await the same day of retribution.

CHAPTER 12.

[v. 1:] "…let us lay aside every burden and tightly-clinging sin…"
Because we see that as many as are saved are saved by faith, let us through faith also set aside every burden of conscience and of sin which is always attacking us, that is, the sin of unfaithfulness. Let us also run patiently to the blessing which has been set before us. Let us not choose for ourselves the method or the way, but let us consider the method, way and teaching of our Gymnasiarch and Agonothetes, Christ. That is, by faith alone let us follow Him who is our Leader in the stadium where we are running in whatever way and by whatever plan He has been leading, just as the ancients about whom we spoke before followed.

This is the cross which is the companion of faith, as the author describes very elegantly here. Here you will wander not at all away from Christ as Leader, when you do not make your own paths, as Isaiah says (58[:13]). For He is the Leader of faith, that is, the beginning and advancement of our every blessing. He is also the Finisher of all our salvation so that you know that nothing remains for our own powers.

Therefore the author is warning carefully here that because of temporal afflictions they not fall away from the faith and the Christian life which faith brings along with it. Thus you see from this one passage that which the whole epistle regards.

He also says "tightly," for sin always clings to us very tightly, but Christ carefully put aside that burden.

[v. 4:] "You have not yet resisted to bloodshed…"
    Some of you have had possessions taken from you. Some of you have been taken prisoner and thrown into prison. Yet you have not yet felt death, by which you might bear witness of Christ. Also, He scourges every son, etc. This is what Paul says [2 Tim. 3:12]: "All who lead a godly life in Christ will suffer persecution." [v. 8:] "Those who don't want to be chastened are bastards."

[v. 11:] "…but grievous, etc."
    It sometimes appears to a person in temptation that God has abandoned him. He is also alluding to those things which are said in Isaiah 35 about strengthening.

[v. 12:] "[Lift up] the hands which hang down…"
    That is, when you begin to feel faint, be strengthened in God. Moreover, the author has said these things metaphorically.

[v. 17:] "He did not find a place for repentance."
    The repentant wailing of Esau is properly the repentance of the ungodly, but that is not repentance before God, because they are bemoaning the loss of property and the anguish of heart in which they now feel and have fallen into the judgment of God. If they were able to be delivered from this anguish, they would hold God in contempt forever, something which history makes very clear. After all, who has wept with great wailing before his father and then went away and married a third wife who was hateful to his father? So also Cain wanted that dread into which he had fallen to be gone, but he was unable to ask from his heart for forgiveness of his sin.
    Thus Saul, caught up in anguish as he was, did not implore that his contempt for God be forgiven, although he wanted his anguish to go away. Because he saw no other remedy, he ended his life

with his sword, just as Judas did with a noose. Who doesn't see that Judas then was sorry for what he had done? Because the judgment of God was causing him inner anguish, he was unable to ask for pardon for his sin.

These frightening examples should terrify those who think that repentance lies in their hands as often as they wish, as if the faith which alone delivers us is human righteousness, and not, rather, the righteousness of God.

The repentance of Pharaoh is well-known. Whenever God chastised him, he would demand God to ask him to deliver His people. So also the evil spirits wished to be delivered, who nevertheless were unable to ask for forgiveness. So also the foolish virgins wished to enter into the wedding, but they do not ask for pardon for their foolishness, that is, for their lack of faith (as we read in Psa. 14[:1]: "The fool has said, etc.") In fact, elsewhere we read that they knew nothing other than their own merits. Holy virgins without oil? Those specious hypocrites ask: "Lord, didn't we prophesy in Your name?"

[v. 25:] "See that you not despise Him…"

The author is comparing those quite horrendous things which happened in the strengthening of the ancient Law with the grace which happens to us in the strengthening of the invisible kingdom of heaven when we believe. The result is that he infers the same thing which he had inferred before; namely, that if the earthly things which the people were seeing at that time could not be despised with impunity because they belonged to God and were from heaven, how much more can these things which are not of this world not be despised with impunity?

[v. 26:] "…whose voice then shook the earth…"

This was fulfilled when Christ was preached to the Jews

and Gentiles with the great disturbance of the earth. We still see this commotion until the figure of this world perishes completely and every kingdom is given to the people of the saints according to the prophecy of Daniel. [ch. 7] That external worship of God had to perish at some time, for it was a worship in the elements of this world, and those perish. But the kingdom which is spirit alone cannot perish.

CHAPTER 13.

[v. 1:] "Let brotherly love continue."

In this chapter, the author is writing very Christian admonitions.

[v. 8:] "Jesus Christ, [the same] yesterday and today…"

That is, on this account have no fear that the teaching of Christ is changing or perishing, as the wicked say.

[v. 10:] "We have an altar on which, etc."

The invisible altar is Christ, who is the same High Priest as we saw above. God accepts no offering except upon this altar, that is, through Christ, as Peter says (1.2[:5]). God accepts no prayers and we receive nothing from Him except on this altar. Christ says, [John 14:14]: "If you ask the Father anything in My name, He will give it to you." Lest you are dreaming here of another altar (although these words are clear), he is not speaking about anointed stones, but about an altar which is different from that of the ancient Law. The author explains himself later and says [v. 15]: "Through Him, therefore, we offer, etc."

But it is clear that he is not speaking here about the Sacrament of the Eucharist when he speaks about eating from this altar, for Christians do not have another altar beside Christ. For the veneration and receiving of that Sacrament of the body of Christ there is no need for an altar except for those who have made a sacrifice out of the testament of Christ. It is an external Sacrament with which external hands are dealing in some external place. To it we bring nothing, whether it be a wood or stone table, unless you should say that Christ sinned, who is believed to have eaten from a wood table or that it is a sin when we give the Sacrament in their own homes to those who are about to die, etc.

But note carefully, namely, that "they who serve this tabernacle have no right to eat from this altar." [v. 11] In the Law "those who used to serve the altar would live from the altar," just as Paul cites it in 1 Cor. 9[:13]; so he is bringing up a simile to show that ministers of the Word are permitted to eat at the expense of their hearers. They would eat of the meat and bread which people had offered. However, no one is permitted to eat from this altar which is Christ. In fact, no one may eat from it who has abandoned the tabernacle of Moses, that is, who puts the worship of God into the class of the external things of this world or who seeks his salvation through the righteousness and works of the Law, much less who seeks it through the works of human traditions.

That you may understand this, see the words which are written in John 6[:29]: "This is the work of God, etc.," something which is a very appropriate figure here, for they have regard for nothing else, as the author shows from Num. 19. You see, when Christ entered into the invisible holy of holies through His own blood, He wanted the Romans to burn His body outside the city on the cross as a burnt offering to God, and indeed a very sweet-smelling one, but nevertheless disgraceful as far as the world is concerned. In the same way, at that time they did not burn with glory on the altar of the Law the bodies of animals slain for sin, through whose blood the high priest entered into the holy of holies. They did this rather when they would, as a disgrace, throw those bodies outside the settlement and burn them so that they even believed that those who burned them were unclean, for this was still a figure.

The author therefore says [v. 13]: "Let us therefore go out with Jesus," outside the elements of this world and endure the disgrace (while in the meantime hypocrites and self-righteous people are glorious to the world according to the elements of the world) that we may finally die to the whole world along with Christ.

THE END
OF THE ANNOTATIONS OF JOHANNES
BUGENHAGEN OF POMERANIA
TO [SOME] EPISTLES OF PAUL.

THE RESURRECTION AND ASCENSION OF OUR LORD JESUS CHRIST ACCORDING TO THE FOUR EVANGELISTS[1]

by

JOHANNES BUGENHAGEN OF POMERANIA

translated by

The Rev. Dr. Richard J. Dinda, Prof. Em.

---

1   Translator's note: This document was attached to a dissertation titled: "THE ANNOTATIONS OF JOHANNES BUGENHAGEN OF POMERANIA ON THE PAULINE EPISTLES."

In the interest of clarity, I have chosen to treat it as a separate document, although the original composite work indicates by the page numbering that the two essays were originally between the same covers and counted as a single volume. There is no real title page nor any dedicatory letter nor introductory note to the reader. I have placed marginal references to cited texts in the body of this harmony.

1 Cor. 15[:3-4]: "Christ died for our sins according to Scriptures. He was buried and rose again on the third day according to Scriptures."

Acts 10[:40-41]: "God raised Him on the third day and caused Him to be seen not by all people but by witnesses whom God had foreordained, by the apostles, who ate and drank with Him after he rose from the dead."

Acts 1[:3]: "He then showed Himself as living to those and this with many proofs when for forty days He appeared to them, and spoke to them about the kingdom of God."

Acts 10[:42-43]: "He commanded them to preach to the people and bore witness that He was the one whom God had appointed to be the judge of the living and the dead. To Him all the prophets bore witness that whoever believed in Him would receive the remission of sins through His name."

Acts 4[:11-12]: "He is that stone whom the builders rejected, and who was made into the capstone. There is no salvation in any other, for no other name has been given under heaven among men by which we must be saved."

Acts 2[:24]: "But, having been freed from the pains of death because it will be impossible for death to hold Him, He appeared to His own."

We shall now open these subjects to the extent that we may, on the basis of the words of the Evangelists.

I decided to place this preface from Paul and from the Acts of the Apostles first. Note, however, that the Evangelists do not write everything, but they individually wrote what they saw. Often, when they write about something that occurred, they are unconcerned about the order of that occurrence and do not speak of the order. Therefore, what some have written quite obscurely others wrote more clearly.

"WHEN THE SABBATH HAD PASSED, Mary Magdalene and the other Mary, who is said to be the mother of James, and Salome and Johanna, and with them the rest who had come with Jesus from Galilee, bought spices and prepared them to come and anoint Jesus, for they had rested on the Sabbath according to the commandment."

The Sabbath had passed. During the evening of the Sabbath, then, they did the buying and preparing because they were permitted to work. Moreover, they had prepared nothing in the evening of Friday. This is contrary to Bede, because according to Luke [24:1], the Sabbath after the burial of Christ was dawning and the women were inactive because of the commandment which is Lev. 23[:32]: "From evening to evening you will celebrate your Sabbath."

"MOREOVER IN THE EVENING OF THE SABBATH," which was dawning into the first day of the week; that is, early in the morning, in deep night when it was still dark, on the first day of the week or, as Mark says [16:2], "after the sun had risen," at first light on the first day of the week, the women came to the tomb carrying the spices which they had prepared.

"Furthermore, the evening, etc." That is, when the Sabbath had turned into night, which night turns into Sunday. However, because Mark said: "After the sun had risen," namely, when the light of day which was close to the sun was appearing. Otherwise he would not have said "at first light," something which Augustine noted with reference to his harmony of the Evangelists.

"AND BEHOLD, THERE APPEARED A GREAT EARTHQUAKE, for an angel of the Lord came down from heaven. He approached and rolled the stone away from the doorway and began to sit upon it. Moreover, his appearance was like lightning and his clothing was as white as snow. Because of their fear of him, the guards were stricken and became like dead men." [Mat. 28:2]

Just as Christ shook the earth when he died, so also He shook it when He rose again. This He did because He didn't want the earth to be ignorant of what He was doing to save it.

"MOREOVER, THE WOMEN BEGAN TO SAY to each other: 'Who will roll the stone away from the doorway of the tomb for us?' You see, it was a very large stone. When they had taken a look, they saw that the stone had been rolled away from the tomb. They entered the tomb, but they didn't find the body of the Lord Jesus. They became mentally confused and came out of the tomb. Behold, two men in gleaming robes stood close to them (that is, their clothes gleamed like lightning). Because the women were terrified, they turned their faces to the ground. The men said to them: 'What is this? Why are looking for the living among the dead? (as if He who was truly living were still among the dead). He is not here. He has risen.

"'Remember that He told you, when He was in Galilee, saying: "The Son of Man must be surrendered into the hands of sinful people and be crucified and rise again on the third day."' And the women remembered. When they returned from the tomb, they announced all those things to the eleven and all the rest, and they began to say those things to the apostles, but their words seemed mad to the apostles and they didn't believe the women.

"Mary Magdalene, however, ran and went to Simon Peter and to that other disciple whom Jesus loved and said to them: 'They have taken the Lord away from His tomb, and we don't know where they have put Him.' Peter got up and went out, and that other disciple went with him, and they came to the tomb. The two were running together, and that other disciple ran more swiftly than Peter and reached the tomb first. When he had bent down, he saw the linen strips set aside, but he didn't go in. Then Simon Peter, who had followed him, came and entered the tomb. He saw only the linen strips and the cloth that had been around His head, but the latter had been folded and was set apart by itself.

"Then that other disciple who had reached the tomb first also entered, and he saw and believed, for they still did not know the Scripture that He had had to rise from the dead. The disciples therefore wondered at what had happened and went back again to themselves (that is, to their home)."

"Moreover, Mary was standing near the tomb weeping just outside it. While she was weeping, she bent over [and looked] inside the tomb and saw two angels clothed in white sitting one at the head and the other at the foot in the place where they had placed Jesus. The said: 'Woman, why are you weeping?' She said to them: 'They have taken away my Lord, and I don't know where they have put Him.'

"When she had said this, she turned around and saw Jesus standing there, but she didn't know that it was Jesus. Jesus said to her: 'Woman, why are you weeping. For whom are you looking?' She thought He was the gardener and said to Him: 'Sir, if you have carried Him away, tell me where you put Him and I shall take Him away.' Jesus said to her: 'Mary.' She turned to Him and said: '*Rabboni* (which is to say, 'Master').' Jesus said to her: "Don't touch Me, for I have not yet ascended to My Father."'

Jesus is touched by faith, as you read about the woman suffering the flow of blood. Therefore He forbade Mary to touch Him because she did not believe that Christ had been glorified. That is what He added: "For I have not yet ascended to My Father"; that is, "I have not yet ascended and been glorified, and I have not yet ascended as far as you are concerned, that is, you do not yet believe this very thing."

"But go to My brothers and tell them…"

You see, once Jesus had obtained His kingdom and was glorified, He was not embarrassed to call us "brothers," just as the Epistle to Hebrews, c. 2[:11–12] and Psa. 22[:22], explain.

"I AM ASCENDING TO MY FATHER and to your Father, to My God and to your God."

As He is by nature His Son, He calls God His "Father"; so as truly Man, He calls the Father His "God." Cyril writes this: "Here I also understand that Christ is calling Him His 'Father,' because according to His humanity he was adopted, for He immediately compares Himself to us when He adds '…and Your Father.'" For this reason He called us His "brothers" above.

From Mark: "This was that Mary Magdalene, from whom Jesus had cast out seven evil spirits. When He had risen, He appeared first to her very early in the morning on the first day of the week. She went and told the disciples who had been with Him and who were mourning and weeping that she had seen the Lord and that she had spoken to Him. When they had heard that He was alive and that she had seen Him, they didn't believe her."

Out of His dispensation, people were seeing the Lord not in the due glory of His body but in His first likeness that you not think that a different body from what He had assumed from the Virgin had risen, and that you not think that some other body had been crucified and had died. Otherwise, people could not have seen Him in the glory of His resurrection, which you might understand easily from Mat. 17[:2], where we have a preview of the glory of the resurrection in His shining body.

"AND WHEN THEY HAD HEARD, etc." That He might sufficiently prove His death and resurrection, He did not quickly ascend.

From Mark: "MOREOVER, WHEN THE WOMEN had entered, they saw a young man clad in a white robe and sitting on the right side, and they became frightened. (This was an angel of the Lord.) But he said to them: 'Don't be afraid, for I know that you are looking for Jesus of Nazareth, who was crucified. He is not here. He is risen, just as He said. Come and see the place where they placed the Lord. But go out quickly and tell His disciples and Peter…'"

The angel names Peter separately. Otherwise, because he had denied Christ, he might have thought that he was not included in the number of the disciples.

"'…that He has risen from the dead. And, behold, He will go ahead of you into Galilee and there you will see Him, just as He said to you. Now I have told you.' The women left and quickly fled from the tomb with great fear and joy and began to run to announce that to the disciples. Trembling and shock were holding them, and they were saying nothing to anyone, for they were frightened. When they had gone to announce these things to the disciples, behold, Jesus met them and said: 'Greetings.' They approached Him and grasped His feet and worshipped Him. Then Jesus said to them: 'Don't be afraid. Go and announce to My brothers that they should go into Galilee, and they will see Me there.'"

Because these women saw and believed, Jesus did not forbid them to touch Him.

"When they [the women] had gone away, behold, some of the guards came into the city and announced to the chief priests all the things that had happened. Those priests gathered together with the elders and developed a plan whereby they gave a large amount of money to the soldiers and told them: "Say that His disciples came during the night and stole Him while we were sleeping. If the governor will have heard of this, we shall persuade him [that this is true] and we shall see to your safety. They took the money and did just as they had been instructed. This is the story that is still told today."

The disciples were terrified before the death of Christ—how might they steal the body while the soldiers were keeping watch and the tomb had been sealed, or how might they not waken the soldiers when they rolled so great a stone from its place, or how might they carry off the body without the linen clothes, or how they might strip off the grave cloths from the body, smeared as they were with myrrh? Against their will, therefore, they confessed to each other: "Christ is not in the tomb. The Jews now should sing, etc. The lie remains with the Jews, but the truth remains with us." As Augustine says in his commentary on Psa. 55: "Such were the blind Jews that they believed an absolutely unbelievable lie. They believed the testimony of those who were sleeping. It was either false that they were sleeping, and they should not have believed the lie; or it is true that they had been sleeping and didn't know what had happened."

"THE LORD WAS ALSO SEEN BY CEPHAS" (1 Cor. 15[:5]), on the very day of the resurrection (Luke 24[:36]).

REGARDING THE EVENING OF THE DAY OF THE RESURRECTION.

"AND BEHOLD, TWO OF THOSE were going on the same day to a village called Emmaus, which was about eleven kilometers from Jerusalem." [Luke 24:13] The rest of this episode is in Luke [24:14–32].

"And in the same hour [those two] stood up and returned to Jerusalem and found the eleven who had gathered together and all who were with them. They said: 'The Lord truly has risen and has appeared to Simon (that is, to Peter).'" [Luke 24:33–34]

Although John says that Thomas was absent; Augustine thinks (*On the Harmony of the Evangelists*) that the question is resolved in this way: Thomas was "absent" before He came to be seen. I answer it in this way, namely, that "the eleven" is posited for the apostles, for at that time they were all included under this title, although they were called "the twelve" before. Paul himself calls the apostles under the title "the twelve" (1 Cor. 15[:5]). "Next," Paul says, "He appeared to the twelve," as the Greek words read consistently, according to Erasmus, which among the Latins was regularly translated as "the eleven," by those who did not pay attention to this custom of naming. John also says [20:24]: "Thomas, one of the twelve," that is, one of the apostles, etc.

"THEN THEY BEGAN TO TELL the things that had happened along the way and how they had recognized Him from the breaking of bread, but they did not believe them." [Luke 24:35] "Moreover, it was the evening of that day which was the first day of the week, and in the place where the disciples had gathered, they had locked the doors because of their fear of the Jews." [John 20:19] "While they were saying these things, Jesus Himself came while the disciples were eating. He stood in the midst of them and said: 'Peace be to you,' and He rebuked them for their unbelief and hardness of heart because they had not believed those who had seen Him." [Mark 16:14]

"PEACE BE TO YOU." This greeting befits Him who is the Bestower of peace, and whose children are "the peacemakers" (Mat. 5). He Himself is the Peace of all. He had left peace, and He brings back peace.

"SHOCKED and frightened as they were, however, they kept thinking that they were seeing a ghost; but Jesus said to them: 'Why are you upset, and why do thoughts rise up in your hearts? Look at My hands and My feet, for I am He. Touch Me and see, for a ghost does not have flesh and bones, as you see that I have.' And when He had said this, He showed them His hands, feet, and side. The disciples therefore rejoiced at having seen the Lord. He therefore said to them again: 'Peace be to you. As the Father has sent Me, so also I send you.'" [Luke 24:37–39]

"As the Father, etc." "Let no one take this honor for himself, etc." (Heb. 5[:4]). He says: "As the Father, etc.," and in this way discloses to them the ministry of His apostolate and the greatness of their power. "In the same way," that is, to call sinners to repentance, to heal those who are sick in mind and body, that you may do not your will but the will of Him who is sending you.

"WHEN HE HAD SPOKEN THESE WORDS, He breathed on them and said to them: 'Receive the Holy Spirit. Whose soever's sins you forgive, they are forgiven them, and whose soever's sins you retain, they are retained." [John 20:22–23]

Receive the Holy Spirit." Some people boast of their power in vain without the Spirit.

"BECAUSE THEY STILL did not believe because of their joy and amazement, He said to them: 'Have you anything to eat here?' And they brought Him a piece of broiled fish and of a honeycomb. He took it and ate it before their eyes; and He said to them: 'These are the words which I spoke to you when I was with you, namely, that all the things which were written in the Law of Moses and in the Prophets and in the Psalms about Me had to be fulfilled.' Then He opened their minds that they might understand Scripture. And He said to them: 'So it was written, and thus it was necessary for Christ to suffer and rise again from the dead on the third day and that repentance and remission of sins be preached in His name among all nations, beginning from Jerusalem. In addition, you are witnesses of these matters.'" [Luke 24:40–48]

A WEEK AFTER THE PASSOVER.

"MOREOVER, THOMAS, one of the twelve, who was called 'Didymus,' was not with them when Jesus came, etc." (John 20[:24] to the end of the chapter).

Thomas surely received the Holy Spirit according to the intent of Christ as He gave the Spirit. Read something quite similar in Num. 11[:10ff.].

THE ACCOUNT OF THE WEEK AFTER OR OF THE OCTAVE OF THE PASSOVER.

"AFTERWARD Jesus revealed Himself again in Galilee at the Sea of Tiberias, but He revealed Himself in such a way, etc." (John 21[:14]). This was now the third time that Jesus revealed Himself to His disciples after He had risen from the dead. When they had eaten, Jesus said to Simon, "Son of Jonas, do you love Me more than these?' etc." (to the end of the chapter).

"Moreover, the eleven disciples went off into Galilee to the mountain which Jesus had appointed for them." [Mat. 28:16] "There He appeared to more than five hundred brethren at the same time, many of whom are still living, but some have fallen asleep." [1 Cor. 25:6] "When they had seen Him, they worshipped Him, but some had doubts. And Jesus came up to them and said: 'All power in heaven and on earth has been given to Me. Go therefore into the whole world and, as you preach the Gospel, teach all nations. Baptize them in the name of the Father and of the Son and of the Holy Spirit. Teach them to observe all things which I have commanded you,'" that is, you ought not preach off the top of your head, but preach what you have heard from Me.

"Behold, I am with you all the days until the end of the age. He therefore who will have believed and will have received baptism will be saved, but the person who will not have believed will be damned" (Mat. 28:20, Mark 16:16). "And these signs will follow those who have believed: through My name they will cast out evil spirits, they will speak in new tongues, they will pick up snakes, and, if they may have drunk something poisonous, that will not harm them. In addition, they will lay their hands on the sick, and they will receive healing." [Mark 16:17-18]

"Next, James saw him" (1 Cor. 17[:7]).

SUMMARY OF THE ACCOUNT OF THE RESURRECTION ALONG WITH THE ACCOUNT OF THE ASCENSION.

In Acts 1, after He had been afflicted with suffering, before He was again taken up on high, He had revealed Himself alive to His apostles, and this with much evidence when over a period of forty days He was seen by them. He spoke to them about the kingdom of God and opened their minds that they might understand Scripture. He gathered them into one place and "commanded them not to leave Jerusalem but to wait for the promise of the Father, saying: 'Behold, I shall send upon you the promise of My Father about which you have heard from Me. But stay in the city of Jerusalem until you have been clothed with power from on high'" (Luke 24[:49]). "'Because John baptized you with water, you will be baptized with the Holy Spirit in a few days after these things.'

"When they therefore had gathered together there, they began to inquire of Him, saying: 'Lord, You will not restore the kingdom of Israel at this time, will You?'" (Acts 1[:5–6]).

We understand this to mean the carnal kingdom which at that time had been wiped out. And the Lord answered in such a way that you might understand that that kingdom of Israel was going to be restored fully and completely, that is, with a believing people, at the final resurrection.

"MOREOVER, HE SAID TO THEM: 'It is not your business to know the times and seasons the Father has established by His own power, but you will receive power after the Holy Spirit has come upon you; and you will be My witnesses not only in Jerusalem but in all Judea, Samaria and finally, to the ends of the earth'" (Acts 24[:7–8]).

"Moreover, He led them out into the area of Bethany, lifted His hands on high and blessed them. (That is, He prayed for their well-being.). While He was blessing them (He had already spoken enough to them after the resurrection.), He happened to depart from them" (Luke 24[:50–51])."And as they watched, He was taken up on high; and a cloud hid Him from their eyes" (Acts 1[:9]). "… and He sat at the right hand of God" (Mark 16[:19])."When they had their eyes fixed on the sky as He was leaving, behold, two men dressed in white stood close to them and said: 'Men of Galilee, why are you standing here looking up into the sky? This Jesus who has been taken up into heaven from you will come in like manner as you have seen Him going up into heaven" (Acts 1[:10–11])."Then they worshipped Him and returned to Jerusalem with great joy (Luke 24[:53]), from the mount which is called 'Olivet,' which is a Sabbath day's journey from Jerusalem." (A Sabbath day's journey is as far as the Jews were allowed to travel on the Sabbath.)

"When they had arrived, they went up into the dining room where they were staying, namely, Peter, James, John, Andrew, Philip, Thomas, Bartholomew, Matthew, James the son of Alpheus, Simon the Zealot, and Judas, the son of James. They were all continuing in prayer and entreaty together with the women and Mary, the mother of Jesus, and His brothers (that is, kinsmen)" (Acts 1[:12–14]). "They kept staying in the temple continually and they praised and blessed God. Amen." [Luke 24:53]

"AND IN THOSE DAYS Peter stood up in the midst of the disciples (There was a crowd of about one hundred twenty people.) and said: 'Men and brothers, etc.'" He spoke about the election of Matthias (Acts 1[:15–26]).

"And when the fifty days were completed, they all were together in the same place, and there came a sudden sound from heaven like the assault of the coming of a violent wind, etc." (Acts 2[:1–2]).

Signs appeared from heaven when the Gospel was confirmed on Mount Zion, just as signs from heaven appeared when the Law was confirmed on Mount Sinai. Here, however, the Spirit was given, but He was not given through the Law. Here people come to their senses and are converted to God, but in the giving of the Law they were terrified and kept running away from God. With reference to that Law of the Spirit, Isaiah [2:3] and Micah [4:2] prophesied: "The Law will come forth from Zion, and the Word of the Lord from Jerusalem, etc."

Read the whole book of the Acts of the Apostles and the writings of the apostles, and you will learn what the disciples accomplished, clad as they were with power from on high. Mark [16:20] includes all these things in a few words: "Then the disciples departed and preached everywhere as the Lord worked with them and strengthened His Word through the miracles which followed."

I am instructing you with the few words of this harmony of mine in which I did not follow Augustine, Jerome, nor Ambrose, although I have noted a few points from them. Rather, I followed the Gospels themselves. I see that I have assisted not a little those who suspect that the Evangelists wrote contrary things with the result that some once did not even accept the last chapter of Mark, according to Jerome, as if that chapter were opposed to the rest of the Evangelists, but it is not.

Thus, then, the time of the first sight of the tomb, when the women came, all the Evangelists write in harmony. Next, they write in various ways of those things which the women saw, but those cover only two accounts. Luke and John write the one, and Matthew and Mark the other. However, Mark forces whom they make first when he says: "He appeared first to Mary Magdalene." Look! You have in the harmony in a few words what seemed to be very different. Thus you will be offended neither in the various appearances of the angels nor in other matters things which were appearing to be different, as, for instance, when you understand that the angel, fearsome in appearance, who was sitting upon the stone appeared only to the soldiers in Matthew. But why does Mary Magdalene, who had already seen that the Lord had risen, go to the tomb again? I say, she went with the others and desired to see often the One she had seen, or she merely wanted to see the tomb again, something which Matthew said as if in passing. For this reason, it is not so much she as her friends who were still doubting about that which Mary Magdalene perhaps had revealed to them and who hear: "He is not here. Come, etc." Therefore it will not be necessary to suspect more than one Mary Magdalene in the Evangelists.

Furthermore, this Mary Magdalene was a Galilean; but we never find Mary, the sister of Lazarus, called "Magdalene" in the Gospel accounts, for she was also not a Galilean but a Judean.

In the evening, Jesus appeared to the apostles who had gathered together. But Thomas was absent. Second, He appeared on the eighth day from the resurrection, when Thomas was present. Third, a few days after week of the Passover, He appeared in Galilee at the Sea of Tiberias. For that reason, John writes: "This was now the third time, etc." This order which John wrote clearly demands that we understand these things after that happened which Matthew writes about the mountain of Galilee where I believe the more than five hundred brothers were present, about which episode Paul writes. Who of the disciples did not wish to be present there where he had heard his Christ was going to appear, for the rumor was already going around among them from what the angels had told the women and the disciples of Christ and from their remembrance of the words which Christ had spoken, especially because Christ had appointed a specific mountain to them, as Matthew writes?

I also believe that He appointed a specific day, and I suspect that the mountain was Mount Tabor, where already before He had given a sign of His resurrection. He was unwilling to appear to so many before the news of His completed resurrection had reached many. Matthew also indicates between the lines that others were present in addition to the apostles when he says: "…but some of them doubted." Tell me, please, who of the apostles at that time doubted when all of them believed, before they went up to Galilee? Therefore they did not have a correct understanding as to what Mark wrote about the day of His ascension: "Later (or next) He appeared to the eleven as they were eating, etc.," because of what follows: "After He had spoken to them, He was taken up into heaven, etc." This happened during the evening of the day of the resurrection, something which Augustine also says about the harmony of the Evangelists.

Also, some people are not noticing from that passage that Mark is not writing a continuous account, but is covering briefly what the Lord had done or said before His ascension. For those words: "Go into all the world, etc.," appear from Matthew to have been spoken on the mountain of Galilee, unless you say they were spoken more often than that one time.

But what follows, namely: "After He had spoken, etc.," do not understand as coming soon after the aforementioned words but after all the words which He spoke during those forty days, according to Luke in Acts, unless you also understand that, soon after the episode on the Mount of Olives, the disciples went out to preach everywhere, because these words follow: "Moreover, they went out, etc.," something which the Acts of the Apostles does not allow. At that time, therefore, Mark wrote that summary of the things which Christ had done after His resurrection.

In fact, Luke wove together his Gospel so that you think that Christ ascended the night following the day of His resurrection. In fact, had Luke not said a single phrase in Acts, namely, "…for forty days," we would still not know on what day Christ ascended. Nowhere more than here, therefore, is it obvious how many things are lacking from the all the activities of Christ of which all the Evangelists wrote scarcely an abridgement, as even John admits at the end of his Gospel.

THE END.

www.ingramcontent.com/pod-product-compliance
Lightning Source LLC
Chambersburg PA
CBHW050548160426
43199CB00015B/2584